The Secret Wars

Volume I

Intelligence, Propaganda and Psychological
Warfare, Resistance Movements, and Secret Operations,
1939-1945

The Secret Wars: A Guide to Sources in English

Volume I: Intelligence, Propaganda and Psychological Warfare, Resistance Movements, and Secret Operations, 1939–1945

Volume II: Intelligence, Propaganda and Psychological Warfare,
Covert Operations, 1945–1980

Volume III: International Terrorism, 1968–1980

The Secret Wars: A Guide to Sources in English

Volume I

Intelligence, Propaganda and Psychological Warfare, Resistance Movements, and Secret Operations, 1939–1945

MYRON J. SMITH, JR.

With an Historical Introduction by
LYMAN B. KIRKPATRICK, JR.

ABC-Clio

Santa Barbara, California

Oxford, England

Library of Congress Cataloging in Publication Data

Smith, Myron J
    The secret wars, a guide to sources in English.
    (War/peace bibliography series; no. 12-   )
    Includes index.
    CONTENTS: v. 1. Intelligence, propaganda, and psychological war-
fare, resistance movements, and secret operations, 1939-1945.
    1. Military intelligence — Bibliography. 2. Espionage — Bibliog-
raphy. 3. Psychological warfare — Bibliography. 4. World War, 1939-
1945 — Underground movements — Bibliography. 5. World War,
1939-1945 — Secret service — Bibliography. 6. Commando troops —
Bibliography. 7. Guerrilla warfare — Bibliography. 8. Terrorism —
Bibliography. I. Title.
Z6724.I7S63 [UB250] 016.3553'43   79-25784
ISBN 0-87436-271-7

American Bibliographical Center—Clio Press
2040 Alameda Padre Serra
Santa Barbara, California 93103

Clio Press, Ltd.
Woodside House, Hinksey Hill
Oxford OX1 5BE, England

Manufactured in the United States of America

The War/Peace Bibliography Series

RICHARD DEAN BURNS, EDITOR

This Series has been developed in cooperation with the Center for the Study of Armament and Disarmament, California State University, Los Angeles.

 # 1 *Songs of Protest, War & Peace*
A Bibliography & Discography
R. SERGE DENISOFF

 # 2 *Warfare in Primitive Societies*
A Bibliography
WILLIAM TULIO DIVALE

 # 3 *The Vietnam Conflict*
Its Geographical Dimensions, Political
Traumas & Military Developments
MILTON LEITENBERG & RICHARD DEAN BURNS

 # 4 *Modern Revolutions and Revolutionists*
A Bibliography
ROBERT BLACKEY

 # 5 *The Arab-Israeli Conflict*
A Historical, Political, Social
& Military Bibliography
RONALD M. DEVORE

About the War/Peace Bibliography Series

With this bibliographical series, the Center for the Study of Armament and Disarmament, California State University, Los Angeles, seeks to promote a wider understanding of martial violence and the alternatives to its employment. The Center, which was formed by concerned faculty and students in 1962-63, has as its primary objective the stimulation of intelligent discussion of war/peace issues. More precisely, the Center has undertaken two essential functions: (1) to collect and catalogue materials bearing on war/peace issues; and (2) to aid faculty, students, and the public in their individual and collective probing of the historical, political, economic, philosophical, technical, and psychological facts of these fundamental problems.

This bibliographical series is, obviously, one tool with which we may more effectively approach our task. Each issue in this series is intended to provide a comprehensive "working," rather than definitive, bibliography on a relatively narrow theme within the spectrum of war/peace studies. While we hope this series will prove to be a useful tool, we also solicit your comments regarding its format, contents, and topics.

RICHARD DEAN BURNS
SERIES EDITOR

Other Bibliographies by Myron J. Smith, Jr.

Navies in the American Revolution. Vol. I of the American Naval Bibliography Series.

The American Navy, 1789–1860. Vol. II of the American Naval Bibliography Series.

American Civil War Navies. Vol. III of the American Naval Bibliography Series.

The American Navy, 1865–1918. Vol. IV of the American Naval Bibliography Series.

The American Navy, 1918–1941. Vol. V of the American Naval Bibliography Series.

The European Theater. Vol. I of *World War II at Sea: A Bibliography of Sources in English.*

The Pacific Theater. Vol. II of *World War II at Sea: A Bibliography of Sources in English.*

General Works, Naval Hardware, Home Fronts, Special Studies, and the "All Hands" Chronology (1941–1945). Vol. III of *World War II at Sea: A Bibliography of Sources in English.*

General Works, European and Mediterranean Theaters of Operations. Vol. I of *Air War Bibliography, 1939–1945: English-language Sources.*

The Pacific Theater; Airpower, Strategy and Tactics; Escape, Evasion, Partisan, and POW Experiences. Vol. II of *Air War Bibliography, 1939–1945: English-language Sources.*

Multi-theater Studies and the Air Forces. Vol. III of *Air War Bibliography, 1939–1945: English-language Sources.*

The Aircraft. Vol. IV of *Air War Bibliography, 1939–1945: English-language Sources.*

World War I in the Air: A Bibliography and Chronology.

Cloak-and-Dagger Bibliography: An Annotated Guide to Spy Fiction, 1937–1975.

Air War Southeast Asia, 1961-1973: An Annotated Bibliography and 16 mm Film Guide.

Men-at-Arms: A Fiction Guide.

The Rise of the Soviet Navy, 1941–1978: A Guide to Sources in English.

With Robert C. Weller. *Sea Fiction Guide.*

for Ron and Ruth Champagne, teachers,
scholars, colleagues, friends

Contents

It is just as legitimate to fight an enemy in the rear as in the front.
The only difference is in the danger.
—John S. Mosby
War Reminiscences (1887)

Selected Chronology

The citations in this chronology were chosen to reflect "secret war" activities of the World War of 1939–1945 as a whole. Specific illustrations demonstrate the breadth of events transpiring "behind-the-scenes" and are arranged by month within the year of occurrence. Many more examples could have been chosen; however, some limitation had to be imposed on selections in order that the chronology not rival the bibliography in size.

1939   **(September)** Nazi party intelligence service (*Sicherheitsdienst* or S.D.) agents wearing Polish uniforms and led by Mjr. Alfred Naujocks attack the German radio station at Gleiwitz in an incident calculated to provide cover for Hitler's invasion of Poland.

Germany invades Poland bringing on World War II; within days, France and Britain declare war on the Third Reich.

The German *Reichssicherheitshauptamt* (RSHS) is established by order of Himmler to coordinate the work of the Gestapo, S.D., and Kripo.

German radar, about which the Allies know little, detects a force of 29 RAF bombers en route to attack German Navy ships in the Heligoland Bight; the electronic warning allows Luftwaffe Me-109's to intercept and down 7 English warplanes.

Sidney Cotton forms the first Royal Air Force reconnaissance outfit, the Photographic Development Unit.

Lt. Cmdr. Eric Feldt, Royal Australian Navy, arrives in New Guinea to establish a chain of coastwatching stations.

William Joyce arrives in Berlin, offers his service to Joseph Goebbels at the German Ministry of Propaganda, and is soon broadcasting to Britain as "Lord Haw-Haw."

By Executive Order, President Franklin Rossevelt defines the Federal Bureau of Investigation (FBI) as America's top civilian counterespionage agency.

(October) German double agent John Owen ("Snow") provides the British, upon his capture, with information on German wireless codes and cipher procedures.

The German Navy radio intelligence service B-Dienst, which has cracked the British naval codes, alerts the remainder of the Kriegsmarine that the convoy system is being adopted for the protection of Allied ocean commerce.

Luftwaffe aerial reconnaissance of Scapa Flow demonstrates the weaknesses which allow Guenther Prient to penetrate the base with *U-47* and sink H.M. battleship *Royal Oak*; for years thereafter, the rumor persists that Prient was aided by a German agent or English traitor.

From Oslo, German military intelligence (Abwehr) agent Hermann Kempf alerts his chief, Admiral Wilhelm Canaris, of British plans to move on Norway.

(November) An anonymous source provides British intelligence with the "Oslo Report"—the first information on German rocket experiments at Peenemünde.

Stewart Menzies succeeds the late Admiral "Quex" Sinclair as chief of the British foreign espionage organization MI-6.

In an unsuccessful attempt to assassinate Adolf Hitler, anti-Nazi Germans plant a bomb in a Munich beerhall which fails to detonate until after the Fuehrer has kept a speaking engagement.

German S.D. agents under Walter Schellenberg kidnap 3 British agents from Holland, accusing them of instigating the unsuccessful attempt on Hitler at Munich; the event is known as the "Venlo Incident."

Hans Frank issues a decree instituting Jewish ghettos in Poland's major cities; these enclaves would become a hotbed of Jewish resistance.

(December) British bombers begin the dropping of propaganda leaflets or "nickels" on Germany.

1940   **(January)** General Tadeusz Bor-Komorowski assumes command of the underground in southern Poland.

(February) To cover preparations for their Scandinavian invasion, the Germans mount a successful deception campaign designed to convince the world of a pending move into Rumania.

(March) Disguised as a Swedish vessel, the German ship *Theseus* patrols the Norwegian coast relaying data obtained by Abwehr agents inland.

(April) German troops invade Denmark and Norway; by nurturing fifth columns, the Abwehr plays a hand in the successful invasions.

The Kriegsmarine B-Dienst deciphers 30–50 per cent of all coded British naval messages sent during the Norwegian campaign.

(May) An RAF photo Spitfire reports German tanks assembling in the Ardennes.

Germany invades France and the Low Countries.

In the first important "Ultra" intelligence, obtained as the result of working with a captured Enigma cipher machine, the Allies learn of orders to the German Sixth Army which result in the Nazi breakthrough at Sedan, France.

The escape-fostering arm of British intelligence, MI-9, is formed in London under Brigadier Norman Crockatt; it will later maintain and assist a large network of escape routes throughout Occupied Europe and into the Far East.

(June) In a memo, Prime Minister Winston Churchill calls for the creation of special raiding forces; these will later be called Commandos.

The British Directorate of Combined Operations is established.

In the first Commando mission, three British officers land near Boulogne and conduct a short reconnaissance.

France falls; many Allied soldiers escape to Britain via Dunkirk.

A French escape group led by André Postel-Thinay begins secreting out British soldiers left behind at Dunkirk.

President Roosevelt issues an Executive Order giving the FBI responsibility for foreign intelligence and counterintelligence in South America via its Special Intelligence Service.

(July) Ultra intercepts provide the British with the disposition and order of battle for German Luftflottes 2, 3, and 5.

A coded message from Hitler's headquarters (H.Q.) to the German Army, Navy, and Air Force is intercepted in Britain and decoded on the Enigma cipher machine; this "Ultra" message provides Churchill and the British war establishment with its first data on "Operation Sea Lion."

Prime Minister Churchill establishes the Special Operations Executive (SOE), placing it secretly under Hugh Dalton's Ministry of Economic Warfare.

A force of 100+ British Commandos unsuccessfully attempt to raid German-held Guernsey in the English Channel.

The RAF Photographic Reconnaissance Unit (PRU) is established under Coastal Command.

The British Security Co-ordinator (BSC), William Stephenson, opens his intelligence network in New York; aside from aiding the FBI and later the OSS, the BSC would attempt to discredit American neutralist groups and individuals and seek ways of thrusting the U.S. into the war before Pearl Harbor.

(August) British air leaders Dowding and Park are appraised of the existence of Ultra and its potential for use in the upcoming Battle of Britain.

An Ultra intercept alerts the British to Luftwaffe chief Goering's orders for his air force to overcome the RAF as quickly as possible; the Enigma machine also delivers up the Reichmarshal's precise "Eagle Day" orders.

After a slow start in July, the Battle of Britain rages; English leaders continue to monitor both their Enigma machine and the screens of their radar.

Luftwaffe warplanes mount a concentrated series of attacks on British radar stations in an effort to knock out the English "eyes;" four are damaged and one put out of action, the latter feat skillfully concealed from German reconnaissance.

The British Naval Intelligence Division begins a security check which leads to a change in naval ciphers presently being read by the Kriegsmarine B-Dienst.

Under Mjr. Roman Czerniawski, "Interallié" is the first major resistance network established in France after the German occupation.

The U.S. Army Signal Intelligence Service, under cryptologist William Friedman, makes the first complete solution of a Japanese "Magic" communication via the "Purple" cipher machine, a Japanese version of the German Enigma.

(September) Ultra continues to deliver to the British Goering's air plans-of-the-day, including orders for a night raid on London.

Abwehr agents Karl Meier and Rudolph Waldberg are captured in Kent; Waldberg is executed two days later, the first Nazi spy to die in Britain during the war.

The W-Branch of the British counterespionage service, MI-5, is established to coordinate the dissemination of false information.

The Intelligence Staff section (A-2) is established in the U.S. Army Air Corps by administrative direction.

(October) In New York, BSC head William Stephenson, in cooperation with the FBI, arranges for the Mexicans to confiscate $3 million in Italian funds en route to Mexico from the U.S. and earmarked to pay for Abwehr intelligence operations.

(November) The British learn of the upcoming German raid on Coventry via Ultra.

The First SOE agent to be parachuted into France refuses to jump making the mission a failure.

Paul Thummel ("René") reveals to London, via the Czech Resistance, German plans to invade Russia in the spring of 1941.

Claire Chennault receives unofficial U.S. permission to form a band of mercenary flyers to aid China; the group will become known as the American Volunteer Group (AVG) or "Flying Tigers."

(December) SOE and Norwegian patriot Lief Larsen establish the Royal Norwegian Navy's Special Service ("Shetland Bus") to run agents, arms, and supplies to the Norwegian underground.

Photo planes of No. 3 PRU begin taking pictures which reveal that RAF bombers are not hitting their targets.

1941   **(January)** The Double Cross (XX) Committee of British MI-5 is formed to pass false information to Germany via "turned" agents.

Orde Wingate's "Gideon Force" begins four months of guerrilla campaigning in Ethiopia, leading to the evacuation by Italians of several important positions.

The U.S. discloses to Britain the means for deciphering the Japanese Purple code.

BSC chief William Stephenson gives FBI boss J. Edgar Hoover a selection of intercepted letters from an anonymous German spy operating in America; this leads to an intensive FBI counterespionage operation.

(February) RAF photo planes deliver the first proof that German radar stations ("Freya") are in France.

HMS *Fidelity*, a "Q" ship, begins conducting clandestine sabotage missions along the south coast of France.

In one of the first examples of Jewish resistance, a Jewish Action Group engages members of the Defense Troop (W.A.) of the Dutch S.S. who have entered the Jewish quarter of Amsterdam.

Via Ultra, the British learn that General Erwin Rommel will command German units being sent to North Africa.

The first SOE agent is flown into Poland.

The Foreign Broadcast Monitoring Service is established within the U.S. Department of Commerce.

(March) Soviet agent Alexander Foote ("Jim") sends the first of his 6,000 messages to Moscow from his apartment in Lausanne, Switzerland.

British Commandos raid Norway's Lofoten Islands destroying the local fish-oil stocks and factories and bringing back additional parts of an Enigma machine.

Between this month and December, only 4 of 227 coded messages sent by the Japanese delegation in Washington to Tokyo are missed by the American intercept service.

(April) From Switzerland Soviet agent Rudolf Roessler ("Lucy") passes information to Moscow on the impending German invasion—the data is ignored.

Via Ultra, the British learn of German plans to invade Crete.

As the result of Ultra intercepts, the British Mediterranean Fleet defeats an Italian force in the Battle of Cape Matapan.

German forces invade Yugoslavia and Greece.

(May) The position of the German battleship *Bismarck* is revealed to the British by RAF reconnaissance and Ultra intercepts; the pride of the Kriegsmarine is sunk.

German forces capture Crete; British Commandos, under Robert E. Laycock, unsuccessfully attempt to raid Nazi positions on the island.

Vietnamese nationalist groups combine under Ho Chi Minh to form the League for the Independence of Vietnam (Vietminh); this resistance organization will come to spy for and receive supplies from the American OSS.

In Washington, D.C., German agent Count Friedrich Douglas ("Dinter") learns of and reports on U.S. plans to occupy Iceland and Greenland.

(June) Working for MI-9, Albert-Marie Guerisse ("Pat O'Leary") runs an escape line between southern France and Spain.

From Japan, Soviet agent Richard Sorge sends word to Moscow concerning German plans to invade Russia.

The Soviet Red Orchestra spy network in Berlin, headed by Harro Schulze-Boysen, an employee of the Reich Air Ministry, begins sending Moscow the first of 500 radio reports.

From Switzerland, Soviet agent Otto Puenter transmits to Moscow the date for "Operation Barbarossa," the German invasion.

In four days over the airways from Switzerland, the Soviet

network in Brussels headed by Leopold Trepper sends 500 messages to Moscow.

German troops invade Russia in "Operation Barbarossa"; having ignored all warnings, the Soviets are completely surprised.

Of three British Desert Commando units which attempt to raid Vichy French airfields in Syria, only that led by Geoffrey Keys is successful.

Lt. Cmdr. Joseph J. Rochefort opens the U.S. Navy Combat Intelligence Unit in Hawaii, charged with communications intelligence against the Japanese navy.

As the result of a counterespionage operation begun with information from the BSC, the FBI arrests 33 on charges of being German agents.

(July) In an effort to keep alive the spirit of resistance in Occupied Europe, BBC News Director Douglas Ritchie ("Colonel Britton") launches the "V Campaign" over the airways.

The Vichy security police, *Service d'Ordre Legionnaire* or *Milice*, is formed by collaborator Joseph Darnand.

A dozen U.S. State Department officials arrive in French North Africa to monitor a U.S.-Vichy trade agreement; later, under Robert Murphy and William Eddy, they would provide data to the OSS.

In a broadcast to the Russian people, Stalin calls for total resistance and the formation of partisan units.

The Central Committee of the Russian CPSU issues a decree on "The Organization of the Struggle in the Enemy Rear."

Yugoslav guerrillas mount their first attack, ambushing German soldiers in Serbia.

William J. Donovan is designated U.S. Co-ordinator of Information by President Roosevelt.

(August) Andreé de Jongh establishes the Comet escape line out of Brussels. Operating from a trawler, British Commandos under John Appleyard explore the Vichy French coastal areas of West Africa to determine if German U-boats are operating from them.

Cardinal Archbishop Graf Clemens von Galen denounces Nazi confiscation of Catholic Church property and murder of the feeble-minded; growing increasingly anti-government in his sermons, the "Lion of Munster" is watched—but never arrested—by the Gestapo.

Some 30 GRU agents are dropped behind German lines near Gomel to conduct sabotage and intelligence operations; most of these Russians are killed by Wehrmacht soldiers.

British XX agent Dusko Popov ("Trycycle") arrives in New York to advise the U.S. about possible Japanese plans for Pearl Harbor, but is turned away by J. Edgar Hoover.

(September) Ivone Kirkpatrick becomes Controller of the European Service of the BBC, which is in charge of propaganda broadcasts.

British XX agents Olaf Klausen and Jack Berg ("Mutt and Jeff") report to the Abwehr on a proposed but bogus British plan to invade Norway.

Col. Maurice Buckmaster becomes chief of the French (F) Section of SOE.

The NKVD forms special commando forces for unusual assignments.

Capt. D. H. Hudson and 11 agents of SOE-Cairo are landed "blind" on the Montenegrin coast in the first mission designed to aid Mihailovic's Chetniks.

Mjr. Gen. Dawson Olmstead succeeds Mjr. Gen. Joseph O. Mauboigne as chief of the U.S. Army Signal Corps.

(October) The Cipher Branch of the German OKW breaks the American military attaché ("Black") code.

Aircraft of the Soviet 6th Air Regiment denote the beginnings of the German move against Moscow.

Employing 4 captured German tanks, Yugoslav Partisans attack Kraljevo.

Yugoslav guerrilla chiefs Tito and Mihailovic meet at Brajichi to negotiate co-operation; the talks break down and the Partisans and Chetniks become deadly enemies.

Soviet spy Richard Sorge is arrested by the Kempei tai in Tokyo after scoring a number of espionage successes.

(November) The first SOE sabotage team is parachuted into Holland.

Led by Hugo Bleicher, Abwehr agents raid the Paris H.Q. of the Interallié network capturing 21 members, including Mjr. Czerniawski ("Armand") and Mathilde Carré ("The Cat"); Carré becomes a double agent and assists Bleicher in wrecking the remainder of her group.

Lt. Col. Geoffrey Keys and his Desert Commandos unsuccessfully attempt to assault a house thought to be the Field Marshal's H.Q. at Beda Littoria and kill Rommel.

As the Red Army battles a German panzer corps approaching Rostov, Russian partisans harass its rear and seize part of the city.

Yugoslav Chetnik head Mihailovic engages in talks with the Germans and begins collaboration with the Italians, a fact not known to the Allies.

Prior to departure from Japan, the Imperial Navy Pearl Harbor strike force disguises its movements by changing communications call signs and sending fake messages.

(December) Abwehr agents take three Soviet agents at a villa outside Brussels, but miss the two most important, Leopold Trepper and Victor Sukulov.

Italian frogmen operating from mini-subs sink H.M. battleships *Valiant* and *Queen Elizabeth* in Alexandria Harbor.

Via transport provided by the Long Range Desert Group, men of Mjr. David Sterling's Special Air Service destroy 90 Axis aircraft on the ground in Libya.

Dr. Leopold Kühn and his sister Ruth signal Japanese agent Otojiro Okudo as to the ongoing success of the Pearl Harbor attack.

Messages designed to alert Pearl Harbor arrive from Washington after the raid.

The FBI arrests 733 Japanese aliens in the U.S. considered to be security risks.

The U.S. Office of Censorship under Byron Price is established by Executive Order.

1942   **(January)** Marie M. Fourcade leads the Alliance Intelligence Service, an SOE network code named "Noah's Ark," which will spirit Gen. Henri Giraud out of France and provide data on German ground, air, and V-weapons order-of-battle in France during the next two years.

SOE agent Peter Churchill arrives in southern France to supply funds to a local resistance group.

Abwehr agent and Spanish military attaché to Washington, Col. José Garcia sends a 20-page report to Germany on the Roosevelt-Churchill meeting of December, 1941, with a complete list of the "Arcadia" decisions.

Soviet partisans and Red Army troops hold open the Vitebsk supply corridor.

(February) British airborne Commandos attack the German Freya radar station at Bruneval, France, bringing away a vital component.

SOE agent Pierre de Vemecourt aids Abwehr agent Mathilde Carré, formerly a British agent, to escape to Britain where she turns once more; uncertain, the English eventually jail her.

Via Ultra, English generals learn the exact details of Rommel's planned attack at Médenine and are able to repulse it.

SOE agent Xan Fielding is sent into Crete to assist in the organization of the island's resistance movement.

Aided by FBI agents, Brazilian police arrest German spy Josef J. J. Starziczny in Rio de Janeiro and take 86 other agents around the country, breaking up 6 radio espionage rings.

(March) British Combined Forces personnel attack the St. Nazaire dock gates.

Captured SOE Dutch agent Hubertus Lauwers is forced by Col. H. J. Giskes, head of Abwehr Dept. 3 (counterintelligence) in Holland, to broadcast false data to Britain which will attract additional agents into German hands; in beginning "Operation North Pole," Giskes will eventually see "the complete rolling up of the Allied espionage/sabotage effort in the Netherlands."

Within two weeks of Lauwers' messages, 8 SOE agents are parachuted into the hands of Abwehr Dept. 3.

The Economic Warfare Division of the U.S. London embassy is established.

Royal Navy escort vessels introduce High Frequency/Direction Finding ("Huff Duff") apparatus into the Battle of the Atlantic; by triangulating with various ship and shore stations, this process allows the Allies to pinpoint the location of U-boats employing their radios.

Czech agent Paul Thummel ("René") is arrested by the Gestapo in Prague.

Orde Wingate arrives in Burma to take charge of guerrilla operations against the Japanese; he sets to work raising a force of raiders who will become famous as the "Chindits."

(April) Having returned to France on another mission, SOE agent Pierre de Vemecourt is captured and sent to Colditz prison.

French Gen. Henri Giraud escapes a German prison and makes his way to Gibraltar via Vichy.

Mjr. Gen. George V. Strong is named Assistant Chief of Staff, U.S. Army, G-2 (intelligence).

(May) Agents of the French group *Organization Civile et Militaire* (OCM) forward to London, via Gilbert Renault ("Colonel Remy"), the first map of Hitler's Atlantic Wall.

After this month, all SOE agents coming into Holland are taken by Col. H. J. Giskes' counterespionage net.

Mjr. Eigil Boich-Johansen, working for SOE and the Danish Military Resistance organization known as "the Princes," effects the escape to Britain of former Danish Foreign Minister Christmas Moller and his family.

Abwehr agent and future famous minister Dietrich Bonhoffer explains the anti-Hitler underground to English Bishop Bell of Chichester during a meeting in Stockholm.

British-trained Chez agents bomb the car of Reinhard Heydrich; the S.S. Protector of Bohemia and Moravia dies within a week from infection.

As the result of Magic intelligence, the U.S. Navy is able to obtain a draw in the Battle of the Coral Sea and break up a planned Japanese occupation of Port Moresby, New Guinea.

Purple/Ultra intelligence reveals the Japanese plan for Midway.

(June) The U.S. Office of Strategic Services (OSS) is established under Gen. William J. Donovan.

The Allied Combined Intelligence Committee is established, comprised of the U.S. Joint Intelligence Staff and the British Joint Intelligence Committee.

In a secret London deal over spheres of influence, the OSS assumes primary responsibility for subversion in North Africa, China, Korea, the South Pacific, and Finland while the SOE assumes predominance in India, West Africa, the Balkans, and Middle East; Western Europe will be considered joint territory while neither will operate in General MacArthur's Southwest Pacific.

As the result of Purple/Ultra intelligence, the U.S. Navy wins the Battle of Midway, considered the turning point in the Pacific war.

The U.S. Navy cedes Japanese diplomatic solutions to the Army, giving over its files and Purple machine.

Working for the Soviet network headed by Semion Kremor, Klaus Fuchs begins stealing Allied atomic secrets.

Four German saboteurs land near Amagansett, R.I., and are quickly caught by Coast Guard sentries; south of

Jacksonville, Fla., four others land and are all taken in hand by the FBI within two weeks.

(July) Ernst Kaltenbrunner succeeds the assassinated Reinhard Heydrich as chief of the German RSHA.

SOE agent Yvonne Rudellat ("Jacqueline") helps the French Resistance blow up a power station and 2 locomotives before she is captured by the Gestapo.

The Allied Intelligence Bureau is established in Brisbane under the auspices of MacArthur's G-2 chief Mjr. Gen. Charles A. Willoughby; this inter-Allied group will perform all of the kinds of duties taken on elsewhere by OSS or SOE.

The Office of War Information is established within the U.S. Office of Emergency Management.

(August) Soviet agent Harro Schulze-Boysen of the Red Orchestra is arrested by the Gestapo in his Reich Air Ministry office.

British Combined Forces and Canadian troops in strength equal to a division raid the French coastal town of Dieppe.

SOE agent Peter Churchill lands by Parachute near Montpellier, France, where he is to act as leader of a team to organize and coordinate resistance groups in the area.

OSS agent Donald Coster tells several French friends in North Africa that the Allies will land in Dakar; the deception plan is soon passed to the Germans.

Via Ultra, the British learn of Rommel's plans for an attack at El Alamein.

By Fuehrer Directive 46, the S.S. is given responsibility for all German anti-partisan operations.

Prominent Soviet partisan leaders meet in Moscow.

U.S. Marines invade Guadalcanal; invaluable intelligence and rescue aid will be provided by the Yanks and the Australian Coastwatchers scattered throughout the Solomons.

The U.S. 2nd Marine Raider Battalion, under Lt. Col. Evans Carlson, raids Makin Island.

Guerrilla activities on Cebu Island, Philippines, come under the control of Harry Fenton and James H. Cushing; a clandestine radio station run by Lt. Col. Buillermo Nakar on Luzon is shut down by his capture.

(September) Wallace Carroll arrives in London to direct European operations for the U.S. Office of War Information.

From Bern, Soviet agent Otto Puenter warns Moscow of the dissolution of the Red Orchestra spy network in Berlin.

The Glomfjord power station is blown up by 10 British and 2 Norwegian Commandos; attempting to escape to Sweden, 7 men are captured—and later executed.

The Allied Translator and Interpreter Section, G-2, is established in General MacArthur's Southwest Pacific area.

(October) Hitler issues his infamous "Commando Order," calling for the execution of all captured sabotage parties "whether or not in uniform."

Once again, cryptanalysts of the German B-Dienst crack the British naval cipher leading to a period of increased submarine sinkings; for example, as the result of intercepts, U-boats sink 15 steamers from Atlantic convoy SC-107.

British Commandos raid Sark.

Mark Clark and Robert Murphy contact sympathetic Vichy leaders in Algeria in an effort to determine the French response to an Allied invasion.

Greek Republican EDES guerrillas conduct a successful ambush of an Italian convoy in the Louros Gorge.

The Philippine Sub-section of the Allied Intelligence Bureau is established.

Col. Claude Thorpe, who has organized guerrilla resistance in the Zambales Mountain area of Luzon, is caught by the Japanese and shot.

By this month, Col. Wendell W. Fertig has established a cohesive guerrilla organization on Mindanao.

(November) Abwehr agents arrest top Soviet spy Leopold Trepper in Paris; the Russian elects to collaborate resulting in the destruction of most Soviet spy nets in France and of the French Communist Resistance.

As a result of the German propaganda campaign in glorification of the U-boat, the Abwehr reaches the conclusion that the Allies have little shipping capacity left.

RAF bombers begin delivery to France of the propaganda tabloid "L'Amérique en Guerre."

Many French army personnel band together to form the *Organisation de Résistance de L'Armée.*

Allen Dulles is attached to the American legation in Bern as a special assistant, under which cover he begins to conduct operations for the OSS.

To aid in persuading Vichy forces of Allied good intentions, the British, via the Aspidistra radio transmitter, and

Americans, via a transmitter on the battleship *Texas*, broadcast propaganda and psychological warfare (psywar) messages into North Africa.

Rommel reports his plight after eight days of combat in the Battle of El Alamein and Hitler orders him to hold firm; Ultra delivers both messages to the British.

Allied forces land in French North Africa; the Germans mount a rapid reinforcement of Tunisia, a move told to the Allies by Ultra.

German troops enter and secure the Unoccupied Zone of Vichy, France.

In a pair of gliders, 30 specially trained engineer troops unsuccessfully attempt to land in Norway to destroy the Norsk Hydro heavy water plant; all are killed in glider crashes or executed upon capture.

The scattered elements of the Yugoslav Partisans are formed, by Tito, into the National Libertion Army.

Tito's guerrillas capture the important town of Bihach, south of Zagreb; since June, the Partisans have liberated a sixth of Yugoslavia.

Greek Communist ELAS guerrillas successfully raid the Italian-garrisoned Gorgopotamos viaduct south of Lamia.

SOE agent Ronald Seth is captured in Estonia.

Radio station KFS in San Francisco makes contact with guerrilla units in northern Luzon and on Panay.

OSS Detachment 101, under Lt. Col. William R. Peers, begins guerrilla operations in Burma, eventually recruiting and supporting a special army of Kachin tribesmen.

(December) In "Operation Frankton," twelve Commandos in canoes attack shipping in Bordeaux harbor sinking 4 vessels and damaging 2 others.

In a plan to cripple the English economy code named "Operation Bernard," the Abwehr prints large amounts of counterfeit British currency; the plan is never executed, however, the funds are sometimes used to pay spies, e.g., "Cicero."

Fourteen captured members of the Soviet Red Orchestra spy net are tried in Germany; thirteen are executed.

Aided by reconnaissance and Ultra intercepts, Allied aircraft begin to attack German points in Tunisia.

Brig. Gen. Robert A. McClure arrives in North Africa to take charge of American psywar operations.

S.S. Obergruppenfuehrer Erich von dem Bach-Zelewski is appointed to command all German anti-partisan units on the Eastern front.

1943 **(January)** The Special Warfare Branch of the U.S. Office of Naval Intelligence, under Captain Ellis M. Zacharias, begins psywar broadcasts designed to demoralize the Axis navies.

Gen. McClure's PsyWar Branch in Algiers begins to employ leaflets against Italian units in North Africa.

Allied aircraft begin dropping shipments of arms to Tito's Partisans.

Hitler decrees that German soldiers cannot be tried for atrocities committed while fighting partisans; the Allies and partisans take a different view.

In an unsuccessful effort to slow deportations, Jewish partisans in Warsaw attack armed elements of the S.S.

Jesse A. Villamor and five Filipinos arrive on Negros Island to coordinate the guerrilla movement and maintain contact with Australia.

(February) To escape forced labor drafts, thousands of Frenchmen begin escaping to the hills and woods to form Marquis bands; these undertake guerrilla warfare against the Germans and Vichy with the help of SOE/OSS.

Captured members of the Soviet Red Orchestra spy network continue to be tried in Germany; in total, over half of the 100 imprisoned agents are executed.

The White Rose student revolt in Munich is ruthlessly crushed by the Gestapo.

The Allies learn, via Ultra, of the amalgamation of Axis forces in North Africa and of growing tensions between German and Italian generals.

Ultra and regular intelligence channels fail to provide warning of Rommel's surprise assault at Kasserine Pass.

Reich propaganda minister Joseph Goebbels reveals to the German people the defeat of the 6th Army at Stalingrad; he cleverly seeks to put a moral victory in place of a great disaster by calling for total mobilization and renewed faith in the Fuehrer.

The German 3rd Panzer Army assaults the Soviet partisan center in the Surazh Rayon area, northeast of Vitebsk, in "Operation Kugelblitz."

The Indian 77th Brigade (Chindits) under Orde Wingate begins guerrilla operations in Burma, cutting the Mandalay-Myitkyina rail lines.

The Japanese begin an anti-guerrilla campaign against the OSS supported Kachin Rangers in north Burma.

(March) As a result of Ultra intelligence on German radar troops, British Prof. R. V. Jones works out the co-ordinates of German V-l test flights resulting in reconnaissance flights over Peenemünde.

The first SOE arms drop is made to the French Marquis.

A bomb placed in Hitler's transport plane by German army officers fails to detonate.

British MI-9 agent Albert-Marie Guerisse ("Pat O'Leary") is arrested in Toulouse by the Gestapo.

Flemming B. Muus arrives in Denmark to take over leadership of the resistance.

As a result of B-Dienst cryptanalysis, German U-boats sink 21 ships from Allied Atlantic convoy HX-229.

Ultra intercepts allow the Allies to sink a large number of German supply submarines in the Atlantic.

Dutch SOE agent Pieter Dourlein is caught attempting to land in Holland.

Under air and artillery attack, Tito's Partisans escape Axis encirclement at the Neretra River, capturing 15 Italian tanks.

XX agent Lily Sergueiev persuades the Germans to give her a radio to report on British invasion buildups—becoming the only woman in Abwehr history entrusted with her own clandestine radio.

The Chief of Staff of the Central Staff of the Partisan Movement, Lt. Gen. Pantiliemon K. Ponomarenko, is attached to the Soviet Army General Staff.

The U.S. Army Counterintelligence Corps (CIC) captures the records of the Italian secret service.

(April) Abwehr Colonel Rudolph von Gersdorff unsuccessfully attempts to assassinate Hitler in Berlin.

Abwehr counterintelligence expert Hugo Bleicher captures SOE agents Odette Sansom and Peter Churchill near Annecy, France.

Abwehr agent Dietrich Bonhoffer is arrested by the Gestapo.

The Conseil National de la Résistance (CNR) is established in France combining major insurgent parties.

The Reich Ministry of Propaganda begins promising the German people impressive victories through the use of "secret weapons."

In an effort to confuse the Germans as to the impending Allied invasion of Sicily, a corpse bearing secret but bogus papers about a proposed invasion of the Balkans is purposefully put into Nazi hands (via the Spanish) from a British submarine in "Operation Mincemeat."

From Switzerland, Soviet agent Rudolf Roessler ("Lucy") provides Moscow with data on the upcoming German offensive code named "Citadel."

S.S. troops under Jurgen Stroop move into the Warsaw Ghetto and meet strong and armed Jewish resistance.

In an effort to split the Allies, Goebbels reveals the Katyn Massacre, placing blame for it on the Soviets.

Russian partisans cut every rail line leading out of Bryansk.

Via Purple/Ultra, the Allies learn of an inspection tour by Admiral Yamamoto and arrange for his aerial assassination.

(May) The CNR recognizes Gen. De Gaulle as political leader of all elements within and outside France.

The final SOE agent is taken in Holland as the result of "Operation North Pole"—37 have been captured in all.

With the German B-Dienst reading their radio traffic, British naval leaders again change their cipher.

Via Ultra the Allies learn the Luftwaffe evacuation plans for Tunisia; as a result, fighters of the Northwest African Air Force are able to down large numbers of Ju-52's and Me-323's.

The German operation against resistance in the Warsaw Ghetto begun in April ends with S.S. claims of 56,000 Jews liquidated in combat for the loss of 70 soldiers.

The Germans open the first of five anti-partisan drives in Russia timed to end with the opening of "Operation Citadel."

In "Operation Schwartz," twelve Axis divisions with air support launch an unsuccessful effort to destroy four trapped Yugoslav Partisan divisions.

Cmdr. Charles Parsons makes the first of several clandestine visits to guerrilla bands in the Philippines.

The first Chindit campaign is completed in Burma.

(June) Air Vice-Marshal Basil Embry assumes command of RAF No. 2 Bomber Group, whose Mosquitos would later make a number of precision raids in support of resistance groups—occasionally with Embry participating.

Photo interpreters at the British Center for Aerial Assessment discover mysterious rockets in PRU reconnaissance pictures of the German research station at Peenemünde on the Baltic.

Allied warplanes drop 35 million propaganda leaflets on Sicily, Sardinia, Pantelleria, and southern Italy.

Via Ultra, the Allies learn the complete Axis order of battle in Sicily.

The location of the German forward H.Q. in Sicily is pinpointed for the Allies by Ultra; as a result, the place is subsequently hit by RAF bombers.

In the Gestapo's greatest coup, agents capture Jean Moulin and the leadership of the CNR at Caluire.

SOE agent Noor Inayat Khan ("Madeleine") arrives near Le Mans by "Moon Squadron" Lysander.

British Commandos under Mjr. John Appleyard mount a close reconnaissance of Pantelleria island.

Polish Home Army Command S. Rowecki is arrested by the Germans in Warsaw; he is subsequently succeeded by his deputy, Bor-Komorowski.

In "Operations Animals," Greek guerrillas attack German targets throughout the country to help convince the Germans, along with "Operation Mincemeat," that the next Allied drive in the Mediterranean would be aimed at Greece and not Sicily.

The Philippine Regional Section of the Allied Intelligence Bureau, under Col. Courtney Whitney, is established to aid Filipino guerrillas.

Abwehr agent Hans R. L. Harnisch aids in the coup which overthrows the Argentine government of President Castillo.

(July) In the first U.S. propaganda raids on Germany, 8th Air Force bombers drop 486 tons of leaflets on Cassel and Kiel.

S.S. officer Otto Skorzeny forms the German Friedenthal Special Formation, modeled after the British Commandos, to conduct special missions.

German aerial reconnaissance reveals the Allied invasion force en route to Sicily too late to affect the forthcoming invasion.

As a result of Ultra intelligence, Gen. Patton is able to make his famous dash to Palermo.

The U.S. Army CIC seizes German radar and wireless transmitter codes during the Sicilian invasion.

Lt. Col. William O. Darby's Rangers capture Castelventrano and its airfield on Sicily.

Polish exile Premier Sikorski is killed in a mysterious plane crash near Gibraltar.

Soviet Supreme Command orders the partisans to start an all-out "rail war."

German forces launch "Operation Citadel," but as a result of intelligence from "Lucy," the Russians are ready to meet it.

The Office of Economic Warfare is established within the U.S. Office of Emergency Management.

(August) Via Ultra the Allies learn the complete order of battle for German forces in southern Italy.

The Enigma cipher machine also tells the Allies the route of march of German reinforcements moving into southern Italy; as a result, they are heavily attacked by planes of the Northwest African Air Force.

S.S. Capt. Otto Skorzeny and 90 of his commandos rescue Mussolini from a prison high in the Apennines.

A Luftwaffe radio reconnaissance unit in Greece detects U.S. bombers taking off from Benghazi and alerts the defenses of Ploesti; as a result, the Americans lose 53 B-24 Liberators.

Despite SOE assistance, guerrillas of the Albanian Front and National Liberation Movement begin to battle each other.

In an effort to undermine the Nazi regime, Soviet propagandists establish the Free Germany National Committee and its subsidiary, the Union of German Officers.

The German advance of "Operation Citadel" is turned into a military disaster.

Soviet partisans attack German supply lines behind German Army Group Centre laying over 4,100 demolitions on railways.

(September) U.S. and British aircraft begin delivery of arms and supplies to the French Marquis in "Operation Carpetbagger."

An SOE mission, comprising Pierre Brossolette and Edward Yeo-Thomas, is landed in France to reconstitute the CNR.

Royal Navy mini-subs known as "X-craft" damage the German battleship *Tirpitz* in a Norwegian fjord.

The British 2nd and 41st Commando and the U.S. 1st, 3rd, and 4th Ranger Battalions participate in the Salerno landings and campaign.

Brig. Fitzroy Maclean, chief of Britain's military mission to Tito's Partisans, is parachuted into Yugoslavia.

Employing canoes launched from a submarine, 13 Australian commandos sink 4,000 tons of shipping in Singapore Harbor.

Allied Intelligence Bureau agents are slipped into New Britain.

(October) Famed Commando leader Robert E. Laycock

succeeds Lord Mountbatten as chief of the British Combined Operations.

The first SOE agents are dropped to make contact with the Marquis.

SOE agent Noor Inayat Khan ("Madeleine") is betrayed to the Germans by an unknown French woman.

Liberators of the U.S. 422nd Bomb Sqn. are assigned solely to propaganda leaflet missions from England.

French and Moroccan troops, plus a small OSS party, gain control of Corsica.

Soviet partisans wreak havoc on railways the Germans are employing to bring reinforcements into the Nevel area.

In "Operation Zeppelin-North," Abwehr agents are dropped behind Russian lines; taken by the NKVD, the initial spies are used in a Soviet-version of the German "North Pole" operation in Holland, to lure by radio additional Nazi operatives to their deaths.

Yugoslav Chetniks destroy a vital rail bridge over the Drina River in eastern Bosnia.

The OSS assembles a fleet of small vessels to run supplies from southern Italy to the Yugoslav Partisan base on the island of Vis.

Allied Intelligence Bureau agent Emegdio Cruz tours the Philippines compiling data about the Japanese puppet government.

Col. Rupert K. Kangleon assumes command of guerrilla units on Leyte.

AIB agents under L. H. Phillips establish a clandestine radio station on Mindoro.

(November) Via Ultra the Allied learn that Field Marshal Rommel has been sent to inspect Atlantic Wall defenses.

French agent Michael Hollard reports to London on German "ski sites" (V-1 emplacements) being constructed in Northern France and aimed at Britain.

The French CNR is reconstituted under the leadership of Georges Bidault.

Swiss counterespionage agents arrest Soviet radio operator Alexander Foote in Lausanne; skipping bail, he makes his way to Moscow via Paris and Cairo.

S.S. troops under Erich von dem Bach-Zelewski launch "Operation Heinrich" against Russian partisans in the Rossono region.

Fighting erupts between the Greek guerrilla forces EDES

and ELAS; in "Operation Panther," German troops attack units of both Greek factions exacting a heavy toll among the partisans.

(December) The London group of SOE and the Special Operations Branch of OSS-London are formed into a single H.Q. known as SOE/SO.

The Psychological Warfare Division of the Allied Expeditionary Force is established in London.

Col. Noel Wild activates the Anglo-American Deception Unit at SHAPE H.Q.

British aerial photography expert Constance Babington-Smith definitely identifies the pilotless planes (V-1) located earlier on "ski ramps."

Elyesa Bazna ("Cicero"), valet of the British ambassador in Ankara, provides the Germans with a transcript of the proceedings of the Allied Tehran Conference and other documents; the Abwehr considers them plants by British intelligence and ignores them.

Working in the U.S., Soviet spy Klaus Fuchs begins 2½ years of atomic espionage at Los Alamos, passing his information on through American traitor Harry Gold.

1944   **(January)** The Vichy Militia battles the Savoy Marquis.

MI-6 dispatches an informant to Spain to provide complete, but false, intelligence about Allied invasion plans; the data is ignored by the Germans who refuse to believe it.

British X-craft carry out a beach reconnaissance of Normandy.

Gen. Alexander von Falkenhausen convinces Field Marshall Rommel to join anti-Hitler conspiracy.

The British Landing-craft Obstruction Clearance Unit (frogman) school is opened on the North Devon coast.

The first Inter-Allied special mission ("Operation Union"), led by British officer H. H. A. Thachthwaite and U.S. Marine Peter Ortis, is parachuted into the Rhone valley.

RAF Transport Command increases supply flights in support of the French Resistance.

U.S. Rangers and British Commandos participate in the Anzio landing.

The OSS Fifth Army Detachment locates the first German reinforcements at Anzio and determines the direction of the main enemy counterattack.

Italian partisans form the unified Committee of National Liberation of Upper Italy (CLNAI).

Soviet partisan bands move into the Pripyat marshes en route towards Kovel and Lutsk.

The British 9th Commando raids Hvan, Yugoslavia.

An Abwehr secretary in Ankara defects to the Americans exposing the Cicero operation.

In their first Pacific appearance, frogmen of the U.S. Pacific Fleet Underwater Demolition Unit explore the beaches of Kwajalein.

Velvalee Dickinson is arrested by the FBI as a Japanese spy.

The FBI and BSC expose German operations in Argentina forcing the country to break relations with the Third Reich.

(February) Allied reconnaissance aircraft begin an extensive reconnaissance of the French Channel coast.

In "Operation Jericho," RAF Mosquitos of No. 140 Wing bomb Amiens jail to free French Resistance prisoners.

Having escaped Haaren prison back in August 1943, SOE agent Pieter Dourlein finally reaches England, where he is unable to persuade his commander that the Dutch network has been compromised.

Abwehr chief Canaris meets Wehrmacht G-2 boss Col. Alexis von Roenne to discuss the possibilities of an Allied invasion of France; a review of all available data convinces the two that any landing will come in the Pas de Calais area.

The defection of several Abwehr agents and the failure of military intelligence to provide data as to Allied intentions at Anzio gives Himmler the chance to create a scandal which brings Hitler to dismiss Admiral Canaris as chief of the Abwehr.

In "Operation Ratweek," SOE/SO launches a Europe-wide operation aimed at assassinating senior Gestapo officers.

SOE agent Nancy Wake ("Madame Andrée") is parachuted into the Auvergne to aid the Marquis.

Capt. Knut Hankelid and several companions from Norwegian Resistance sink a train ferry in Lake Tinnsjo, successfully destroying the results of all German heavy water production then en route to the Reich.

The British persuade the Greek guerrilla forces EDES and ELAS to agree to an armistice in their civil war.

All British aid to the Yugoslav Chetniks is halted.

J. Edgar Hoover persuades the White House to block an exchange of missions between the OSS and NKVD fearing an influx of Soviet spies into America.

Acting on FBI information, Chilean police arrest German agent Bernardo Timmerman and break up the PQZ radio espionage network.

Mjr. Gen. Clayton Bissell succeeds Gen. George Strong as U.S. Army Assistant Chief of Staff, G-2.

(March) The Psychological Warfare Division of SHAPE begins a campaign of challenge to the Luftwaffe designed to increase interceptions of American bombers and increasing numbers of "kills" for escorting fighters.

In "Operation Fortitude," the Allies in England launch a massive deception campaign, including the establishment of a bogus army under Gen. Patton, designed to convince the Germans that any invasion would come elsewhere than Normandy.

Gen. De Gaulle proclaims the unification of all French Resistance forces under Gen. P. J. Koenig's *Forces Françaises de l'Intérieur* (FFI).

The Communist Action Group in Rome blows up 32 German police; in reprisal, 355 Italian hostages are excuted in the Ardeatine Caves.

The Polish underground reports German missile tests being held at Blizna.

Capt. Salvador Abcede assumes command of all guerrilla units on Negros Island, P.I.

Supported by the 1st Air Commando, the second Chindit raid into Burma begins; returning from an inspection of his organization's progress, Brig. Orde Wingate is killed when his plane crashes into a mountain.

The U.S. 5307th Regiment (Provisional), nicknamed "Merrill's Marauders" after its commander, Brig. Gen. Frank Merrill, unsuccessfully attempts to envelop Inkangahtawang, Burma.

(April) Via Ultra the Allies learn of a special German H.Q. near Amiens designed to control V-1 operations.

A team of British XX agents headed by Luis Calvo ("Garbo") floods Germany with bogus data on the Allied buildup in Britain.

A Vichy police report showing considerable damage caused to railroads by the French Resistance reaches London via SOE/SO, bringing about renewed SHAPE interest in the possible contribution of the FFI in the upcoming invasion.

After considerable soul searching, Allied leaders and Gen. Pierre Koenig of the FFI agree that aerial attacks on strategic targets in French towns must be made without regard to civilian losses.

In an effort to slow German labor drafts, RAF Mosquitos of No. 613 Squadron attack the Dutch Central Population Registry.

Abwehr Col. H. J. Giskes radios London and boldly announces the end of the *Englandspiel* ("England Game"), also known as "Operation North Pole," whereby he had compromised and captured all SOE agents landing in Holland.

Mussolini's puppet government in northern Italy announces the death penalty for all captured partisans.

The German Third Panzer Army launches "Operation Regenschauer" and "Operation Fruehlingsfest" against the Ushachi Partisan Republic, a large guerrilla colony in Russia, smashing it within a month.

The Greek Communist ELAS attacks the weaker republican EKKA and destroys it.

As a result of Ultra intelligence, the British 14th Army forms air-supplied boxes and defeats the Japanese in the battles of Imphal and Kohima.

(**May**) The German Abwehr is abolished with the OKW retaining some of its functions within the newly formed Mil. Amt.

Via Ultra the Allies learn that 50 V-1 sites are operational in France; the American and British air forces begin "Operation Crossbow" in an effort to destroy them.

XX agent Hans Hansen ("Tate") radios false data to Germany on British train traffic reinforcing the idea of an Allied invasion in the Pas de Calais area.

Responding to the Allied psywar campaign against the Luftwaffe, Reich Propaganda Minister Goebbels begins an internal propaganda operation designed to inflame the German people over American and British aerial atrocities.

Gen. Karl Dittmer of the German General Staff makes several psywar broadcasts to the German people telling them that the Reich is being "encircled" and laying the groundwork for a new psychology and policy of strategic defense.

The combined British-American SOE/SO is redesignated Special Force Headquarters (SFHQ) and is given the task of handling FFI problems in northern France; a separate counterpart, Special Project Operations Center (SPOC) is formed to look after resistance affairs in southern France.

Via Ultra the Allies learn of German plans to hold their panzer forces in Normandy as a reserve.

The BBC communicates orders, via its "Personal Messages" code some of which has been broken by the Germans, to the FFI concerning its assistance to the Allies on D-Day; these communications bring a general Marquis uprising all over France, much of it premature and put down by the Wehrmacht and S.S.

SHAPE G-2 incorrectly reports that Allied air raids on the French rail system have been unsuccessful.

S.S. Gen. Walter Schellenberg becomes head of a unified German secret service designed to replace the defunct Abwehr.

The Norwegian Resistance group known as the "Oslo Squad," under Gunnar Sonsteby, raids the firm of Watson Norsk destroying three tabulating machines about to be employed by the Germans to speed up their forced labor draft.

Despite Ultra intelligence which reveals German weak points, Gen. Mark Clark fails in his attempt to reach Rome.

Compromised, the British XX network in Portugal run by Dusko Popov ("Trycycle") collapses.

The German Third Panzer Army opens "Operation Kormoran" against Soviet partisans in the Minsk area claiming 13,000 Russian casualties within a month.

SOE agents successfully kidnap Gen. Heinrich Kreipe, German commander of the Crete garrison.

S.S. glider troops and parachutists nearly succeed in capturing Tito at Drvar.

A large number of AIB agents are landed on Samar and Mindanao by submarine.

Merrill's Marauders and Kachin Rangers of OSS Detachment 101 capture Myitkyina airfield in Burma; the Kachin Rangers also gain temporary possession of Washang, east of Myitkyina.

(June) Allied forces invade Normandy.

Three-man teams ("Jedburghs") are sent into France to provide communications and leadership aid to the FFI; larger units, U.S. Operational Groups and British Special Air Service forces, are sent in for independent tactical movement or use in stiffening the FFI.

Via Ultra the Allies learn of German reactions to the Normandy invasion, including troop and panzer movements, defensive plans, and withdrawals.

Via Ultra the Allies learn of German orders to France

directing the commencement of the V-1 campaign against Britain.

The 4th French SAS battalion arrives northeast of Vannes to foster an armed revolt against the Germans.

Alerted by Ultra, Allied fighter-bombers attack the German 7th Army as it moves on Bayeux.

The *État-Major des Forces Française de l'Intérieur* (EMFFI) is established in London under Gen. Koenig to co-ordinate Allied activities in support of the FFI; representatives on the staff come from the SFHQ, SOE, OSS, and the French intelligence group, BCRA.

As the V-1's are sent toward Britain, the German Propaganda Ministry in broadcasts in the Reich population, impresses the retaliatory nature of the weapon.

On D-Day, 27 million Allied propaganda leaflets are dropped on the Channel coast between Brittany and the Zuider Zee.

U.S. 8th Air Force bombers drop 300 tons of supplies to FFI forces in four areas of southern France.

Having learned via Ultra of the German evacuation of Rome, Gen. Clark's troops occupy the city.

The Italian partisan Committee of National Liberation of Northern Italy forms its military arm, the Volunteers of Liberty Corps.

Soviet partisans place over 5,000 charges on roads and railways behind the German Second and Fourth Armies.

The American Observer Group ("Dixie Mission"), under OSS Col. David Barret, is sent into the Communist-controlled areas of northern China where it will gather intelligence and assist downed flyers.

(July) Via Ultra, the Allies learn that Hitler has taken personal command over the whole western theater; the Enigma machine also reveals German orders to move the V-weapons launching facilities inland from the Pas de Calais.

RAF Mosquitos of No. 140 Wing destroy the Gestapo barracks at Bonnevil, France.

The Marquis "Republic of Vercours" is destroyed by the Germans in a desperate combat.

An RAF Dakota arrives in Britain, via Italy from Poland, where it has obtained parts of a German V-2 missile supplied by Home Army agent.

Via an agent, the OSS learns the details of the forthcoming German plot against Hitler ten days before it occurs.

Wehrmacht Col. Count Klaus von Stauffenberg places a bomb in Hitler's conference room which explodes, but fails to kill the Fuehrer; thousands of Germans, in addition to the actual plotters, die in reprisal over the unsuccessful July 20 scheme.

Allied psywar organs in London and Moscow beam radio programs to Germany in an effort to discourage the population over the July 20 plot; the Reich Propaganda Ministry and Joseph Goebbels, who took a vital role in maintaining the government during the critical hours, assure the German people that "Providence took the Fuehrer under its gracious protection."

The Norwegian Resistance group known as the Oslo Squad hijacks a German truck containing 75,000 ration cards, turning them over to the Milorg.

Ten GRU agents are parachuted into East Prussia to gather intelligence for the advancing Red Army.

With the opening of the great Russian summer offensive, the Soviet partisan movement begins to go out of business as its members in liberated areas are placed in the Red Army.

Dr. Allen Nunn May begins passing atomic secrets to Soviet agents in Canada.

(August) Via Ultra the Allies learn of Hitler's plan to counterattack the invaders in the Avranches area; as a result, the Allies are able to envelop Von Kluge's 7th army at Falaise and virtually destroy it.

The BBC broadcasts a deception concerning an American division moving south of the Loire.

The Allied scientific intelligence ALSOS Mission is sent to Europe to begin seeking data on German scientific-atomic developments.

Working closely with the FFI, Gen. Patton's 3rd Army liberates Brittany.

The Paris police, by order of the FFI, goes on strike while partisans take over important government buildings and open an armed revolt against the German occupiers; Gen. von Choltitz, German commander in Paris, effects a truce with the FFI in order to remove his troops, however, Communist partisans in Paris break the agreement leading to a resumption of hostilities.

The French revolt in Paris ends when Gen. von Choltitz surrenders the city to Gen. Leclerc.

In preparation for the Allied landing, FFI forces in southern France are placed under the command of Gabriel Cochet; in "Operation Anvil," Allied forces invade southern France.

Allied propagandists in London begin to proclaim that the end of the European war is approaching.

RAF Mosquitos of No. 139 Wing attack the Gestapo barracks at Poitiers and the S.S. saboteur school at Chateau Maulny.

The Polish Home Army raises the standard of revolt in Warsaw; German forces under von dem Bach-Zelewski eventually crush the ghetto defenders on October 2.

Some 250 downed U.S. airmen are rescued by Yugoslav Chetniks.

Prime Minister Churchill meets Yugoslav Partisan leader Tito in Naples.

(September) Allied propagandists proclaim the beginning of the Battle of Germany.

Captured by U.S. troops, Radio Luxemburg is put on the air to rebroadcast psywar programs from New York and London.

The OSS Seventh Army Detachment in France begins infiltrating agents into Germany.

Joseph Goebbels begins to inform the Reich population of the "Morgenthau Plan," a leveling of the country proposed by the U.S. Treasury Secretary as the postwar fate of Germany.

FFI forces capture the southern France communications center of Seez.

SHAPE G-2, MI-6, and the Dutch Resistance warn of the German use of Holland as a rest and reequipment area for troops coming out of France; ignoring this advice and receiving no Ultra warning, Gen. Montgomery proceeds with the disastrous "Operation Market-Garden," an airborne landing at Arnhem.

Special German troops begin launching V-2 missiles at London and Antwerp.

"Operation Carpetbagger," the aerial resupply of the FFI, ends.

Together with three other female SOE agents, Noor Inayat Khan ("Madeleine") is executed in Dachau concentration camp.

Forty-eight SOE agents, nearly all of those sent to Holland in 1942–1943 and caught as a result of "Operation North Pole," are executed in Mauthausen concentration camp.

As a result of Ultra, Gen. Clark's 5th Army begins the successful bypassing of German Apennine defenses and reaches the Lombardy plains and Po River.

In the area between Florence and Bologna, the German 10th Panzer Division destroys the Italian partisan Red Star Brigade.

British Lt. Gen. R. M. Scobie is ordered to assume control of all guerrilla bands operating in Greece.

The British Special Boat Squadron aids in the capture of Patras, off Greece.

Allied intelligence services make an accurate estimate as to the Japanese naval defense of the Philippines.

Mjr. Russell W. Volckmann's guerrillas on Luzon finally establish radio contact with Australia.

(**October**) In "Operation Pegasus," the British MI-9 and Dutch underground rescue many survivors of the 1st Airborne Division who have evaded capture since the Battle of Arnhem.

RAF Mosquitos of No. 140 Wing bomb the Gestapo H.Q. in Aarhus University, Jutland.

The Allies order the partisans of northern Italy to sabotage the main roads of Venetia and hold the Alpine passes; a German counterattack on Monte Grappa disperses a 1700-member guerrilla band.

Led by Otto Skorzeny, S.S. commandos kidnap the son of Admiral Horthy, forcing the Hungarian leader to nullify an armistice between Russia and Hungary.

Yugoslav Partisans assist the Red Army in the capture of Belgrade; unaided, the Partisans take the Dalmatian ports of Dubrovnik and Split.

Led by Mjr. Ivan Lyon, Australian commandos in canoes raid shipping in Singapore Harbor.

Guerrilla units on Leyte assist the American invasion through military action and sabotage.

Intelligence sources and reconnaissance by air and submarine reveal the positions of major Japanese fleet elements leading to the crushing American victory in the Battle of Leyte Gulf.

As OSS agent is parachuted into Siam to contact the Regent of Thailand, Luang Pradit, who is desirous of working as a double agent; as "Ruth," he functions in behalf of the Allies while still technically governing the country for the Japanese.

Famed Soviet agent Richard Sorge is executed in Tokyo.

(**November**) S.S. chief Himmler authorizes captured Russian general Andrei Vlasov's formation of an anti-Stalinist "Committee for the Liberation of the Peoples of Russia"; later outfitted with Russian POW's and other soldiers, Vlasov is given the chance to fight on the eastern front where he causes more concern to the Germans than to the Soviets.

Himmler raises a virulent S.S. raiding group known as the "Werewolves."

Yugoslav partisans take Zara and Šibenik on the Dalmatian coast.

OSS chief Gen. Donovan submits a detailed memo to President Roosevelt outlining a possible U.S. National Intelligence Agency for the period after the war.

(**December**) In "Operation Heinrich," Col. H. J. Giskes arranges for slave laborers to escape to the U.S. 1st Army with false information.

In "Operation Griffin," troops of Otto Skorzeny's 150th Panzerbrigade, dressed as U.S. soldiers, cross U.S. lines to carry out reconnaissance and sabotage during the Battle of the Bulge; the ploy is very successful, although a large number of agents are caught and executed.

Due to extreme security, the Germans are able to launch the surprise Ardennes campaign without radio traffic giving the plan away to Ultra.

Greek guerrillas and British soldiers battle in Athens in a 6-week civil war.

The U.S. 1st Cavalry Division and local guerrillas capture the important Taft-Wright Highway on Samar Island.

Col. David Barret of "Dixie Mission" in north China proposes an OSS-controlled guerrilla force; the idea is turned down by his superiors.

1945   (**January**) Hitler launches a counterattack in Alsace; as the result of Ultra intelligence, the U.S. 7th Army is able to contain it.

British XX agent Hans Hansen ("Tate") radios false data concerning British minefields to German U-boat H.Q. in an effort to counteract the activities of Schnorkel-equipped submarines around the British Isles.

Captured SOE female agents Violette Szabo, Denise Bloch, and Lilian Rolfe are executed by the Germans.

German mini-subs known as Seehund are employed against Allied shipping in the Scheldt estuary.

In support of the American invasion of Mindanao, guerrillas under Col. Wendell Fertig secure the beaches near Bugo, seize the Tagum and Talikub river fronts, and guard Highway #1 for the U.S. 24th Division.

Guerrillas under Robert Lapham assist the U.S. 6th Rangers in freeing 500 Allied internees from Cabanatuan prison camp.

(February) Via Ultra the Allies learn of German plans for defenses on the Siegfried Line; the intelligence leads to British attacks north of the defended area.

In his last successful propaganda coup, Reich Minister of Propaganda Joseph Goebbels invents the "National Redoubt."

The first OSS agent is captured by the Special Command of the German S.D. in Holland.

RAF Mosquitos of No. 140 Wing blast the Gestapo H.Q. in the Shellhause building in Copenhagen.

From his headquarters in Bern, OSS official Allen Dulles begins two months of negotiations which lead to the surrender of northern Italy by S.S. Gen. Karl Wolff.

Luzon guerrillas assist the U.S. 11th Airborne reach and release 2,100 prisoners from the Los Banos concentration camp.

OSS and SOE agents are regularly placed into Siam to aid the resistance of "Ruth," Regent Luang Pradit.

Kachin Rangers of OSS Detachment 101 briefly hold a hill overlooking the Hsenwi-Lashio road in Burma, inflicting losses on the Japanese.

Gen. Donovan's plan for a postwar U.S. intelligence agency is leaked to the press, bringing an editorial storm.

(March) Via Ultra the Allies learn of German dispositions along the Rhine; the information allows troops of Montgomery and Patton to cross almost without incident.

Deposed Abwehr chief Adm. Wilhelm Canaris and agent/minister Dietrich Bonhoffer are executed at Flossenberg concentration camp in Bavaria.

In "Operation Green-Up," a three-man OSS team is parachuted into the area of the so-called "National Redoubt" to reconnoiter the region, sabotage German defense installations, and establish contacts with the Austrian resistance.

The first permanent OSS radio transmitter in Germany is established by a team code named "Chauffeur"; it is located in the silo of a dairy farm near Egensburg.

Supported by U.S. 5th Air Force warplanes, Luzon guerrillas clear the Japanese from Ilocos Norte Province, capturing the towns of San Fernando, Bagnio, Cervantes, Tuguegarao, and taking the Balite Pass.

The Assistant Chief of Staff, G-5, Far East Command, is placed in charge of all clandestine warfare activity in China.

(April) German intelligence chief Schellenberg arranges secret meetings between Himmler and Count Bernadotte of Sweden to discuss an armistice.

The Gestapo school at Odense is destroyed by RAF Mosquitos of No. 140 Wing.

The American ALSOS mission arrives at Hechingen to investigate the German nuclear research effort centered in that town.

OSS agents Carl Wiberg and Hennings Jessen-Schmidt report Hitler's presence in the town of Bernau and from a nearby location watch the RAF destroy the town; the Fuehrer, it turns out, was in his Berlin bunker instead.

OSS agent Sgt. Fred Mayer secures the surrender of key German officials of the Austrian Tyrol, which encourages the "O5" Resistance, under Dr. Karl Gruber to revolt and seize Innsbruck.

The NKVD's Special Section (00) begins to search for German war criminals in Russian-occupied Germany.

Urban partisans stage insurrections in Genoa, Milan, and Turin.

Italian partisans under Count P. B. Delle Stelle capture Mussolini, his mistress, and several supporters; near Dongo, they are executed.

Via Ultra the Allies learn the complete Japanese order-of-battle on Borneo; the data leads to a successful invasion.

With 3,200 men, OSS Detachment 101 begins a 3-month campaign to clear the Japanese from Burma's central Shan States in support of the British advance on Rangoon.

(May) The Russians capture Berlin.

Germany surrenders unconditionally; large numbers of

German intelligence agents and officials, e.g., Schellenberg, Gehlen, Kaltenbrunner, fall into Allied hands while the liberators set free numerous SOE, OSS, and other agents from concentration camps.

Gunnar Sonsteby's Oslo Squad covertly obtains Gestapo records on Norwegian traitors and war criminals.

The NKVD scatters leading captured members of the Reich Chancellery Group into a whole series of camps stretching from Berlin via Poland to Moscow.

In Bern, Japanese Navy Cmdr. Yoshiro Fujimura and agent Dr. Friedrich Hack open unsuccessful peace discussions with Allen Dulles of the OSS.

Capt. Ellis Zacharias and the OWI develop a plan, code named "I-45," for a bold psywar thrust at the Japanese Cabinet, employing propaganda broadcasts from Washington to Tokyo.

U.S. forces wage a psywar campaign against the defenders of Okinawa.

Filipino guerrillas under Col. Wendell Fertig capture Malabang airfield on Mindanao.

Three OSS-controlled guerrilla groups begin operations against Japanese railways, troop movements, and supply dumps in China.

(June) As the result of an Ultra/Purple report, the U.S. submarine *Trenchant* sinks the Japanese cruiser *Ashigara* off Indonesia; throughout the Pacific war, such intelligence has given U.S. submarine wolfpacks the opportunity to destroy large numbers of Nipponese war- and merchant-shipping.

Kachin Rangers of OSS Detachment 101 capture Liolem, Burma, and conclude the clearing of the Shan Hills.

(July) British X-craft sink the Japanese cruiser *Takao* in Singapore Harbor.

OSS Detachment 101 is disbanded; in addition to combat, the unit is credited with having provided almost all intelligence employed by the U.S. 10th Air Force in hitting Burmese targets.

As part of "Operation Carbonado," OSS guerrilla groups seize the high ground near Tanchuk airfield in China.

(August) American OWI psywar experts, under the direction of Capt. Ellis Zacharias, conduct the "I-45" campaign against the Japanese leadership.

OSS agents rescue POW's from various Japanese camps in China.

OSS agents are sent to reconnoiter the area of China held by the Communists and pass their intelligence back to Washington; agent John Birch is executed by Red Guerrillas near Suchow.

Ho Chi Minh and Vo Nguyen Giap march the Vietminh guerrillas into Hanoi and proclaim a provisional government.

Following the dropping of two atomic bombs by the Americans, Japan surrenders unconditionally.

The U.S. Office of War Information is terminated by Executive Order 9608.

(September) The Japanese surrender document is signed in Tokyo Bay; with this ceremony, World War II ends.

Tried for treason for broadcasting German propaganda, John Amery, son of a British Cabinet official, admits his guilt and is convicted in 8 minutes; Amery will hang in December.

OSS agents in Manchuria document the Russian dismemberment of captured Japanese factories.

Soviet cipher clerk Igor Gouzenko defects to the RCMP, revealing a large wartime Russian espionage network in Canada.

The OSS is terminated by Executive Order 9621; the British SOE suffers the same fate within weeks.

Preface

Background

A vast "secret war" was fought around the globe during the years 1939–1945 as part and parcel of that huge conflict known as the Second World War. The role of intelligence, propaganda and psychological warfare, resistance movements, and military special forces was one of the most dramatic and, until recently, lightly regarded aspects of the fight.

Although literature pertaining to these subjects was produced, the emphasis during the first three decades after that conflict was primarily on tales of the battlefield or conference table. Accounts of the secret war appear to have been dismissed as secondary in value and confined almost totally to that half-recognized shadow world of popular spy fiction.

In the late 1960s and early 1970s several events conspired to bring recognition to the secret war of 1939–1945. Principal among these was an ongoing interest in insurgency and counterinsurgency, the investigations of the U.S. intelligence community by Congress and the press, and, most important for this work, the emergence of startling new evidence. The declassification of certain British documents, the revelation of the "Ultra" secret, and the release of OSS archival material brought serious recognition to the importance of the secret war in a way no memoir of general history could. Lack of scholarly interest as a whole was no longer a problem. Conferences to discuss intelligence, as well as very different aspects of the resistance situation, became common. As a result, new titles enter the arena almost monthly, their flow apparently unchecked and the enthusiasm of their authors unrivaled among the producers of Big War literature.

Several years ago when addressing the sea and air services aspects of the conflict, I joined a select group of students who had noticed and were attempting to do something about the dearth of good, useful English-language bibliographies on World War II, either in whole or in part. Unfortunately, the difficulties of control continue to exist on all fronts for English-language sources, even though a few more gallant bibliotroopers have entered the fray.

In my preparation for this work, I found only a few bibliographies in English devoted to the war as a whole and none of any consequence concerned entirely with its secret aspects. Several guides have treated the subject of intelligence from ancient times to the present and at least one (Blackstock/Schaf) is extremely well annotated. Most of these contain at best only a few hundred citations, are unpublished, or are twenty-five or are more years out of date. The principal reason for this state of affairs is that, despite current interest, so little was done bibliographically in Britain or America over the past decades on the war as a whole that few have gotten around to a concentration on its shadowy side.

This is not to say that nothing is being accomplished. The Subcommittee on Bibliography of the American Committee on the History of the Second World War, under the able chairmanship of Ms. Janet Ziegler, has been working on World War II literature control problems for several years. In the non-English language speaking world, interest in the secret war is high, and judging from various foreign pieces examined or described in the foreword to Ms. Ziegler's bibliography, that interest appears to be growing. The *La Libération de la France: Bibliographie*, put out by the Comité d'Histoire de la 2ᵉ Guerre Mondiale, is an excellent example of work being done overseas.

Objectives

This bibliography is intended to serve as a working guide to English-language sources concerning intelligence, propaganda and psychological warfare, resistance, and military special forces of the World War II era written during the years 1939–early 1979. While aimed primarily at scholars and especially graduate and undergraduate students, it should also prove useful to librarians, general readers, and journalists. It may prove also to be interesting to that category of specialized student known as the "World War II enthusiast."

This guide is not definitive, but it attempts comprehensiveness in that virtually all factors concerning the secret war are covered. As a reference tool, it will permit its user to quickly determine what material is available and help him to establish a basis for further research. In general, the items cited are those the user might reasonably expect to find in large university, public, or government libraries. In practice, students should be able to find many of the more recent book titles in small- or medium-sized college or public library collections. Should you be unable to turn up a given reference locally, keep in mind that many items cited are available through interlibrary loan, details of which service can be obtained at your nearest library.

The criteria for selection in this compilation are the same as those employed in my *World War II at Sea: A Bibliography of Sources in English* and *Air War Bibliography Series, 1939–1945*. The following types of published material are represented below: books and monographs, scholarly papers, periodical and journal articles, government documents, doctoral dissertations, and masters' theses. Although much has been included, it was necessary to draw a line somewhere and omit certain kinds of information. Excluded materials include fiction, obvious children's works, newspaper articles (unless reprinted in other works), poetry, and book reviews.

Arrangement

The eight main sections of the table of contents, with their subsections, form a classified subject index to this guide and the key to the manner in which the book is laid out. Within the text, each alphabetically arranged section receives a brief introduction outlining its task and concludes with a note on "further references" designed to guide the user to other sections containing related materials. By and large, references are not repeated from one section to another.

Each citation receives an entry number. These entry numbers run consecutively throughout the guide. An author index keyed to entry numbers is provided. Annotations of a noncritical nature are provided on a few occasions, basically in order to clarify title content. Unnumbered cross-references to joint authors, editors, and spy aliases are provided within the body of the text where appropriate.

Acknowledgments

For their advice, assistance, or encouragement in the formulation, research, and completion of this endeavor, the following persons and libraries are gratefully acknowledged. Their involvement does not necessarily constitute endorsement.

Dr. Dean C. Allard, Head, Operational Archives Branch, U.S. Naval Historical Center

Mr. Robert B. Lane, Director, Air University Library

Hon. John Ashbrook, U.S. House of Representatives Permanent Select Committee on Intelligence

Hon. Edward P. Boland, U.S. House of Representatives Permanent Select Committee on Intelligence

Hon. Birch Bayh, U.S. Senate Select Committee on Intelligence

Dr. Arthur L. Funk, Chairman, American Committee on the History of the Second World War

Mr. Charles E. Wilson, Chief, Plans and Policy Branch, U.S. Central Intelligence Agency

Dr. Walter Pforzheimer, Washington, D. C.

The Association of Former Intelligence Officers, McLean, Virginia

West Virginia University Library

U.S. Navy Department Library

U.S. Air University Library

U.S. Army Military History Institute

Special appreciation is reserved for my colleagues at Salem College without whose backing and aid this project would not have gotten out of file boxes. President James C. Stam and Dean Ronald O. Champagne provided continuous support and encouragement to proceed. The Political Science Department, chaired by Dr. Jesse Kelly and including Dr. David Lynch, provided stimulation, insight, and resources. Mrs. Sara J. Graham, Margaret Allen, Jacqueline Isaacs, and Sara Casey of the Benedum Learning Resources Center staff gave bibliographic and interlibrary loan assistance.

To series editor Richard Burns and publisher Lloyd Garrison go my appreciation for their support and guidance, to say nothing of their endurance.

Finally, hearty thanks is due to Professor Lyman B. Kirkpatrick, Jr., of the Political Science Department of Brown University. A veteran of more than twenty-two years in the intelligence services of America who began his career with the Office of Strategic Services, served as an intelligence staff officer at the headquarters of General Omar Bradley's Twelfth Army Group, and rose to the number-three position, Executive Director, of the Central Intelligence Agency, the professor breathes insight and wisdom into the story of the secret war, the subject of his excellent historical introduction.

The Lessons of History

LYMAN B. KIRKPATRICK, JR.
BROWN UNIVERSITY

It is appropriate that the quotation by John Singleton Mosby opens this volume. When I returned to the United States at the end of World War II after having spent nearly three years in Europe working in various aspects of the "secret wars," I bought a home in Fairfax Courthouse, Virginia, on land that Mosby's Rangers had crossed in March 1863 to capture the Union area Commander Brigadier General H. G. Stoughton, who was asleep in his headquarters about a hundred yards away.

To many, Mosby's Rangers seem the epitome of Secret Warfare: grey ghosts who struck deep behind enemy lines successfully using the support of Southern sympathizers in Union-occupied territory.

Mosby had joined Confederate forces as a private in the 1st Virginia Cavalry. He fought in the first battle at Bull Run, but gained recognition as a scout for Confederate Cavalry Commander J. E. B. Stuart in the famous ride around McClellan's Army in June 1862. He was captured once, but the Union made a major mistake and quickly exchanged him. He was to ride again for Stuart in the march to Gettysburg in June 1863.

Mosby had organized his Partisan Rangers in January 1863 in the Loudon Valley of northern Virginia and from that time until the war ended in April 1865 was constantly engaged in hit-and-run tactics. By the end of hostilities there were eight companies of Partisan Rangers, and during the last winter of the war they were so active in eastern Virginia that the area was called "Mosby's Confederacy." The best efforts of Union cavalry greats such as Sheridan and Custer to catch Mosby or destroy his forces were to no avail as the experienced guerrillas faded into the night or used their greater familiarity with the terrain to escape and evade.

Eighty years later what Mosby had done in Virginia during the American Civil War was being repeated in many parts of the world by armed partisans opposing enemy occupation of their homelands. The twentieth-century irregular of World War II was more likely to be on foot, for aircraft, armored cars, and fast, light tanks had made the cavalry more vulnerable, but in forested areas the horsemen still operated successfully. Modernity changed little but the techniques of the secret warriors.

Whether on foot or mounted, in the cities or rural areas, the men and women fighting the clandestine battles against the regular military forces of the occupiers survived only if they had better intelligence than the enemy. Frequently this was not the case, especially when attacks achieved surprise or there was an unexpected collapse of the defending forces. Then resistance networks had to be established in enemy-occupied territories, usually at a heavy cost in life to the patriots.

The collapse of France in 1940 is illustrative. French intelligence naturally had concentrated its efforts on Germany, the traditional enemy. With the coming to power of Adolf Hitler and the Nazis in 1933 and the clear indications that Germany was violating the disarmament provisions of the Versailles treaty, French intelligence operations were increased and the Deuxième Bureau accurately reported the growing power of the Germans.

In 1935 the Second Bureau warned of the potential of German panzer divisions and presented an accurate description of how they would be used, one that was confirmed by a book published in Germany in 1937, *Achtung! Panzer*, by Heinz Guderian, the man who was to command an armored corps in the May 1940 attack on France. In 1938 French intelligence said Germany had achieved military superiority and warned of the increasing power of the Luftwaffe in the air.

Germany attacked Poland September 1, 1939, and Britain and France declared war on Germany. But aside from sending military missions and words of encouragement there was little the western allies did to aid the Poles: there was not time. General Armengaud, who headed the French military mission to Warsaw, reported to Gamelin, the commanding general in France, on the defeat of what was reported to be a strong Polish army in twenty-three days. Armengaud said that the combined power and speed of the German Panzers and Luftwaffe impeded the maneuverability of the defendrs and broke the chain of command. The Second Bureau presented a similar analysis and added that the first German objective was to destroy the Polish army, not capture Warsaw, and that German Panzers had neutralized fortifications by using tank guns to knock out the machine guns. The report urged that antitank guns be placed in all French fortications.

The intelligence reports and analyses were not accepted by the French High Command, despite the fall of Poland followed in April 1940 by the occupation of Denmark and the conquest of Norway. The French generals still thought in terms of World War I and assumed it would be a long struggle of attrition similar to the trench warfare of

1914–1918. France had massive fortifications in the Maginot Line stretching from the Swiss border north to Longwy. They assumed that mobile forces could defend the border from Longwy to the north, counting on the impenetrability of the Ardennes region and relying on the Belgian and Dutch forces to assist in preventing a reenactment of the Schlieffen Plan of 1914. The French Army was believed to be one of the best in the world and the generals believed that they could bring up reserves and move mobile forces to block German breakthroughs as they had less than a quarter century earlier. In truth, most of the High Command thought they could refight the last war and ignored indications that armor, aircraft, and airborne troops had rendered fixed defenses vulnerable. In 1935 Major Charles de Gaulle had written a book on the requirements of a professional army, arguing against relying on defensive measures and urging development of a fast mobile force of 100,000 volunteers serving six-year enlistments. He predicted attacks by as many as 3,000 tanks that could advance 30 miles per day, and he criticized a military leadership clinging to concepts of the last war. The generals were hostile, the leaders of the Popular Front government even more so, and de Gaulle was removed from the 1936 promotion list.

In the spring of 1940 French intelligence received an increasing number of reports on German troop concentrations in the west, with more and more indications of a major assault across the Ardennes region of Belgium. The Second Bureau reported a heavy buildup of forces in the Trier region. An interception of a German intelligence message indicated that the Wehrmacht High Command wanted to know the road conditions between Sedan and Abbeville, a clear indication of a possible route of attack. On April 30 the French military attaché in Berne reported that the Germans would attack France between May 8 and 10 and that the principal axis of advance would be Sedan. The Dutch passed on reports given to their military attaché in Berlin by Col. Hans Oster of the German Abwehr warning that Hitler planned a major offensive against the West. On May 3 Oster said that Holland would be attacked. At 9:30 on the evening of May 9 Oster told his Dutch friend that the attack would be the next morning at 5:30

Despite the warnings, the French Army was still granting normal leave in early May 1940. There had been no major action on the western front for eight months. Many in France believed that there would be no major battle and that the war would be ended by negotiation. German deception operations helped confuse the Allies. The Abwehr spread rumors in neutral countries that the German people were war-weary and that the army could not mount a major offensive. There also were efforts to mislead as to the principal point of attack. On the one hand, a new attempt at the Schlieffen Plan was mentioned in places where it could be heard by France. Goering publicly said the

Maginot Line would be attacked between May 5 and 15 and that Germany expected to have about 500,000 casualties.

Goering's statement only reinforced the views of Gamelin, who in effect ignored the Second Bureau and made his own intelligence estimates. Gamelin said that the Germans would attack the Maginot Line and claimed that there were twice as many German divisions opposite those fortifications as the Second Bureau reported. He also placed double the number of divisions in the German reserves as the Second Bureau—45 compared to 20—thus underestimating the size of the attacking forces. Not only did the commander-in-chief believe that Sedan would not be the main point of attack and that German armor could not pass through the Ardennes, but he was also confident that Sedan could be defended. Unfortunately for France, Gamelin was wrong and the military intelligence service essentially correct.

The German attack came at dawn on May 10. By May 12 Holland was cut in two and German Panzers had rolled through the "impenetrable" Ardennes and were across the Meuse in France. Two days later German armor was ten miles west of Sedan, which had been occupied virtually unopposed. The same day Holland surrendered. By May 18 the French knew that the Germans were headed for the English Channel, which they reached on the 20th, covering their left flank on the Aisne. By the 24th Allied forces had been split, with the British and some French encircled at Dunkirk. That day Hitler ordered the German ground advance to stop and leave the encircled enemy to the Luftwaffe, apparently at Goering's request. On May 26 the evacuation of the British Expeditionary Force from Dunkirk started and two days later Belgium surrendered. When the evacuation at Dunkirk was completed, 337,000 troops had been saved, of whom 110,000 were French, but all of their equipment was gone. The Germans had estimated that there were only 110,000 in the pocket. On June 11 Churchill shocked the French by suggesting that they not try to defeat the Germans in pitched battles but use guerrilla warfare tactics until the United States entered the war. The French leaders were particularly appalled that the British leader urged them to defend their beloved Paris street by street and house by house. On June 14 the Germans occupied Paris and on June 22 the armistice was signed. France was divided, with Germans occupying the north and a French government installed at Vichy, to last until 1942 when German forces occupied the entire nation. The first phase of a conventional war had ended. Now began the secret war.

France had been defeated not by superior force and strategy alone but also by the ineptitude of its High Command. Germany had made skillful use of secret war techniques. German military intelligence was good, but not omniscient. Nazi use of deception, propaganda, and terror contributed to French confusion and uncertainty. The German Stuka dive-bomber was used not only to destroy defensive positions but also as an instrument of terror to bomb undefended cities and terrorize troop concentrations, even refugee columns. The spreading of rumors conjured visions of a fifth column of enemy operatives: yes, there were enemy agents but not on the vast scale that the uninformed could imagine. Even the division of France after the armistice served to divide the French, who were already seeking scapegoats on whom to blame the defeat.

There had been no time between May 10 and June 22 for French intelligence to establish any stay-behind intelligence networks, nor was there any anticipation in May or early June of 1940 of the potential extent of disaster. Had a French intelligence officer suggested in the spring of 1940 that agents be left behind in eastern France to send reports on the German occupiers to headquarters in Vincennes, Paris, Bordeaux, or wherever, he would have been court-martialled for defeatism. And suddenly it was too late! Their beloved Paris, the heart of France, had fallen. The population was stunned. The military either were in prison camps or by the terms of the armistice had given their word not to resist further. And it was a nation divided not only by the occupiers but by political views and the primary human instinct of survival.

The official Communist Party line was that this was an imperialist war they wanted no part of. After the Nazi–Soviet Pact of August 1939 the Comintern had directed its national sections to cease their anti–Axis crusades, which they did. On August 25 the French Council of Ministers dissolved "of all legality the Communist Party." The head of the party, Maurice Thorez, joined his military unit on the day France declared war on Germany, but within a month he had deserted and made his way to the Soviet Union where he stayed for the duration. He was replaced in France by Jacques Duclos, a longtime Soviet intelligence agent. After the armistice in 1940 the Communists were content to rebuild local organizations while the Germans allowed *L'Humanité,* the party publication, to continue publication.

By late 1940 resistance against the Germans was beginning to be organized, and the inevitable law of action–counteraction set in. As underground groups became more and more evident, German countermeasures increased as the Abwehr expanded operations in France. While France was divided, Abwehr agents obtained information from those wishing to visit friends and relatives in the occupied zone in exchange for travel permits. The major operational base against France was in Wiesbaden with posts in Paris, Dijon, and Lyons and subposts in Cherbourg, Nancy, Toulouse, and Limoges. The Paris post had 328 people, Cherbourg 3; Paris reported to Wiesbaden through a radio station operating from a villa in Neuilly. Abwehr III concentrated on penetrating French resistance groups.

Charles de Gaulle had been taken out of France on a British plane shortly before the armistice. He immediately started to organize Free French forces from London, initially struggling with rival groups in North Africa, including those who would cooperate with the Germans. Ultimately, de Gaulle would prevail, defeating the collaborators and by February 1942 incorporating rival groups into the Forces of Fighting France.

The Communists initially abstained from active resistance, but with the German attack on the Soviet Union on June 22, 1941, they joined the militants. Jacques Duclos started to organize the Franc Tireurs et Partisans, the military arm of the Communist resistance. On August 26 the Russians recognized de Gaulle as chief of all the Free French, and at the same time Moscow urged the peoples of Europe to rise in armed revolt against the Germans. By November 1942 there was agreement between the Communists and the Gaullists for a unified effort in the secret war.

Soviet intelligence continued to operate in France after the German occupation. Leopold Trepper, a Soviet agent who had been an active there since 1932, organized the Simex trading company in Paris, which supplied services to the German construction organization TODT. This provided Trepper with passes to visit military construction projects in the occupied area. For more than two years Trepper and his network provided the Russians with valuable military intelligence on German units in France and Belgium.

British intelligence had lost many assets with the fall of France and in the summer of 1940 started to rebuild. The British had two of their top operators kidnapped by German intelligence on the Dutch border. Winston Churchill directed that a new organization be created to "set Europe ablaze" and the "Special Operations Executive" was organized. The SOE's basic mission was to recruit persons who could infiltrate enemy–occupied territory to organize and help train a secret army to harass the Germans until the Allied armies of liberation arrived and then to raid enemy forces going to the front. By the time the Allies landed in western France in June 1944, hundreds of agents, thousands of tons of arms, ammunition, and explosives, and considerable money had been sent to the underground. Infiltration was by parachute, by light plane, by sea, by border crossers, and by "legal" travelers through neutral countries.

By the end of 1942 the American Office of Strategic Services was ready to enter the secret war in Europe, working out of London and North Africa with the British and French. As preparations for the Allied landings in France neared completion, the OSS, the British SIS and the French BCRA cooperated to recruit, train, and parachute into key transit points in France some fifty intelligence teams whose task was to report on German troop movements at the time of the Allied landing. A similar tripartite arrangement put into place teams for guerrilla operations.

The secret war in Western Europe was fought primarily by the men and women of the occupied countries who knowingly accepted missions involving the ultimate risk. Many paid with their lives in Nazi concentration camps and Gestapo torture cells; the more fortunate died before firing squads. Their contribution to Allied victory was considerable. By 1944 everything the Germans did in France was known in London within hours or days at the most. Considerable credit for this must go to de Gaulle's intelligence service, the Bureau Central de Renseignements et d'Action (BCRA) under Colonel André de Wavrin. In addition to intelligence, the French resistance paramilitary units played a major role in the liberation of Paris in August 1944 and of several departments. Other paramilitary units fought hit-and-run battles with the Germans in other areas of France, committed sabotage to disrupt railways, telephone, and telegraph plus central electrical stations, and harassed the enemy in every way conceivable.

By the spring of 1944 the Germans also were preparing for the Allied landing in France. Members of the pro-Nazi Parti Populaire Français and the Milice and Belgian Rexists were recruited for reconnaissance work. Admiral Canaris, the head of the Abwehr, ordered concentration on stay–behind agents, and one successfully operated in the port of Cherbourg after Allied liberation, reporting on troop movements and the landing of material. But by the end of 1944 with most of France liberated the Germans were parachuting agents into northern France. Over half were killed. During the German offensive in the Ardennes in December 1944 scores of "American–speaking" Germans in U.S. army uniforms were infiltrated to disrupt communications and kill senior officers. Most were caught and executed after summary courts–martial.

By the third year the secret war was being waged in all of the occupied countries. Belgian, Dutch, Danish, and Norwegian resistance was being directed by the intelligence services of their governments-in-exile in London. The North Sea became a highway for many an agent in the guise of a fisherman. Danish resistance performed the remarkable feat of evacuating nearly the entire Jewish population of the nation to the safety of Sweden under the nose of the Nazi occupiers. The Norwegians assisted in stopping the German atom–bomb project with the destruction of heavy-water supplies.

Clandestine operations flourished even in the neutral nations of Switzerland, Spain, and Sweden as intelligence services worked to gain information. Allen Dulles in Switzerland for the American OSS produced much valuable intelligence on Germany and secretly helped to negotiate a surrender of German forces in Italy, where in the north partisans operated on an ever-increasing scale in 1944 and the winter of 1945.

No other partisan effort equaled the scale of that in Yugoslavia. Initially Royalists under Mihailovic competed with the Communist partisans under Tito, but by 1943 the latter held the field. Ultimately, Tito's partisans numbered some 600,000 armed guerrillas in the forests and mountains and occupied 22 German divisions whose aircraft, tanks, and wholesale executions of hostages failed to dislodge or break their will. To the south, in Greece, smaller bands of guerrillas harassed the Germans.

In Eastern Europe a valiant Polish underground army fought the Germans in pitched battle in Warsaw while Russian armies nearby watched its ultimate destruction.

After the German invasion in June 1941 a sizable partisan force, perhaps 30,000, operated in the forests of western Russia harassing the line-of-communications. Partisans captured by the Germans were promptly hanged, but Nazi brutality and mass murders served to build rather than limit guerrilla activity.

In mentioning the Russo–German battles it would be negligent not to mention that perhaps the greatest failure of the war was Stalin's refusal to believe the detailed and accurate reporting of Soviet espionage networks both in Europe and Japan that warned Moscow well in advance when, where, and with what forces the Germans would attack Russia.

In battles in Asia and the Pacific the men and women who operated behind enemy lines made vital contributions. Coastwatchers on Pacific islands provided valuable intelligence and saved flyers. Guerrillas in Burma, such as Orde Wingate's Raiders, Merrill's Marauders, and the OSS 101 Detachment, plus native units, fought behind Japanese lines as did many others in South Asia, in the Philippines, Malaysia, Indo-China, and the Netherlands East Indies.

In a brief foreword such as this it is impossible to do more than indicate a few of the aspects of the secret wars, or to mention some of the nations or peoples involved. The more than two thousand citations in this bibliography will provide the serious scholar with leads to the many sources throughout the world. There is much to learn from secret wars, perhaps nothing as important as the fact that there is no sacrifice too great for people who want to seek their own destiny free of foreign domination.

I/Reference Works

Introduction

The purpose of this section is twofold: first, to present tools that should prove useful in updating this guide and for additional research into the complexities of the 1939–1945 secret wars; second, to point out those titles that in different ways have a general impact either on our topic per se or on the formation of background knowledge for those who wish to deal with it.

Current and retrospective English-language sources relative to this book may be located in the bibliographies and indexes cited in subsection A. Quick overviews and general background information on various aspects of our topic may be found among the encyclopedias and encyclopedia articles and the general war histories reviewed in subsections B and D. Terminology useful in interpreting language or concepts in some of the works cited in this guide may be had through consultation with the sources in subsection C. Users should also be certain to check the footnotes and bibliographies (where provided) in all of the books, scholarly journal articles, dissertations, and documents cited in this guide.

A.   Bibliographies and Indexes

1.   *ABS Guide to Recent Publications in the Social and Behavorial Sciences.* New York: American Behavioral Scientist, 1965.

2.   ———. *Supplements.* Beverly Hills, Calif.: Sage, 1966–.

3.   *Abstracts of Military Bibliography.* Buenos Aires, Argentina: Navy Publications Institute, 1968. v. I–.

4.   *America: History and Life–A Guide to Periodical Literature.* Santa Barbara, Calif.: ABC–Clio Press, 1964–. v. I–.

5.   American Historical Association. *Writings on American History.* Washington, D.C.: U. S. Government Printing Office, 1948–1961.

6.   ———. ———. Milwood, N.Y.: Kraus, 1962–.

7.   ———. Committee for the Study of War Documents. *Guides to German Records Microfilmed at Alexandria.* Washington, D.C.: National Archives, General Services Administration, 1958–. v. I–.

8.   Bayliss, Gwyn M. *Bibliographic Guide to the Two World Wars: An Annotated Survey of English-language Reference Materials.* London and New York: R. R. Bowker, 1977. 578p.

9.   "Bibliography of Cryptography." *American Mathematical Monthly,* L (May 1943), 345–346.

10.   *Biography Index.* New York: H. W. Wilson, 1947–. v. I–.

11.   Blackstock, Paul W., and Frank L. Schaf, Jr. *Intelligence, Espionage, Counterespionage, and Covert Operations: A Guide to Information Sources.* International Relations Information Guide Series, no. 2. Detroit: Gale Research Company, 1978. 255p.

12.   Bloomberg, Marty, and Hans H. Weber. *World War II and Its Origins: A Select Annotated Bibliography of Books in English.* Littleton, Colo.: Libraries Unlimited, 1975. 311p.

13.   *Book Review Index.* New York: H. W. Wilson, 1939–. v. 35–.

14.   "Books and Ideas." In: *Air University Review.* Maxwell Air Force Base, Ala.: Air University, 1959–.

15.   British Museum. Department of Printed Books. *Catalog of Printed Books: Additions.* London: Clowes, 1963–.

16.   Carlson, J. R. "Undercover Guide to the War." *Saturday Review of Literature,* XXVIII (August 25, 1945), 13–14.

17.   Collison, Robert L. *Broadcasting in Britain: A Bibliography.* Cambridge, Eng.: At the University Press, 1961. 32p.

18. *Congressional Record.* Washington, D.C.: U.S. Government Printing Office, 1939–. v. 85–.

19. Cooling, B. Franklin, and Alan Millett. *Doctoral Dissertations in Military Affairs: A Bibliography.* Manhattan: Kansas State University Library, 1972.

20. _____ . _____: *Update.* In: *Military Affairs,* annual April issue, 1973–.

21. *The Cumulative Book Index.* New York: H. W. Wilson, 1939–.

22. Dallin, Alexander, comp. *The German Occupation of the U.S.S.R. in World War II: A Bibliography.* External Research Paper. Washington, D.C.: Office of Intelligence Research, Department of State, 1955. 96p.

23. Devore, Ronald M. *Spies and All That . . . : Intelligence Agencies and Operations, a Bibliography.* Political Issues Series, vol. 4, no. 3. Los Angeles, Calif.: Center for the Study of Armament and Disarmament, University of California, 1977. 71p.

D'Hoop, Jean Marie, jt. compiler. *See* Michel, Henri.

24. *Dissertation Abstracts.* Ann Arbor, Mich.: University Microfilms, 1939–1968.

25. *Dissertation Abstracts International: "A" Schedule.* Ann Arbor, Mich.: University Microfilms, 1969–.

26. Enser, A. G. S. *A Subject Bibliography of the Second World War: Books in English, 1939–1974.* Boulder, Colo.: Westview Press, 1977. 542p.

27. *Foreign Affairs,* Editors of. *Foreign Affairs Bibliography: A Selected and Annotated List of Books on International Relations, 1919–1962.* 4 vols. New York: Harper, 1933–1962.

28. *Forthcoming Books.* New York: R. R. Bowker, 1966–. v. I–.

29. Funk, Arthur L. *The Second World War , a Bibliography: A Select List of Publications Appearing since 1968.* Gainesville, Fla.: American Committee on the History of the Second World War, 1972. 32p.

30. _____ , et al. *A Select Bibliography of Books on the Second World War in English: Published in the United States, 1966–1975.* Gainesville, Fla.: American Committee on the History of the Second World War, 1975. 33p.

31. Galland, Joseph S. *An Historical and Analytical Bibliography of the Literature of Cryptology.* Northwestern University Studies in the Humanities Series, no. 10. Evanston, Ill.: Northwestern University Press, 1945. 209p.

32.   Great Britain. Public Records Office. *The Second World War: A Guide to Documents in the Public Records Office.* Handbook, no. 15. London: H. M. Stationery Office, 1972. 303p.

33.   Harris, William R. *Intelligence and National Security: A Bibliography with Selected Annotations.* Rev. ed. Cambridge, Mass.: Center for International Affairs, Harvard University, 1968. 838p.

Readers should also be aware of Max Gunzenhauser's important but untranslated *Geschichte der Geheimen Nachrichtendienst (Spionage, Sabotage und Abwehr): Literatur Berichte und Bibliographie* (Frankfurt, West Germany: Bernard und Graefe, 1968, 434p).

34.   Hart, Donn V. "Guerrilla Warfare and the Filipino Resistance on Negros Island in the Bisayas, 1942–1945: A Bibliographic Essay." *Journal of Southeast Asian History*, V (Spring 1964), 101–125.

35.   Haven, Violet S., comp. *Espionage Bibliography, 1942.* Washington, D.C.: U.S. Department of Justice Library, 1942. 16p.

36.   *Historical Abstracts: A Quarterly, Covering the World's Periodical Literature.* Santa Barbara, Calif.: ABC–Clio Press, 1955–. v. 1–.

37.   Hellman, Florence S., comp. *Nazi Fifth Column Activities: A List of References.* Washington, D.C.: General Reference and Bibliography Division, Library of Congress, 1943. 42p.

38.   Higham, Robin, ed. *A Guide to the Sources of British Military History.* Berkeley: University of California Press, 1971. 630p.

39.   _____. *A Guide to the Sources of United States Military History.* Hamden, Conn.: Archon Books, 1975. 559p.

40.   _____. *Official Histories: Essays and Bibliographies from Around the World.* Manhattan: Kansas State University Library, 1970. 644p.

41.   Holler, Frederick L., comp. *The Information Sources of Political Science.* 6 vols. Santa Barbara, Calif.: ABC–Clio Press, 1975.

42.   Imperial War Museum, Library. *Bibliography of Espionage and Treason in World War I and II.* London, 1955. 21p.

43.   _____. *Yugoslav Partisans: Selected List of References.* London, 1963. 5p.

44.   *Index to the Times.* London: *The Times,* 1939–.

International Index. See Social Sciences and Humanities Index.

45.   *International Information Service: A Quarterly Annotated Index of Selected Materials on Current International Affairs.* Chicago: Library of International Affairs, 1963–.

46. *International Relations Digest of Periodical Literature.* Berkeley: Bureau of International Relations, University of California, 1950–.

47. Kahn, David. "World War II History: The Biggest Hole [Intelligence]." *Military Affairs,* XXXIX (April 1975), 74–77.

48. *Masters Abstracts.* Ann Arbor, Mich.: University Microfilms, 1962–. v. 1–.

49. Michel, Henri, and Jean Marie D'Hoop. *The Two World Wars: A Selective Bibliography.* Translated from the French. London and New York: Pergamon Press, 1964. 246p.

50. "The Military Library." In: *Military Affairs.* Washington, D.C.: The American Military Institute, 1937–. v. 1–.

Millett, Alan, jt. compiler. *See* Cooling, B. Franklin

51. Miller, Lester L., Jr. *Intelligence Gathering: A Two-part Twentieth Century Bibliography.* Report 5B–52. Ft. Sill, Okla.: U.S. Army Field Artillery School, 1978. 20p.

52. Morton, Louis. "World War II: A Survey of Recent Writings." *American Historical Review,* LXXV (December 1970), 1987–2009.

53. ———. *Writings on World War II.* Washington, D.C.: Service Center for Teachers of History, 1967. 54p.

54. New York Public Library. "The Trojan-horse Bibliography: The European 'Fifth Column' and American Morale–Resistance, 1939–1940." *Bulletin of the New York Public Library,* XLIV (1940), 741–744.

55. ———. Research Libraries. *Subject Catalog of the World War II Collection.* 3 vols. Boston: G. K. Hall, 1977.

56. *New York Times Index.* New York: New York Times Company, 1939–.

57. Ney, Virgil. "Bibliography on Guerrilla Warfare." *Military Affairs,* XXIX (Fall 1960), 146–149.

58. Powe, Marc B. "The History of American Military Intelligence: A Review of Selected Literature." *Military Affairs,* XXXIX (October 1975), 142–145.

59. *Public Affairs Information Service Bulletin.* New York: Public Affairs Information Service, 1945–.

60. RAND Corporation. *Selected RAND Abstracts.* Santa Monica, Calif.: RAND Corporation, 1962–. v. 1–.

61. *Reader's Guide to Periodical Literature.* New York: H. W. Wilson, 1939–. v. 12–.

Schaf, Frank L. Jr., jt. compiler. *See* Blackstock, Paul W.

62. Siehl, George. "Cloak, Dust Jacket, and Dagger." *Library Journal,* XCVII (October 15, 1972), 3277–3282.

63. Smith, Myron J., Jr. *Air War Bibliography, 1939–1945: A Guide to Sources in English.* 5 vols.+ Manhattan, Kan.: Published for the U.S.A.F. Historical Foundation by Military Affairs/Aerospace Historian Publishing, 1976–.

64. _____ . *Cloak-and-Dagger Bibliography.* Metuchen, N. J.: The Scarecrow Press, 1976. 225p.

65. _____ . *World War II at Sea: A Guide to Sources in English.* 3 vols. Metuchen, N. J.: The Scarecrow Press, 1976.

66. *Social Sciences and Humanities Index.* New York: H. W. Wilson, 1939–. v. 8–.

67. *Subject Guide to Books in Print.* New York: R. R. Bowker, 1957–. v. 1–.

68. Tompkins, Dorothy L. C. C. *Sabotage and Its Prevention during Wartime.* Defense Bibliographies. Berkeley: Bureau of Public Administration, University of California, 1951. 53p.

69. United States. Air Force. Air Force Academy, Library. *Unconventional Warfare, Part I: Guerrilla Warfare.* Special Bibliography Series, no. 21. Colorado Springs, Colo., 1962. 39p.

70. _____ . _____ . _____ . *Unconventional Warfare, Part II: Psychological Warfare.* Special Bibliography Series, no. 22. Colorado Springs, Colo., 1962. 37p.

71. _____ . _____ . _____ . *Unconventional Warfare, Part IV: Propaganda.* Special Bibliography Series, no. 30. Colorado Springs, Colo. 1964. 45p.

72. _____ . _____ . Air University. *Air University Index to Military Periodicals.* Maxwell AFB, Ala.: Air University Library, 1949–. v. 1–.

73. _____ . Army. Military History Institute. *The Era of World War II.* Special Bibliography Series, no. 16. 2 vols.+ Carlisle Barracks, Pa., 1977–.

74. _____ . Department of State. *Intelligence, a Bibliography of Its Functions, Methods and Techniques.* Bibliographies no. 33 and no. 331. Washington, D. C., 1948–1949.

A mimeographed 700+ entry project developed by the Office of Strategic Services before its disbandment.

75. _____ . Library of Congress. *Library of Congress Catalog, Books: Subjects. A Cumulative List of Works Represented by Library of Congress Printed Cards.* Washington, D.C.: U.S. Government Printing Office, 1950–.

76. _____ . Superintendent of Documents. *Monthly Catalogue of United States Government Documents.* Washington, D.C.: U.S. Government Printing Office, 1939–.

Weber, Hans H., jt. compiler. *See* Bloomberg, Marty

77. Wiener Library. *Persecution and Resistance under the Nazis* [A Bibliography]. London: Vallentine, 1960. 45p.

78. Ziegler, Janet. *World War II: Books in English, 1945–1965.* Hoover Bibliography Series, no. 45. Stanford, Calif.: Hoover Institution Press, 1971. 224p.

B. Encyclopedias and Encyclopedia Articles

79. Blackstock, Paul W. "Espionage." In: Vol. X of the *Encyclopedia Americana.* International Edition. New York: Americana Corp., 1978. pp. 584–587.

80. Callimakos, Lambros D. "Cryptology." In: Vol. VII of *Collier's Encyclopedia.* New York: Macmillan Educational Corp., 1977. pp. 519–530.

81. _____ . _____ . In: Vol. V of *Encyclopedia Britannica.* Chicago: Britannica Corp., 1974. pp. 322–333.

82. Daugherty, William E. "Psychological Warfare." In: Vol. XIII of *International Encyclopedia of the Social Sciences.* New York: Macmillan Educational Corp., 1968. pp. 46–49.

83. Donovan, William J., "Espionage." By W. J. Don, pseud. In: Vol. XII of *Encyclopedia Brittannica.* Chicago: Britannica Corp., 1954. pp. 459–462.

84. Dupuy, R. Ernest, and Trevor N. *The Encyclopedia of Military History.* Rev. ed. New York: Harper & Row, 1976. 1,488p.

85. Eliot, George F. "Espionage." In: Vol. IX of *Collier's Encyclopedia.* New York: Macmillan Educational Corp., 1977. pp. 312–315.

86. Elting, John R. "Military Intelligence." In: Vol. XVI of *Collier's Encyclopedia.* New York: Macmillan Educational Corp., 1977. pp. 211–214.

87. *Facts on File: A Weekly News Guide with Cumulative Index.* New York: Facts on File, Inc., 1940–. v. 1–.

88. Giddens, Jackson A. "Propaganda." In: Vol. XXII of the *Encyclopedia Americana.* New York: Americana Corp., 1978. pp. 656–659.

89.   Hoover, J. Edgar. "Espionage and Counterespionage." In: Vol. X of the *Encyclopedia Americana.* New York: Americana Corp., 1965. pp. 504–506.

90.   Kahn, David. "Cryptology." In: Vol. VIII of the *Encyclopedia Americana.* New York: Americana Corp., 1978. pp. 276–285.

91.   Keegan, John, ed. *The Rand McNally Encyclopedia of World War II.* Chicago: Rand McNally, 1977. 256p.

92.   *The Marshall Cavendish Illustrated Encyclopedia of World War II.* 25 vols. Hicksville, N. Y.: Marshall Cavendish Corp., 1972.

93.   Parrish, Thomas, ed. *The Simon and Schuster Encyclopedia of World War II.* New York: Simon and Schuster, 1978. 765p.

94.   Ransom, Harry H. "Intelligence and Counterintelligence." In: Vol. IX of the *Encyclopedia Britannica.* Chicago: Britannica Corp., 1974. pp. 679–686.

95.   _____. "Intelligence, Political and Military." In: Vol. VII of *International Encyclopedia of the Social Sciences.* New York: Macmillan Educational Corp., 1968. pp. 415–421.

96.   _____. "Intelligence, Strategic." In: Vol. XV of the *Encyclopedia Americana.* International Edition. New York: Americana Corp., 1978. pp. 246–248.

97.   Reid, Alan. *A Concise Enyclopedia of the Second World War.* Reading, Bucks., Eng.: Osprey, 1974. 234p.

98.   Seth, Ronald. *Encyclopedia of Espionage.* Garden City, N. Y.: Doubleday, 1974. 718p.

99.   Smith, Bruce L. "Propaganda." In: Vol. XII of *International Encyclopedia of the Social Sciences.* New York: Macmillan Educational Corp., 1968. pp. 579–589.

100.   Snyder, Louis L. *Encyclopedia of the Third Reich.* New York: McGraw–Hill, 1976. 387p.

101.   Stessin, Laurence. "Intelligence: Military, Political, and Industrial." In: Vol. XII of the *Encyclopedia Britannica.* Chicago: Britannica Corp., 1972. pp. 347–350.

102.   Wright, Charles R. "Propaganda." In: Vol. XV of the *Encyclopedia International.* New York: Grolier Corp., 1967. pp. 97–99.

C. Dictionaries

Bond, P. S., jt. author. *See* Garber, Max

103. Gale Research Company. *Acronyms and Initialisms Dictionary.* 3d ed. Detroit, 1970. 484p.

104. Garber, Max, and P. S. Bond. *A Modern Military Dictionary.* 2d ed. Washington, D. C.: Bond, 1942. 272p.

105. Luttwak, Edward. *The Dictionary of Modern War.* London: Penguin Books, 1971. 224p.

Otton, Roy, jt. author. *See* Plano, Jack C.

106. Partridge, Eric, ed. *A Dictionary of Forces' Slang, 1939–1945.* Freeport, N. Y.: Books for Libraries, 1970. 212p.

107. Plano, Jack C., and Roy Olton. *The International Relations Dictionary.* New York: Holt, Rinehart & Winston, 1969. 337p.

108. Quick, John. *Dictionary of Weapons and Military Terms.* New York: McGraw–Hill, 1973. 527p.

109. Ruffner, Frederick G., Jr., and Robert C. Thomas, eds. *Code Names Dictionary.* Detroit: Gale Research Co., 1963. 555p.

110. Safire, William. *Safire's Political Dictionary.* 3d ed. New York: Random House, 1978. 845p.

111. Taylor, A. Marjorie. *The Language of World War II.* Rev. ed. New York: H. W. Wilson, 1948. 265p.

Thomas, Robert C., jt, editor. *See* Ruffner, Frederick G., Jr.

112. United States. War Department. Military Intelligence Service. *British Military Terminology.* Washington, D. C., 1943. 210p.

D. General War Histories

113. Adams, Henry H. *1942: The Year That Doomed The Axis.* New York: David McKay, 1967. 544p.

114. _____ . *Years of Deadly Peril: The Coming of the War, 1939–1941.* New York: David McKay, 1969. 559p.

115. _____ . *Years of Expectation: Guadalcanal to Normandy.* New York: David McKay, 1973. 430p.

116. _____ . *Years to Victory.* New York: David McKay, 1973. 507p.

117. Arnold–Foster, Mark. *The World at War.* New York: Stein & Day, 1973. 340p.

118. Bateson, Charles. *The War with Japan: A Concise History.* East Lansing: Michigan State University Press, 1968. 417p.

119. Bergamini, David. *Japan's Imperial Conspiracy.* New York: Morrow, 1971. 1, 239p.

120. Butler, James R. M., ed. *Grand Strategy.* History of the Second World War: United Kingdom Military Series. 6 vols. in 7. London: H. M. Stationery Office, 1957.

121. Calvocoressi, Peter, and Guy Wint. *Total War: The Story of World War II.* New York: Pantheon, 1972. 959p.

122. Churchill, Winston S. *The Second World War.* 6 vols. Boston: Houghton, Mifflin, 1948–1953

Both history and memoir.

123. Collier, Basil. *The Second World War.* New York: Morrow, 1967. 640p.

124. _____ . *The War in the Far East, 1941–1945.* New York: Morrow, 1969. 530p.

125. Davis, Kenneth S. *Experience of War: The United States in World War II.* Mainstream of America Series. Garden City, N.Y.: Doubleday, 1965. 704p.

126. Dennis, Geoffrey P., ed. *The World at War.* 4 vols. London: Caxton, 1951.

127. Dupuy, R. Ernest. *World War II: A Compact History.* New York: Hawthorn, 1969. 334p.

128. *Encyclopedia Americana,* Editors of. *A Concise History of World War II.* New York: Praeger, 1964. 434p.

Esposito, Vincent J., jt. editor. *See* Stamps, T. Dodson

129. Heiferman, Ronald. *World War II.* Secaucus, N. J.: Derbibooks, 1973. 256p.

130. Hoyle, Martha B. *A World in Flames: A History of World War II.* New York: Atheneum, 1970. 356p.

131. Jacobsen, Hans A., and Jurgen Rohwer, eds. *Decisive Battles of World War II: The German View.* New York: Putnam, 1965. 509p.

132. Jarman, Thomas L. *The Rise and Fall of Nazi Germany.* New York: New York University Press, 1956. 388p.

133. Jones, James. *World War II.* New York: Grosset and Dunlap, 1975. 272p.

134. Kirby, S. Woodburn. *The War against Japan.* United Kingdom Military Series. 5 vols. London: H. M. Stationery Office, 1957–1969.

135. Liddell–Hart, Basil. *History of the Second World War.* New York: Putnam, 1970. 768p.

136. MacDonald, Charles B. *The Mighty Endeavor: American Armed Forces in the European Theater in World War II.* New York and London: Oxford University Press, 1969. 564p.

137. Matloff, Maurice, and Edwin M. Snell. *Strategic Planning for Coalition Warfare, 1941–1944.* U.S. Army in World War II: The War Department. 2 vols. Washington, D. C.: Office of the Chief of Military History, Department of the Army, 1953–1959.

138. Michel, Henri. *The Second World War.* Translated from the French. London: Deutsch, 1975. 947p.

139. Preston, Anthony, ed. *Decisive Battles of Hitler's War.* A Quarto Book. London and New York: Hamlyn Publishing Corp., 1977. 256p.

140. Purnell Publishers. *History of the Second World War.* 96 parts. London, 1966–1967.

141. *Reader's Digest,* Editors of. *The Reader's Digest Illustrated History of World War II.* Pleasantville, N. Y.: Reader's Digest Association, 1969. 528p.

142. Reeder, Russel P. *The Story of the Second World War.* 2 vols. London: Meredith, 1969–1970.

Rohwer, Jurgen, jt. editor. *See* Jacobsen, Hans A.

143. *Seventy True Stories of the Second World War.* Beacon Books. London: Odham's Press, 1958. 320p.

144. Shirer, William L. *The Rise and Fall of the Third Reich.* New York: Simon and Schuster, 1960. 1,245p.

Snell, Edwin M., jt. author. *See* Matloff, Maurice

145. Snyder, Louis L. *The War: A Concise History, 1939–1945.* New York: Messner, 1960. 579p.

146. Stamps, T. Dodson, and Vincent J. Esposito, eds. *A Military History of World War II.* 2 vols. Westpoint, N. Y.: Department of Military Art and Engineering, U. S. Military Academy, 1953.

147. Taylor, Alan J. P., ed. *The Second World War: An Illustrated History.* New York: Putnam, 1975. 285p.

148.   *Time Magazine,* Editors of. *Time Capsule: History of the War Years.* 7 vols. in 1. New York: Bonanza Books, 1967.

149.   Toland, John. *The Rising Sun: The Decline and Fall of the Japanese Empire, 1936–1945.* New York: Random House, 1970. 707p.

Wint, Guy, jt. author. *See* Calvocoressi, Peter

150.   Wright, Gordon. *The Ordeal of Total War, 1939–1945.* New York: Harper & Row, 1969. 315p.

151.   Young, Peter. *Atlas of the Second World War.* New York: Putnam, 1974. 288p.

152.   _____ , ed. *Decisive Battles of the Second World War: An Anthology.* London: Barker, 1967. 439p.

Further References

Readers will find a few specialized reference works in certain of the subsections below. See especially section II through V and section VIII, subsection A.

II/Propaganda and Psychological Warfare

Introduction

The references in this section concern the organized effort to panic, subvert, depress, or unnerve World War II populations (military and civilian) through the creative use of truth, lies, or deception. The term "psychological warfare," born of this conflict, has generally come to mean the use of nonviolent propaganda and persuasion aimed at the soldiers and citizens of one side by calculating "machines" of the other. Skillfully employed, as it was by the Reich Ministry of Information and the U. S. Office of War Information among others, "psywar" and propaganda activities could and did depress morale, foster treason, cowardice, and social disorganization, subvert beliefs and ideals, cultivate prejudice and distrust, and divert public opinion among target audiences. Posters, radio broadcasts, pamphlets and leaflets, news releases, loudspeakers, and rumors spread by agents were all means employed by those engaged in the battle for men's minds. These means and methods, many sponsored by such agencies as the OSS, were directly involved in the process of disinformation or "reverse intelligence" and created a corresponding need for analysis of their effects.

The materials listed below demonstrate how propaganda and "psywar" were developed into very potent weapons capable of obtaining specific goals through sycronization with the political, military, and covert efforts of both the Allied and Axis sides.

153. Allied Forces, Supreme Headquarters, Psychological Warfare Division. *The Psychological Warfare Division, Supreme Headquarters, Allied Expeditionary Force: An Account of Its Operations in the Western European Campaign, 1944-1945.* Bad Homburg, Germany, 1945. 278p.

154. "Allied Propaganda to Occupied Europe." *Nation*, CLIX (July 8, 1944), 44-46.

155. Allport, F. H. "Broadcasting to an Enemy Country: What Appeals Are Effective and Why." *Journal of Social Psychology*, XXIII (May 1946), 217-224.

156. Aries, Leonard P. "Propaganda: Its Analysis." In: Harold G. Merriam, *et al.*, eds. *Readings for an Air Age.* New York: Macmillan, 1943. pp. 262-268.

157. *Army Times*, Editors of. *The Tangled Web: True Stories of Deception in Modern Warfare.* Washington, D. C.: Luce, 1963. 199p.

158. Auckland, Reginald G. *Aerial Propaganda over Great Britain.* Sandridge, Herts. Eng.: Auckland, 1963. 43p.

159. _____. "The Leaflet War in the Corridors of Whitehall." *Royal Air Forces Quarterly*, XIV (Autumn 1974), 239-245.

160. Baird, Jay W. *The Mythical World of Nazi War Propaganda, 1939-1945.* Miami, Fla.: University of Miami Press, 1975. 329p.

161. Bayles, William D. "England's Radio Blitz." *Reader's Digest*, XLIV (April 1944), 61-63.

162. Becker, Howard. "The Nature and Consequences of Black Propaganda." *American Sociological Review*, XIV (April 1949), 221-235.

163. Berreman, J. V. "Assumptions about America in Japanese War Propaganda to the United States." *American Journal of Sociology*, LIV (September 1948), 108-117.

164. Bingham, W. V. "Military Psychology in War and Peace." *Science*, CVI (August 22, 1947), 155-160.

165. Black, G. D. "The Keys of the Kingdom: [U.S. Office of War Information] Entertainment and Propaganda." *South Atlantic Quarterly*, LXXV (Autumn 1976), 434-446.

_____ , jt. author. *See* Koppes, C. R.

166. Black, John B. *Organizing the Propaganda Instrument: The British Experience.* The Hague: Nijhoff, 1975. 116p.

167. Boehm, E. H. "Free Germans in Soviet Psychological Propaganda." *Public Opinion Quarterly*, XIV (Summer 1950), 285-295.

168.   Boelcke, Willi A., ed. *The Secret Conferences of Dr.* [Joseph] *Goebbels: The Nazi Propaganda War*, *1939–1945*. New York: E. P. Dutton, 1970. 364p.

169.   Bornstein, Joseph, and Paul R. Milton. *Action against the Enemy's Mind.* Indianapolis: Bobbs–Merrill, 1942. 294p.

170.   Bramstead, Ernest K. *Goebbels and National Socialist Propaganda, 1925–1945.* East Lansing: Michigan State Universtiy Press, 1965. 488p.

171.   Brann, Henry W. "Some Facts of Group Psychology That Endangers Enduring Peace." In: Lyman Bryson, Louis Finkelstein, and R. M. MacIver, eds. *Approaches to World Peace: Fourth Symposium.* New York: Harper, 1944. pp. 232–239.

172.   Briggs, Asa. *The War of Words.* Vol. III of *The History of Broadcasting in the United Kingdom.* London and New York: Oxford University Press, 1970. 766p.

173.   British Broadcasting System. *Annual Reports and Accounts of the British Broadcasting Corporation.* London: H. M. Stationery Office, 1928–. v. 1–.

Consider especially volumes 11–18, 1939–1946.

174.   Brome, Vincent. *Europe's Free Press: The Underground Newspapers of Occupied Lands Described as Far as the Censor Permits.* London: Feature, 1943. 127p.

175.   Burger, H. H. "'Operation Annie': Now It Can Be Told." *New York Times Magazine,* (February 17, 1946), 12–13+.

U.S. Army psychological warfare broadcasts.

176.   Campbell, John P. "D–Day 1943: The Limits of Strategic Deception." *Canadian Journal of History,* XII (December 1977), 207–237.

177.   Carroll, Wallace. *Persuade or Perish.* Boston: Houghton, Mifflin, 1948. 392p.

178.   Cave–Brown, Anthony. *The Bodyguard of Lies.* New York: Harper & Row, 1975. 947p.

179.   Childs, Harwood L., and John B. Whitton, eds. *Propaganda by Short Wave.* Princeton, N. J.: Princeton University Press, 1942. 355p.

Christopher, Stefan, C., jt. author. *See* Dodd, Stuart C.

180.   Colby, Benjamin. *'Twas a Famous Victory: Deception and Propaganda in the War against Germany.* New Rochelle, N. Y.: Arlington House, 1974. 221p.

181. Connors, Michael F. *Dealing in Hate: The Development of Anti–German Propaganda.* London: Britons Publishing Co., 1966. 85p.

182. Conway, J. S. "The German National Reich Church and American War Propaganda." *Catholic Historical Review,* LXII (July 1976), 464–472.

183. Cruickshank, Charles G. *The Fourth Arm: Psychological Warfare, 1939–1945.* London: Davis–Poynter, 1977. 200p.

184. Darnacott, Joseph. *Second World War Posters.* London: Imperial War Museum, 1972.

185. Daugherty, William E., and Morris Janowitz. *A Psychological Warfare Casebook.* Baltimore, Md.: Johns Hopkins University Press, 1958. 880p.

186. Delmer, Sefton. *Black Boomerang.* London: Seeker & Warburg, 1962. 320p.

187. _____. "H. M. G.'s Secret Pornographer." *Times Literary Supplement,* no. 71 (January 21, 1972), 63–64.

188. _____. "The Secret Minutes of Dr. Goebbels." *Times Literary Supplement,* no. 3428 (November 9, 1967), 1063–1064.

189. _____. *Trail Sinister.* London: Seeker & Warburg, 1961. 423p.

190. De Mendelssohn, Peter. *Japan's Political Warfare.* London: Allen and Unwin, 1944. 192p.

191. DeWeerd, Harvey A. "Japan Explains Her War to Her People." *Infantry Journal,* LVII (August 1945), 6–10.

192. Dodd, Stuart C., and Stefan C. Christopher. "The Reaclants Models." In: Alfred de Grazia, *et al.,* eds. *The Behavior Sciences: Essays in Honor of George A. Leindberg.* New York: Behavior Research Council, 1968. pp. 143–177.

Air-dropped psychological warfare leaflets.

193. Doob, Leonard W. "Goebbels' Principles of Propaganda." *Public Opinion Quarterly,* XIV (Fall 1950), 419–442.

194. _____. *Public Opinion and Propaganda.* 2d ed. Hamden, Conn.: Archon Books, 1966. 612p.

195. _____. "The Utilization of Social Scientists in the Overseas Branch of the [U.S.] Office of War Information." *American Political Science Review,* XLI (August 1947), 649–667.

196.   Dover, Cedric. *Hell in the Sunshine*. London: Seeker & Warburg, 1943. 207p.

Japanese propaganda and psychological warfare.

197.   Eagleton, Clyde. "The Unbearable Pressure of Modern War." In: his *Forces That Shape Our Future*. Stokes Lectures, 1943. New York: New York University Press, 1945. pp. 30–56.

198.   Emery, Walter, B. *National and International Systems of Broadcasting: Their History, Operations, and Control*. East Lansing: Michigan State University Press, 1969. 752p.

199.   Erdman, James. *Leaflet Operations in the Second World War: The Story of the How and the Why of the 6,500,000 Propaganda Leaflets Dropped on the Axis Forces and Homelands in the Mediterranean and European Theaters of Operations*. Denver, Colo.:Department of History, University of Denver, 1969. 399p.

200.   _____ . "United States Army Air Force Leaflet Operations in the European Theater of Operations in World War II." Unpublished Ph.D. dissertation, University of Colorado, 1970.

201.   Farago, Ladislas, ed. *German Psychological Warfare*. New York: Putnam, 1942. 302p.

202.   Flershem, R. E. "British Broadcasts in Japanese." *Far Eastern Survey*, XV (November 20, 1946), 359–360.

203.   Freifeld, Sidney A. "Nazi Press Agentry and the American Press." *Public Opinion Quarterly*, VI (Summer 1942), 221–235.

204.   Gask, Roland C. "Japs Do Surrender: Psychological Warfare Somewhere in the China–India–Burma Theater." *Newsweek*, XXIV (October 30, 1944), 31–33.

205.   Gayn, Mark J. "A Million Words of Poison: Domei, the Japanese Army's House Organ." *Saturday Evening Post*, CCXVII (June 16, 1945), 22–23+.

206.   George, Alexander L. *Propaganda Analysis: A Study of Inferences Made from Nazi Propaganda in World War II*. Westport, Conn.: Greenwood Press, 1959. 287p.

207.   "German Wehrmacht Propaganda in World War II." *Military Review*, XXX (May 1951), 103–109.

208.   Gibson, Ralph. *Stop This Fascist Propaganda*. Richmond, New South Wales, Australia: *Richmond Chronicle*, 1943. 16p.

209.   Glasgow, George. "As Germany Sees It." *Contemporary Review*, CLXVII (January 1945), 51–59.

210.   Godwin, George S. *Marconi, 1939–1945: A War Record.* London: Chatto and Windus, 1946. 125p.

211.   Gombrich, Ernest H. J. *Myth and Reality in German Wartime Broadcasts.* Creighton Lecture in History, 1969. London: Athlone Press, 1970. 28p.

212.   Gorham, Maurice. *Sound and Fury: Twenty-One Years in the B.B.C.* London: Percival Marshall, 1948. 248p.

213.   Graves, Harold N., Jr. "European Radio and the War." *Annals of the American Academy of Political and Social Science,* CCXIII (January 1941), 75–82.

214.   _____. "Propaganda by Short Wave: Berlin Calling America." *Public Opinion Quarterly,* IV (December 1940), 601–619.

215.   Gray, George W. "The War of Ideas." In: his *Science at War.* New York: Harper, 1943. pp. 249–274.

216.   Gullahorn, J. T. "Propaganda Techniques in German Documents during World War II." *Sociological and Social Research,* XXX (March 1946), 290–295.

217.   Haffner, Sebastian. *Offensive against Germany.* London: Seeker & Warburg, 1941. 127p.

218.   Hale, Aron J. *The Captive Press in the Third Reich.* Princeton, N.J.: Princeton University Press, 1964. 353p.

219.   Hardy, Alexander G. *Hitler's Secret Weapon: The Managed Press and Propaganda Machine of Nazi Germany.* New York: Vantage Press, 1968. 350p.

220.   Henslow, Miles. *The Miracle of Radio: The Story of Radio's Decisive Contribution to Victory.* London: Evans, 1946. 127p.

221.   Herma, Hans. "Goebbels' Conception of Propaganda." *Social Research,* X (May 1943), 200–218.

222.   Herz, M. F. "Some Psychological Lessons from Leaflet Propaganda in World War II." *Public Opinion Quarterly,* XIII (Fall 1949), 471–486.

223.   Herzstein, Robert E. *The War That Hitler Won: The Most Infamous Propaganda Campaign in History.* New York: Putnam, 1978. 491p.

224.   Hitler, Adolf. "'The Bigger the Lie, the Better': An Excerpt from *Mein Kampf.*"In: William Ebenstein, ed. *Modern Political Thought: The Great Issues.* 2d ed. New York: Holt, 1960. pp. 362–364.

225. Hopkins, George E. "Bombing and the American Conscience during World War II." *Historian,* XXVIII (May 1966), 451–473.

226. Hummel, William C., and K. G. Huntress. *Analysis of Propaganda.* New York: Sloane, 1949. 222p.

227. Hunt, Robert, comp. *Swastika at War.* London: Cooper, 1975. 160p.

Huntress, K. G., jt. author. *See* Hummel, William C.

228. Institute for Propaganda Analysis. "Propaganda Techniques of German Fascism." In: Roger S. Loomis and Donald L. Clark, eds. *Modern English Readings.* 5th ed. New York: Rinehart, 1946. pp. 312–332.

229. *International Propaganda/Communications: Selections from the Public Opinion Quarterly.* New York: Arno Press, 1972. 345p.

First published in 1943.

230. Jablin, J. N. "Axis Radio Propaganda in Tunisia." *Infantry Journal,* LIII (December 1943), 21–22.

231. Jacobs, Lewis. "World War II and the American Film." *Cinema Journal,* VII (Winter 1967–1968), 1–21.

Janowitz, Morris, jt. author. *See* Daugherty, William E.

232. Jones, E. L. "Fighting with Words: Psychological Warfare in the Pacific." *Atlantic,* CLXXVI (August 1945), 47–51.

233. Jones, Ken D., and Arthur F. McClure. *Hollywood at War.* Cranbury, N. J.: A. S. Barnes, 1971. 300p.

234. Judd, Denis. *Posters of World War II.* London: Wayland, 1972. 327p.

235. Kalijarvi, Thorsten V. "Psychological Warfare." In: his *Modern World Politics.* 2d ed. New York: Crowell, 1945. pp. 318–338.

236. Koop, Theodore, F. *Weapon of Silence* [Radio]. Chicago: University of Chicago Press, 1946. 304p.

237. Koppes, C. R., and G. D. Black. "What to Show the World: The Office of War Information and Hollywood, 1942–1945." *Journal of American History,* LXIV (June 1977), 87–105.

238. Krabbe, Henning, ed. *Voices from Britain: Broadcast History, 1939–1945.* London: Allen and Unwin, 1947. 304p.

239. Kris, Ernst, and Hans Speier. *German Radio Propaganda.* London and New York: Oxford University Press, 1944. 243p.

240. _____ , and Nathan Leites. "Trends in Twentieth Century Propaganda." In: Bernard Berelson and Morris Janowitz, eds. *Reader in Public Opinion and Communication.* Enl. ed. Glencoe, Ill.: Free Press, 1953. pp. 278–288.

241. Kumlien, Gunnar D. "The Italian War of Words." *Commonweal,* LXI (December 31, 1954), 351–354.

242. Lavine, Harold, and J. A. Weckster. *War Propaganda and the United States.* New Haven, Conn.: Yale University Press. 1940. 363p.

243. Lean Edwart T. *Voices in the Darkness: The Story of the European Radio War.* London: Seeker & Warburg, 1943. 243p.

244. Leighton, Alexander H. *Human Relations in a Changing World: Observations on the Use of the Social Sciences.* New York: E. P. Dutton, 1949. 354p.

Leites, Nathan, jt. author. *See* Kris, Ernst

245. Lerner, Daniel. *Sykewar: Psychological Warfare against Germany, D–Day.* New York: Stewart, 1949. 377p.

246. _____ , ed. *Propaganda in War and Crisis.* New York: Stewart, 1951. 500p.

247. Lerner, Max. *Propaganda in Our Time.* In: his *Ideas For the Ice Age: Studies in a Revolutionary Era.* New York: Viking Press, 1941. pp. 184–190.

248. Linebarger, Paul M. A. "The British–German Radio War." In: Steuart H. Britt, ed. *Selected Readings in Social Psychology.* New York: Rinehart, 1950. pp. 460–465.

249. _____ . *Psychological Warfare.* Washington, D. C.: Infantry Journal Press, 1948. 259p.

250. _____ . _____ . 2d ed. New York: Duell, Sloan and Pearce, 1954. 318p.

251. _____ . "Psychological Warfare in World War II." *Infantry Journal,* LX (May–June 1947), 36–39, 41–46.

252. Lipman, Samuel. "German Wartime Broadcasts." *Commentary,* LXIII (March 1977), 72–75.

253. London, Kurt "Methods of Indoctrination." In: his *Backgrounds of Conflict: Ideas and Forms in World Politics.* New York: Macmillan, 1948. pp. 103–129.

German propaganda.

254.   Luckmann, L. D. "Foreign Policy by Propaganda Leaflet." *Public Opinion Quarterly,* IX (Winter 1945), 428–429+.

McClure, Arthur F., jt. author. *See* Jones, Ken D.

255.   McKenzie, Vernon. *Here Lies Goebbels!* London: Joseph, 1940. 319p.

256.   _____ . "United Nations Propaganda in the United States." *Public Opinion Quarterly,* VI (September 1942), 351–362.

257.   McLaine, Ian. *Ministry of Morale: Home Front Morale and the* [British] *Ministry of Information in World War II.* London: Allen and Unwin, 1979. 344p.

258.   Mahoney, Thomas. "Words That Win Battles: Psychological Warfare." *Popular Science,* CXLVI (June 1945), 121–123+.

259.   Margolin, Leo J. *Paper Bullets: A Brief History of Psychological Warfare in World War II.* New York: Froben, 1946. 149p.

Margolin, Victor, jt. author. *See* Rhodes, Anthony

260.   Martelli, George. "The Propagandist's Propaganda." *Encounter,* XLII (March 1974), 47–52.

261.   Mayer, Stanley L., ed. *Signal: Hitler's Wartime Picture Magazine.* Englewood Cliffs, N. J.: Prentice Hall, 1976. 192p.

262.   Maynard, Richard A., ed. *Propaganda on Film: A Nation at War.* New York: Hayden Books, 1975. 147p.

263.   Meaney, J. W. "[German] Propaganda as Psychical Coercion." *Review of Politics,* XIII (January 1951), 64–87.

264.   Meerloo, Abraham M. "Treason and Traitors." In: his *Aftermath of Peace: Psychological Essays.* New York: International University Press, 1946. pp. 11–29.

Lord Haw Haw and Tokyo Rose.

265.   Menefee, S. C. "Propaganda Wins Battles: Our Psychological Campaign in the Mediterranean." *Nation,* CLVIII (February 12, 1944), 184–186.

266.   _____ . "Japan's Psychological Warfare." *Social Forces,* XXI (May 1943), 425–436.

267.   Meo, L. D. *Japan's Radio War on Australia, 1941–1945.* Carlton, Victoria, Australia: Melbourne University Press, 1968. 300p.

268. Michie, Allan A. "War as Fought by Radio." *Reader's Digest,* XXXVI (June 1940), 17–21.

269. Miller, Clyde R. "Radio and Propaganda." *Annals of the American Academy of Political and Social Science,* CCXIII (January 1941), 69–74.

270. Miller, William. "Talking Them Out of It: Psychological Warfare." *Collier's,* CXIV (August 19, 1944), 23+.

Milton, Paul R., jt. author. *See* Bornstein, Joseph

271. Morella, Joseph, *et al. The Films of World War II.* Secaucus, N. J.: Citadel Press, 1973. 249p.

272. Morgan, Brewster. "'Operation Annie': [The U.S.] Army Radio Station That Fooled the Nazis by Telling Them the Truth." *Saturday Evening Post,* CCXVIII (March 9, 1946), 18–19+.

273. Morris, B. S. "War and the Psychological Services." *Fortnightly,* CLXVIII (August 1947), 112–118.

274. Neumann, Franz. "Propaganda and Violence." In: his *Behemoth: The Structure and Practice of National Socialism, 1933–1944.* Rev. ed. New York and London: Oxford University Press, 1944. pp. 436–440.

275. "Nickelling: Propaganda Leaflets." *New Yorker,* XXI (April 8, 1945), 16–17.

276. Nippon Hoso Kyokai. *The History of Broadcasting in Japan.* Tokyo, 1967. 423p.

277. "'Operation Annie.'" *Time,* XLVII (February 25, 1946), 68+.

278. Padover, Saul K. "Japanese Race Propaganda." *Public Opinion Quarterly,* VII (Summer 1943), 191–204.

279. Painton, Frederick C. "Fighting with Confetti: How the Army's Psychological Warfare Branch Works and How It Saved American Lives in the Sicilian Campaign." *Reader's Digest,* XLIII (December 1943), 99–101.

280. Paul, Oscar. *Underground Europe Calling.* London: Gollancz, 1942. 160p.

Radio.

281. Paulu, Burton. *British Broadcasting.* Minneapolis: University of Minnesota Press, 1956. 457p.

282. Perry, John. "War Propaganda for Democracy." *Public Opinion Quarterly,* VI (September 1942), 437–442.

283.   Perry, Ralph B. "The Right and Wrong of Propaganda." In: his *Our Side Is Right.* Cambridge, Mass.: Harvard University Press, 1942. pp. 53–78.

284.   Pollard, J. A. "Words Are Cheaper Than Blood: Overseas O.W.I. and the Need for a Permanent Propaganda Agency." *Public Opinion Quarterly,* VII (Fall 1945), 283–304.

285.   Possony, Stefan T. "Needed—A New Propaganda Approach to Germany." *Public Opinion Quarterly,* V (Fall 1942), *passim.*

286.   Powell, Robert. "War by Leaflet." *Living Age,* CCCLVII (December 1939), 326–329.

287.   Prange, Gordon W. tler's Speeches and the United States. New York: Oxford University Press, 1941. 32p.

288.   _____ , ed. *Hitler's Words.* Washington, D.C.: American Council on Public Affairs, 1944. 400p.

289.   Pringle, H. F. "The Baloney Barrage Pays Off: The Psychological Warfare Section's Paper Offensive." *Saturday Evening Post,* CCXVII (March 31, 1945), 18–19+.

290.   "Psychological Warfare: The O.W.I. Runs a School for Propagandists." *Life,* XV (December 13, 1943), 81–84.

291.   Pyle, Norman R. "A Study of United States Propaganda Efforts and Pro-Allied Sentiments in Argentina during World War II." Unpublished Ph.D. dissertation, Georgetown University, 1968.

292.   Qualter, Terence H. *Propaganda and Psychological Warfare.* New York: Random House, 1962. 172p.

293.   Reiners, Wilfred O. *Soviet Indoctrination of German War Prisoners, 1941–1956.* Cambridge, Mass.: Center for International Studies, Massachusetts Institute of Technology, 1959. 80p.

294.   Rennie, J. O. "Dr. Goebbel's Awkward Squad." *Atlantic,* CLXXII (September 1943), 107+.

295.   Rhodes, Anthony, and Victor Margolin. *Propaganda: The Art of Persuasion—World War II.* New York: Chelsea House, 1976. 318p.

296.   Riess, Curt. "The Germans Don't Know They're Beaten." *New York Times Magazine,* (February 4, 1945), 5+.

297.   _____ . "Planned Chaos, the Nazi Goal." *New York Times Magazine,* (April 22, 1945), 10–11+.

298.   Rigby, Charles A. *War on the Short Waves.* London: Cole, 1944. 68p.

299.   Robbs, Peter H. "Aerial Propaganda Leaflets." *World War II Journal*, III (January–February 1976), 29.

300.   Roetler, Charles. *The Art of Psychological Warfare, 1914–1945*. New York: Stein & Day, 1974. 199p.

301.   Rolo, Charles J. *Radio Goes to War: The Fourth Front*. New York: Putnam, 1942. 293p.

302.   _____. "Radio War on the U.S.A." *American Mercury*, LII (January 1941), 67–74.

303.   _____. "The Strategy of War by Radio." *Harper's Magazine*, CLXXXI (November 1940), 646–649.

304.   Romulo, Carlos P. "Japan Exploits Our Lost Face." *New York Times Magazine*, (October 10, 1943), 8+

305.   Roucek, Joseph. *Axis Psychological Strategy against the United States*. Hempstead, N.J.: Hofstra College, 1942. 23p.

306.   _____. "The Nature of Public Opinion and Propaganda." In: his *Twentieth Century Political Thought*. New York: Philosophical Library, 1946. pp. 354–382.

307.   Rubin, Bernard. "Propaganda and Ideological Conflicts, 1917–1945." *Contemporary Review*, CCI (February 1962), 92–98.

308.   Rupp, Leila J. *Mobilizing Women for War: German and American Propaganda, 1939–1945*. Princeton, N.J.: Princeton University Press, 1978. 243p.

309.   Rutherford, Ward. *Hitler's Propaganda Machine*. New York: Grosset and Dunlap, 1978.

310.   Sava, George. *War without Guns: The Psychological Front*. Toronto, Canada: Ryerson Press, 1943. 156p.

311.   Schultz, Sigrid. "Invasion Lies." *Collier's*, CXIII (March 25, 1944), 11–12+.

German propaganda.

312.   Seth, Ronald. *The Truth-benders: Psychological Warfare in World War II*. London: Frewin, 1969. 204p.

313.   Shils, E.A. "Cohesion and Disintegration in the Wehrmacht in World War II." In: Bernard Berelson and Morris Janowitz, eds. *Reader in Public Opinion and Communication*. Enl. ed. Glencoe, Ill: Free Press, 1953. pp. 407–422.

Caused by propaganda and psychological warfare.

314.   Sington, Derrick, and Arthur Weidenfeld. *The Goebbels Experiment: A Study of the Nazi Propaganda Machine.* London: Murray, 1942. 260p.

315.   Smith, Arthur L., Jr. "Life in Wartime Germany: Colonel [Otto] Ohlendorf's Opinion Service." *Public Opinion Quarterly,* XXXVI (Spring 1972), 1–8.

316.   Smith, Bruce L., *et al. Propaganda, Communication, and Public Opinion: A Comprehensive Reference Guide.* Princeton, N.J.: Princeton University Press, 1946. 435p.

317.   Speier, Hans. "Morale and Propaganda." In: Hans Speier and Alfred Kähler, eds. *War in Our Time.* New York: Norton, 1939. pp. 299–326.

318.   _____ . "Nazi Propaganda and Its Decline." *Social Research,* X (September 1943), 337–357.

319.   _____ . "War Aims in Political Warfare." *Social Research,* XII (May 1945), 157–180.

_____ , jt. author. *See* Kris, Ernst

320.   "Station Atlantik: The Phoney Station Set Up by the British." *New Yorker,* XXI (October 13, 1945), 20–22.

321.   Steel, Richard W. "Preparing the Public for War: Efforts to Establish a National Propaganda Agency, 1940–1941." *American Historical Review,* LXXV (October 1970), 1640–1653.

322.   Taylor, Edmond. *Strategy of Terror: Europe's Inner Front.* Boston: Houghton, Mifflin, 1940. 278p.

323.   Tell, Rolf, ed. *Nazi Guide to Nazism.* Washington, D.C.: American Council on Public Affairs, 1942. 191p.

324.   Thompson, Dorothy. *Listen, Hans!* Boston: Houghton, Mifflin, 1942. 292p.

325.   Thum, Gladys, and Marcella Thum. *The Persuaders: Propaganda in War and Peace.* New York: Atheneum, 1972. 213p.

326.   Unger, Aryeh L. "The Public Opinion Reports of the Nazi Party." *Public Opinion Quarterly,* XXIX (Winter 1965–1966), 565–582.

327.   United States. Congress. House. Special Committee on Un-American Activities. *Investigation of Un-American Propaganda Activities in the United States: Hearings.* 78th Cong., 2d sess. 3 vols. Washington, D.C.: U.S. Government Printing Office, 1944.

328. _____ . Foreign Broadcast Information Service. *The Foreign Broadcast Information Service in Retrospect, 1941–1971.* Washington, D.C., 1971. 56p.

329. _____ . War Department. Information and Education Division, Research Branch. *Studies in Social Psychology in World War II: Prepared and Edited under the Auspices of a Special Committee of the Social Science Research Council.* 4 vols. Princeton, N.J.: Princeton University Press, 1949–1950.

330. Valcher, W. H., Jr. "Combat Propaganda against the Japanese in the Central Pacific." Unpublished Ph.D. dissertation, Stanford University, 1950.

331. "The Voices of Freedom." *U.S. Army Talks*, IV (September 16, 1945), 1–31.

332. Von Strempel, Heribert. "Confessions of a German Propagandist." *Public Opinion Quarterly*, X (Summer 1946), 216–233.

333. Wales, H. G. Q. "Buddhism as a Japanese Propaganda Instrument." *Free World*, V (May 1943), 428–432.

334. Walker, David E. *Civilian Attack.* London: Chapman, Hall, 1943. 124p.

Propaganda and psychological warfare.

335. Warburg, James P. *Unwritten Treaty.* New York: Harcourt, 1946. 186p.

Psychological warfare.

Weidenfeld, Arthur, jt. author. *See* Sington, Derrick

336. Weinberg, Gerhard L. "Hitler's Image of the United States." *American Historical Review*, LXIX (July 1964), 1006–1021.

337. Weinburg, Sydney. "What to Tell America: The Writers' Quarrel in the Office of War Information." *Journal of American History*, LV (June 1968), 73–89.

338. Wells, Robert D. "Persuading the U-boats." *U.S. Naval Institute Proceedings*, XC (1964), 52–59.

Allied psychological warfare broadcasts.

339. Whitton, John B. "War by Radio." *Foreign Affairs*, XIX (April 1941), 584–596.

_____ , jt. editor. *See* Childs, Harwood L.

340. Wildes, Harry E. "The War for the Mind of Japan." *Annals of the American Academy of Political and Social Science*, CCXCIV (July 1954), 1–7.

341. Wilkinson, Marc. *World War II Radio Broadcasts.* Las Vegas, Nev.: Byzantine Press, 1978.

342. Winkler, Alan M. *The Politics of Propaganda: The Office of War Information, 1942–1945.* Yale Historical Publications Miscellany, no. 118. New Haven, Conn.: Yale University Press, 1978. 230p.

343. Zeman, Zbynek A. B. *Nazi Propaganda.* London and New York: Oxford University Press, 1964. 226p.

Further References

Readers will find a few additional references to the use of propaganda and psychological warfare in section I, subsections B and D, above, section VII below, and in the individual biographies of Joseph Goebbels and Ellis M. Zacharias in section VIII, subsection B.

III/Intelligence: General Works and Secret Services

Introduction

Intelligence, for our purposes, means basically information from various sources that has been sifted and evaluated. Such data may or may not be usefully employed. Since World War II, intelligence has generally come to be classified into three categories: 1) national–strategic, 2) combat–tactical, and 3) counterintelligence.

National–strategic intelligence seeks to give insight into the intentions and capabilities of an enemy state. Combat–tactical intelligence provides data on opposing military forces valuable in planning or mounting campaigns or battles. During the war, the distinction between these two categories tended to blur on occasion but was far clearer than it is today in the nuclear age. Counterintelligence, largely a police function, focuses on the process of gathering information as well as the protection of one's own secrets while frustrating the intelligence-gathering process of an opponent, especially one operating in your nation or sphere. Occasionally, counterintelligence can be a positive factor in providing information about a foe. One of the war's most successful counterintelligence operations was the "North Pole" affair perpetrated by the Germans in the Low Countries.

The citations presented in subsection A were grouped there for emphasis on national–strategic intelligence and the spy/counterspy process as a whole. Those accounts not directly devoted to the war all contain segments relative to the conflict. There is overlap between the theoretical and operational.

Scientific, technical, communications, and electronic intelligence is the topic for subsection B. There is great overlap between national–strategic and combat–tactical intelligence here as well as between theory and operations. Because of the great current interest in such subjects as "Ultra" and "Magic," however, the majority of these titles have been segregated in one convenient location.

National espionage and counterespionage agencies are treated in subsection C. The spy/counterspy organizations of seven Allied and Axis nations are surveyed with organizational emphasis. Here one can find references to the OSS, the Gestapo, and the NKVD among others in both agency stories and more general institutional histories or certain political biographies (e.g., Hitler). Most of the citations in this subsection are rich in biographical and operational detail as well.

A. General Works

344. Boucard, Robert. *The Secret Services of Europe.* Translated from the French. London: S. Paul, 1940. 260p.

345. Clark, Ronald W. *Great Moments in Espionage.* New York: Roy Publishers, 1964. 126p.

Deindorfer, R. G., jt. author. *See* Rowan, Richard W.

346. DeLaunay, Jacques. *The Secret Diplomacy of World War II.* Translated from the French. New York: Simmons–Boardman, 1963. 175p.

347. Dulles, Allen W. *The Craft of Intelligence.* New York: Harper, 1963. 277p.

348. _____ , ed. *Great True Spy Stories.* New York: Harper, 1968. 393p.

349. Elliott-Bateman, Michael. *Intelligence–Subversion–Resistance.* Vol. I of *The Fourth Dimension of Warfare.* New York: Praeger, 1970. 181p.

350. Farago, Ladislas. *Burn after Reading: The Espionage History of World War II.* New York: Walker, 1961. 319p.

351. _____ . *The War of Wits: The Anatomy of Espionage and Intelligence.* New York: Funk & Wagnalls, 1954. 379p.

352. Felix, Christopher. *A Short Course in the Secret War.* Toronto, Canada: Clarke, Irwin, 1963. 314p.

353. FitzGibbon, Constantine. *Secret Intelligence in the 20th Century.* London: Hart–Davis, 1976. 350p.

354. Gribble, Leonard R. *Famous Feats of Espionage.* London: Barker, 1972. 153p.

355. Haldane, Robert A. *The Hidden War.* New York: St. Martin's Press, 1978. 224p.

356. Halter, Jon C. *Top Secret Projects of World War II.* New York: Messner, 1978. 192p.

Includes top-secret missions.

357. Haswell, Chetwynd J. D. *Spies and Spymasters: A Concise History of Intelligence.* London: Thames & Hudson, 1977. 176p.

358. Ind, Allison. *A History of Modern Espionage.* London: Hodder and Stoughton, 1965. 288p.

359. _____ . *A Short History of Espionage.* New York: McKay, 1963. 337p.

360.   Irwin, William H., and Thomas M. Johnson. "The Spy: What He Does and How" *Science Digest,* XIV (September 1943), 87–92.

361.   _____. *What You Should Know about Spies and Saboteurs.* New York: Norton, 1943. 227p.

362.   Johnson, Brian D. G. *The Secret War.* New York and London: Methuen, 1978. 352p.

Johnson, Thomas M., jt. author. *See* Irwin, William H.

363.   Kahn, David. "Intelligence." American Committee on the History of the Second World War, *Newsletter,* no. 11 (December 1973), 6–8.

364.   Komroff, Manuel. *True Adventures of Spies.* Boston: Little, Brown, 1954. 220p.

365.   Lawson, Donald. *The Secret World War II.* New York: Watts, 1978. 118p.

366.   McRory, George W. *Strategic Intelligence in Modern European History.* Washington, D. C., 1957. 74p.

367.   Newman, Bernard. *Epics of Espionage.* New York: Philosophical Library, 1951. 270p.

368.   Palmer, Raymond. *The Making of a Spy.* New York: Crescent Books, 1978. 144p.

369.   Pawle, Gerald. *The Secret War, 1939–1945.* New York: Sloane, 1957. 297p.

370.   Perles, Alfred, ed. *Great True Spy Adventures.* New York: Arco Press, 1957. 210p.

371.   *Reader's Digest,* Editors of. *Secrets and Spies: Behind-the-Scenes Stories of World War II.* Pleasantville, N. Y.: Reader's Digest Association, 1964. 576p.

372.   _____. *Secrets and Stories of the War: A Selection of Articles and Book Condensations in Which the Reader's Digest Records the Second World War.* 2 vols. Pleasantville, N. Y.: Reader's Digest Association, 1963.

373.   Rowan, Richard W. *Spy Secrets.* New York: Buse Publications, 1946. 112p.

374.   _____. *Terror in Our Time: The Secret Service of Surprise Attack.* New York: Longmans, Green, 1942. 438p.

375.   _____, and R. G. Deindorfer. *Secret Service: 33 Centuries of Espionage.* London: Kimber, 1969. 786p.

376.   Schaf, Frank L., Jr. *The Evolution of Modern Strategic Intelligence.* Research Study. Carlisle Barrcks, Pa.: U. S. Army War College, 1965. 698p.

377.   Seth, Ronald. *The Art of Spying.* New York: Philosophical Library, 1957. 183p.

378. _____ . *Spies at Work: A History of Espionage.* New York: Philosophical Library, 1955. 234p.

379. _____ . *True Book about the Secret Service.* London: Muller, 1953. 142p.

380.   Singer, Kurt D., ed. *Three Thousand Years of Espionage: An Anthology of the World's Greatest Spy Stories.* Englewood Cliffs, N. J.: Prentice–Hall, 1948. 384p.

381. _____ . *The World's Best Spy Stories: Fact and Fiction.* Toronto, Canada: Ryerson Press, 1954. 342p.

382. _____ . *More Spy Stories.* London: Allen and Unwin, 1955. 224p.

383.   Stoney, T. B. *Spies and Saboteurs: How They Work.* New York: Authentic Publications, 1943. 96p.

384.   United States. Navy Department. Office of the Chief of Naval Operations, Office of Naval Intelligence. *Espionage, Sabotage, Conspiracy: German and Russian Operations, 1940–1945.* Washington, D. C., 1947. 191p.

385.   Wasserman, Benno. "The Failure of Intelligence Predictions." *Political Studies,,* VIII (June 1960), 156–169.

386.   Zlotnick, Jack. *National Intelligence.* Rev. ed. Washington, D. C.: Industrial College of the Armed Forces, 1964. 75p.

Further References

A few relative additional works supplemental to this section will be found in section I, subsection D, above, section IV, and section VIIA below as well as in the collected biographies in section VIII, subsection A.

B. *Cryptography, Ultra, and Technical Intelligence*

1. Cryptography

387. Ardman, Harvey. "U. S. Code-breakers vs. Japanese Code-breakers in World War II." *American Legion Magazine* (May 1972), 18–23, 38–42.

388. Bond, Raymond, T., ed. *Famous Stories of Code and Cipher.* New York: Collier Books, 1965. 383p.

389. Farago, Ladislas. *The Broken Seal: The Story of "Operation Magic" and the Pearl Harbor Disaster.* New York: Random House, 1967. 439p.

390. Gaines, Helen. *Cryptanalysis: A Study of Ciphers and Their Solutions.* New York: Dover Books, 1939. 230p.

391. Kahn, David. *The Codebreakers: The Story of Secret Writing.* New York: Macmillan, 1967. 1,164p.

The definitive work.

392. _____. "German Military Eaves-droppers." *Cryptologia* (October 1977), 378–380.

393. _____. "Modern Cryptology." *Scientific American*, CCXV (July 1966), 38–46.

394. _____. "The Significance of Codebreaking and Intelligence in Allied Strategy and Tactics." *American Committee on the History of the Second World War*, *Newsletter*, no. 17 (May 1977), 3–4.

395. _____. "The Significance of Codebreaking in Allied Strategy and Tactics." *Cryptologia*, (July 1977), 209–222.

396. "Magic Was the Word for It." *Time*, XLVI (December 17, 1945), 20–22.

397. Maskelyne, Jasper. *Magic—Top Secret.* London and New York: Kegan Paul, 1949. 191p.

398. Paul, Doris A. *The Navajo Code Talkers.* Philadelphia, Pa.: Dorrance, 1973. 170p.

399. Pratt, Fletcher. *Secret and Urgent: The Story of Codes and Ciphers.* Garden City, N. Y.: Blue Ribbon Publishing Co., 1942. 282p.

400. Shannon, Claude E. "Communication Theory of Secrecy Systems." *Bell System Technical Journal*, XXVIII (1949), 656–715.

401. Smith, Lawrence D. *Cryptography: The Science of Secret Writing.* New York: Dover Publications, Inc., 1955. 164p.

402. _____ . "Secret Messages Vital in War." *Science Digest,* XIV (July 1943), 15–20.

403. United States. Department of Defense. *The "Magic" Background of Pearl Harbor* [February 14 to December 7, 1941]. 8 vols. Washington, D.C.: U.S. Government Printing Office, 1977–1978.

404. _____ . Navy and War Departments. *The Magic Documents: Summaries and Transcripts of the Top-secret Diplomatic Communications of Japan, 1938–1945.* 14 reels, 35mm microfilm. Washington, D.C.: University Publications of America, 1979.

405. Van Der Rhoer, Edward. *Deadly Magic.* New York: Scribner, 1978. 225p.

406. Wickware, F. S. "Secret Language of War: Breaking the Japanese Code before Pearl Harbor." *Life,* XIX (November 26, 1945), 63–64+.

2. Ultra

407. Bell, Ernest L. *An Initial View of "Ultra" as an American Weapon.* Keene, N. H.: T.S.U. Press, 1977. 110p.

408. Bethell, Nicholas. "After 'The Last Secret.'" *Encounter*, XLV (November 1975), 82–88.

409. Blumenson, Martin. "Intelligence and World War II: Will 'Ultra' Rewrite History?" *Army,* XXVIII (August 1978), 42–48.

410. Cave–Brown, Anthony. *The Bodyguard of Lies.* New York: Harper & Row, 1975. 947p.

411. Cook, Don. "On Revealing 'The Last Secret.'" *Encounter*, XLV (July 1975), 80–86.

412. Deavours, C. A., and James Reeds. "The Enigma—Historical Perspective." *Cryptologia,* (October 1977), 381–391.

413. Deutsch, Harold C. "The Historical Impact of Revealing 'The Ultra Secret.'" *Parameters,* VII (March 1977), 16–32.

414. Dunn, Walter S., Jr. "The 'Ultra' Papers." *Military Affairs,* XLII (October 1978), 134–136.

415. FitzGibbon, Constance. "'The Ultra Secret': Enigma in the War." *Encounter*, XLIV (March 1975), 81–85.

416. Howard, Michael. "'Ultra' Variations." *Times Literary Supplement,* no. 3872 (May 28, 1976), 641–642.

417. Korbonski, Stefan. "The True Story of 'Enigma': The German Code Machine in World War II." *East European Quarterly,* XI (Summer 1977), 227–234.

418. Lewin, Ronald. *"Ultra" Goes to War: The Secret Story.* New York: McGraw–Hill, 1979. 360p.

419. Montagu, Ewen E. S. *Beyond "Top Secret Ultra."* New York: Coward–McCann, 1977. 192p.

Reeds, James, jt. author. *See* Deavours, C. A.

420. Rosengarten, Adolph G., Jr. "With 'Ultra' from Omaha Beach to Weimar Germany—A Personal View." *Military Affairs*, XLII (October 1978), 127–133.

The author was chief of G–2 for the U.S. 1st Army.

421. Spiller, Roger J. "Some Implications of 'Ultra.'" *Military Affairs*, XL (April 1976), 49–54.

422. Stafford, David A. T. "'Ultra' and the British Official Histories: A Documentary Note." *Military Affairs,*, XLII (February 1978), 29–31.

423. United States. Army Air Forces. *"Ultra" and the History of the United States Strategic Air Force in Europe vs. the German Air Force.* Washington, D.C.: University Publications of America, 1979. 300p.

Reprinting of a formerly classified study.

424. Winterbotham, Frederick W. *The Ultra Secret.* New York: Harper & Row, 1974. 199p.

3. Technical Intelligence

425. Ablett, Charles B. "Electronic Warfare: A Modern Weapons System." *Military Review*, XLVI (November 1966), 3–11.

426. Bar–Zohar, Michael. *The Hunt for German Scientists.* Translated from the French. New York: Hawthorn Books, 1967.

427. Baxter, James P., III. *Scientists against Time.* Boston: Little, Brown, 1948. 473p.

Boas, Marie, jt. author. *See* Guerlac, Henry

428. Bond, Donald. *Radio Direction Finders.* New York: McGraw–Hill, 1944. 287p.

429. Bush, Vannevar. *Modern Arms and Free Men: A Discussion of the Role of Science in Preserving Democracy.* New York: Simon and Schuster, 1949. 273p.

430. Carne, Daphne. *The Eyes of the Few.* London: Macmillan, 1960. 238p.

Radar.

431.   Carroll, John M. *Secrets of Electronic Espionage.* New York: E. P. Dutton, 1966. 224p.

Communication, electronic, and radar techniques, hardware, and countermeasures.

432.   Clark, Ronald W. *The Rise of the Boffins.* London: Phoenix House, 1962. 268p.

433.   Dunlap, Orrin E. *Radar: What It Is and How It Works.* New York: Harper, 1948. 268p.

434.   Eggleston, Wilfrid. *Scientists at War.* London and New York: Oxford University Press, 1951. 291p.

435.   Ford, Brian J. *Allied Secret Weapons.* Ballantine's Illustrated History of the Violent Century. New York: Ballantine Books, 1971. 160p.

436.   _____ . *German Secret Weapons.* Ballantine's Illustrated History of the Violent Century. New York: Ballantine Books, 1969. 160p.

437.   Goudsmet, Samuel. *Alsos.* New York: Henry Schuman, 1947. 259p.

U. S. scientific intelligence agents probe newly liberated areas of Western Europe seeking data on German atomic research.

438.   Gray, George W. "Electric Warfare." In: his *Science at War.* New York: Harper, 1943. pp. 111–141.

439.   Green, Constance M., Harry C. Thomson, and Peter C. Roots. *The Ordnance Department: Planning Munitions for War.* United States Army in World War II: The Technical Services. Washington, D. C.: Office of the Chief of Military History, Department of the Army, 1955. 542p.

Technical intelligence covered in chapters 7 and 9.

440.   Guerlac, Henry, and Marie Boas. "The Radar War against the U-boat." *Military Affairs,* XIV (Summer 1950), 99–111.

441.   Harrod, Roy F. *The Prof: A Personal Memoir of Lord Cherwell.* London: Macmillan, 1959. 281p.

442.   Hezlet, Arthur. *Electronics and Sea Power.* New York: Stein & Day, 1976. 318p.

443.   Hoover, J. Edgar. "The Enemy's Masterpiece of Espionage: The Microdot Process." *Reader's Digest,* XLVIII (April 1946), 1–6.

444.   Horne, Charles F. "Report of the Board Convened to Consider and Report on Radar and Countermeasures Equipment." Unpublished paper, Operational Archives, U. S. Naval Historical Center, 1945. 142p.

445. "'Huff Duff' vs. the U-boat." *Electronic Warfare,* VIII (May–June 1976), 71+.

446. Moore, Frederick L. "Radio Countermeasures." *Air University Quarterly Review,* II (Fall 1948), 57–66.

447. O'Connell, Jerome A. "Radar and the U-boat." *U. S. Naval Institute Proceedings,* LXXXIX (1963), 53–65.

448. Page, Robert M. *The Origin of Radar.* Garden City, N.Y.: Anchor Books, 1962. 196p.

449. Pash, Boris T. *The ALSOS Mission.* New York: Award House, 1966.

Paszek, Lawrence J., jt. editor. *See* Wright, Monte D.

450. Price, Alfred. *Instruments of Darkness: The History of Electronic Warfare.* New, enl., and rev. ed. London: Macdonalds and Jane's, 1977. 284p.

451. _____. "The Radio War." *RAF Flying Review,* XVIII (June 1963), 25–27+.

British vs. German airborne radar.

452. Reit, Seymour. *Masquerade: The Amazing Camouflage Deceptions of World War II.* New York: Hawthorn Books, 1978. 255p.

453. Rolya, William I. "Intelligence, Security, and Electronic Warfare." *Signal,* XXXII (March 1978), 15–17.

Roots, Peter C., jt. author. *See* Green, Constance M.

454. Rowe, Albert P. *One Story of Radar.* Cambridge, Eng.: At the University Press, 1948. 207p.

455. Saville, Gordon P. "Electronics in Air Defense." *Signal,* IV (September–October 1949), 5–7.

456. Saward, Dudley. *The Bomber's Eye.* London: Cassell, 1959. 264p.

457. Smith, Harry F. "Flak Evasion." *Electronic Warfare,* II (April–May 1970), 18–19+.

458. Terrell, Edward. *Admiralty Brief: The Story of Inventions That Contributed to Victory in the Battle of the Atlantic.* London: Harrap, 1958. 240p.

Thomson, Harry C., jt. author. *See* Green, Constance M.

459. Thurbon, M. T. "The Origins of Electronic Warfare." *Journal of the Royal United Service Institute for Defence Studies,* CXXII (September 1977), 56–63.

460. United States. Army. Far East Command, Military Intelligence Section. *History of Technical Intelligence: Southwest and Western Pacific Areas, 1942–1945.* 2 vols. Tokyo, Japan: U. S. Army Technical Information Center, 1945.

461. _____ . _____ . _____ . *Operations of the Technical Intelligence Unit in the Southwest Pacific Area.* 1 vol. Tokyo, Japan: U. S. Army Technical Information Center, 1948.

462. _____ . Joint Board on Scientific Information Policy. *Electronics Warfare: A Report on Radar Countermeasures.* Washington, D.C., 1945. 38p.

463. _____ . _____ . *Radar: A Report on Science at War.* Washington, D.C., 1945. 53p.

464. _____ . National Defense Research Committee, Division 15. "Electronic Warfare History, World War II." *Electronic Warfare,* IV (Summer, Fall 1972), 20+, 20–22+.

465. _____ . Navy Department. Office of the Chief of Naval Operations, Naval Technical Mission, Europe, Historical Section. "Office of Naval Operations Technical Mission to Europe." Unpublished paper, Operational Archives, U. S. Naval Historical Center, 1945. 280p.

466. _____ . _____ . Pacific Fleet and Pacific Ocean Area. "Japanese Radar." *Cincpac–Cincpoa Weekly Intelligence, Supplement,* I (1944), *passim.*

467. Vosseller, Aurelius B. "Science and the Battle of the Atlantic." *Yale Review,* New Series XXXV (June 1946), 667–681.

468. Waddington, Conrad H. *OR in World War II: Operational Research against the U-boat.* London: Elek, 1973. 253p.

469. Watson–Watt, Robert A. *The Pulse of Radar.* New York: Dial Press, 1959. 438p.

470. Wilhelm, Donald. "Radar, the Super Sleuth." In: John D. Ratcliff, ed. *Science Year Book of 1944.* Garden City, N. Y.: Doubleday, 1945. pp. 89–93.

471. Wright, Monte D., and Lawrence J. Paszek, eds. *Science, Technology, and Warfare: Proceedings of the Third Military History Symposium Held at the U. S. Air Force Academy, 8–9 May 1969.* Washington, D. C.: Published for the Office of Air Force History by the U. S. Government Printing Office, 1971. 221p.

Further References

Users can locate additional references to these specialized aspects of World War II intelligence by checking works in section I, subsections B, C, and D, above, and section III, subsection C, section IV, V, and VII below. Biographies of a few prominent individuals may be found by checking over the introductory material designated III:B in section VIII, subsection B, below.

C. Secret Services: Espionage and Counterespionage Organizations

1. Great Britain

472.   Bulloch, John. *MI 5: The Origin and History of the British Counterespionage Service.* London: Barker, 1963. 206p.

473.   Busch, Tristan. *Secret Service Unmasked.* London: Hutchinson, 1950. 272p.

474.   Collier, Basil. *The Defence of the United Kingdom.* History of the Second World War: United Kingdom Military Series. London: H. M. Stationery Office, 1957. 557p.

Cookridge, E. H., pseud. *See* Spiro, Edward.

Deacon, Richard, pseud. *See* McCormick, Donald

475.   "The Double-cross System: British Intelligence." *Newsweek,* LXXVIII (November 22, 1971), 58+.

476.   Felstead, Sidney T. *Intelligence: An Indictment of a Colossal Failure.* London: Hutchinson, 1941. 253p.

477.   Haswell, Chetwynd J. D. *British Military Intelligence.* London: Weidenfeld and Nicolson, 1973. 262p.

478.   Hinsley, Frank H., *et al. History of British Intelligence in the Second World War: Volume I.* London: H. M. Stationery Office, 1979. 600p.

479.   Langelaan, Henry. *The Masks of War.* Garden City, N. Y.: Doubleday, 1959. 283p.

480.   McCormick, Donald. *A History of the British Secret Service.* By Richard Deacon, pseud. New York: Taplinger, 1970. 440p.

481.   Macrae, Stuart. *Winston Churchill's Toy Shop.* New York: Walker, 1971. 228p.

Secret weapons department MD–1.

482. Masterman, John C. *The Double-cross System in the War of 1939–1945.* New Haven, Conn.: Yale University Press, 1972. 203p.

483. Peis, Günter. *The Mirror of Deception: How Britain Turned the Nazi Spy Machine against Itself.* Translated from the German. London: Weidenfeld and Nicolson, 1977. 190p.

484. Spiro, Edward. *Secrets of the British Secret Service: Behind-the-Scenes of the Work of British Counterespionage during the War.* By E. H. Cookridge, pseud. London: Low, Marston, 1948. 216p.

485. Wade, G. A. *Intelligence and Liaison.* Training Series. London: Gale and Polden, 1942. 36p.

2. Germany

486. Allied Expeditionary Forces. Supreme Headquarters. Office of the Assistant Chief of Staff, G–2, Counter-intelligence Subdivision, Evaluation and Dissemination Section. *The German Intelligence Services.* By Hugh Trevor–Roper. London, 1944. 32p.

487. _____ . _____ . _____ . _____ . _____ . Rev. ed. London, 1945. 30p.

488. Bartz, Karl. *The Downfall of the German Secret Service.* Translated from the German. London: Kimber, 1956. 202p.

489. Bender, Roger J., and Hugh P. Taylor. *Uniforms, Organization, and History of the Waffen SS.* 2 vols. London: Scott, 1969–1970.

490. Bracher, Karl D. *The German Dictatorship.* Translated from the German. New York: Praeger, 1970. 553p.

491. Brissard, André. *The Nazi Secret Service.* Translated from the French. New York: Norton, 1974. 320p.

Collins, Frederick L., jt. author. *See* Hoover, J. Edgar

492. Crankshaw, Edward. *Gestapo: Instrument of Tyranny.* New York: Putnam, 1956. 275p.

493. De Jong, Louis. *The German Fifth Column in World War II.* Translated from the Dutch. Chicago: University of Chicago Press, 1956. 308p.

494. Delarue, Jacques. *The Gestapo: A History of Terror.* Translated from the French. New York: Morrow, 1964. 384p.

495. Felstead, S. Theodore. *Germany and Her Spies: A Story of the Intrigues of the Nazis.* London: Hutchinson, 1940. 232p.

496.   Fest, Joachim C. *Hitler.* Translated from the German. New York: Harcourt, 1974. 844p.

Much on the use of the secret instruments.

497.   Graber, G. S. *History of the SS.* New York: McKay, 1978. 244p.

498.   Great Britain. War Office. *Manual on the German Secret Services and British Countermeasures.* London: H. M. Stationery Office, 1944.

499.   _____ . _____ . *The Trials of German Major War Criminals.* 26 vols. London: H.M. Stationery Office, 1948.

The Nuremberg documents contain much on German secret services and counterespionage efforts.

Hagen, Walter, pseud. *See* Hoettl, Wilhelm

500.   Hale, Aron J. "The German Secret Service." *Virginia Quarterly Review,* XLVIII (Winter 1973), 126–131.

501.   Hoettl, Wilhelm. *The Secret Front: The Story of Nazi Political Espionage.* By Walter Hagen, pseud. Translated from the German. New York: Praeger, 1954. 327p.

502.   Höhne, Heinz. *The Order of the Death's Head: The Story of Hitler's SS.* Translated from the German. New York: Ballantine Books, 1971. 786p.

503.   Hoke, Henry R. *It's a Secret.* New York: Reynal, 1946. 312p.

504.   Hoover, J. Edgar. "New Tricks of the Nazi Spies." *American Magazine,* CXXXVI (October 1943), 28–29+.

505.   _____ , and Frederick L. Collins. "Hitler's Spies Are Experts." *Collier's,* CXI (April 24, 1943), 12+.

506.   Institute für Zeitgeschichte. *Anatomy of the SS State.* New York: Walker, 1968. 614p.

507.   International Military Tribunal. *Trial of the Major War Criminals before the International Military Tribunal, Nuremberg, 14 November 1945–10 October 1946.* 42 vols. Nuremberg, Germany, 1947.

508.   Irving, David, ed. *Breach of Security: The German Secret Intelligence File on Events Leading to the Second World War.* London: Kimber, 1968. 216p.

509.   Keegan, John. *Waffen SS: The Asphalt Soldiers.* Ballantine's Illustrated History of the Violent Century. New York: Ballantine Books, 1970. 160p.

510.   Lennhoff, Eugen. *Agents of Hell: Himmler's Fifth Column.* London: Hutchinson, 1940. 157p.

511.   Manvell, Roger. *SS and Gestapo: Rule by Terror.* Ballantine's Illustrated History of the Violent Century. New York: Ballantine Books, 1969. 160p.

512.   Meldal–Johnsen, Trevor, and Vaughn Young. *The Interpol Connection: An Inquiry into the International Criminal Police Organization.* New York: Dial Press, 1978. 320p.

From the days when it was chaired by Reinhard Heydrich.

513.   Neave, Airey. *On Trial at Nuremberg.* Boston: Little, Brown, 1979.

The author took evidence against the S.S. and Gestapo.

514.   Neumann, Franz. "The Rise of Himmler, the Police, and SS." In: his *Behemoth: The Structure and Practice of National Socialism, 1933–1944.* Rev. ed. London and New York: Oxford University Press, 1944. pp. 540–550.

515.   Neumann, Peter. *The Black March: The Personal Story of an SS Man.* New York: Sloane, 1959. 312p.

516.   Newman, Bernard. *Secrets of German Espionage.* New York: Ryerson Press, 1940. 288p.

517.   Paetel, K. O. "Why the Wehrmacht Fights On: Gestapo Espionage." *Nation,* CLIX (October 14, 1944), 437–438.

Peis, Günther, jt. author. *See* Wighton, Charles

518.   Reitlinger, Gerald R. *The SS: Alibi of a Nation, 1922–1945.* New York: Viking Press, 1957. 502p.

519.   Rigg, Robert B. "Of Spies and Specie." *Military Review,* XLII (August 1962), 13–21.

520.   Russell, Edward F. L. *The Scourge of the Swastika: A Short History of Nazi War Crimes.* By Lord Russell of Liverpool. New York: Ballantine Books, 1961. 244p.

521.   Speer, Albert. *Inside the Third Reich.* New York: Macmillan, 1970. 596p.

522.   _____. *Spandau: The Secret Diaries.* New York: Macmillan, 1976. 463p.

Much on Himmler, Goebbels, the S.S., and the Gestapo.

523.   Stein, George H. *The Waffen SS: Hitler's Elite Guard at War, 1939–1945.* Ithaca, N. Y.: Cornell University Press, 1966. 330p.

524. Sydnor, Charles W. *Soldiers of Destruction: The SS Death's Head Division, 1933–1945.* Princeton, N.J.: Princeton University Press, 1977. 371p.

Taylor, Hugh P., jt. author. *See* Bender, Roger J.

525. Toland, John. *Hitler.* 2 vols. Garden City, N. Y.: Doubleday, 1976.

Much on Germany's secret instruments of terror.

Trevor–Roper, Hugh, author. *See* Allied Expeditionary Forces

526. United States. Chief of Counsel for the Prosecution of Axis Criminality. *Nazi Conspiracy and Agression.* 8 vols. Washington, D.C.: U.S. Government Printing Office, 1946.

527. _____ . _____ . _____ : *Supplement A–B.* 2 vols. Washington, D. C.: U. S. Government Printing Office, 1947.

528. Whitman, Philip. "The Black Terror Called Gestapo: Its Agents Are Spread All over Europe and There Is No Appeal from Their Grim Actions." *New York Times Magazine,* (February 8, 1942), 5+.

529. Wighton, Charles, and Günther Peis. *Hitler's Spies and Saboteurs.* New York: Holt, 1958. 285p.

530. Windrow, Martin C. *The Waffen SS.* Reading, Berkshire, Eng.: Osprey, 1971. 40p.

Young, Vaughn, jt. author. *See* Meldal–Johnsen, Trevor

3. Soviet Union

531. Dallin, David J. *Soviet Espionage.* New Haven, Conn.: Yale University Press, 1956. 558p.

532. Deriabin, Petr S. *Watchdogs of Terror: Russian Bodyguards from the Tsars to the Commisars.* New York: Arlington House, 1972. 448p.

533. Heilbrunn, Otto. *The Soviet Secret Services.* New York: Praeger, 1956. 216p.

534. Hingley, Ronald. *The Russian Secret Police.* London: Hutchinson, 1970. 305p.

535. Höhne, Heinz. *Codeword Direktor: The Story of the Red Orchestra.* Translated from the German. London: Pan Books, 1973. 256p.

536. Lewytzkyji, Borys. *The Uses of Terror: The Soviet Secret Police, 1917– 1970.* Translated from the Russian. New York: Coward–McCann, 1972. 349p.

537. Peyroles, Jacques. *The Red Orchestra.* By Gilles Perrault, pseud. Translated from the French. New York: Simon and Schuster, 1969. 512p.

538.   Reinhardt, Guenther. "Hitler Aide—Stalin Spy." *Plain Talk*, III (August 1949), 24–28.

539.   Seth, Ronald. *The Executioners: The Story of SMERSH*. New York: Hawthorn Books, 1967. 199p.

540.   _____ . *Unmasked! The Story of Soviet Espionage*. New York: Hawthorn Books, 1965. 306p.

541.   Sinevirskii, Nikolai. *SMERSH*. Translated from the Russian. New York: Holt, 1950. 253p.

Slusser, R. M., jt. ed. *See* Wolin, Simon

542.   United States. Central Intelligence Agency. *The Rote Kapelle [Red Orchestra]: The CIA's History of Soviet Intelligence and Espionage Networks in Western Europe, 1936–1945*. Washington, D. C.: University Publications of America, 1979. 450p.

543.   White, John B. *The Soviet Spy System*. London: Grey Walls Press, 1948. 133p.

544.   Wolin, Simon, and R. M. Slusser, eds. *The Soviet Secret Police*. New York: Praeger, 1957. 408p.

4. United States

545.   Alcorn, Robert H. *No Banners, No Bands: More Tales of the O.S.S.* New York: McKay, 1965. 275p.

546.   _____ . *No Bugles for Spies: Tales of the O.S.S.* New York: McKay, 1962. 209p.

547.   Alsop, Stewart J. O., and Thomas Braden. *Sub Rosa: The O.S.S. and American Intelligence*. New York: Reynal, 1946. 237p. Rpr. 1964.

548.   Bellamy, F. R. "Treasury Traps Spies." *American Mercury*, LXXXVIII (May 1944), 617–622.

Braden, Thomas, jt. author. *See* Alsop, Stewart J. O.

549.   Cave–Brown, Anthony, ed. *The Secret War Report of the O.S.S.* New York: Berkley/Medallion Books, 1976. 586p.

550.   Chamberlain, John. "O.S.S." *Life,* XVI (November 19, 1945), 119–130.

551.   Chandler, Harriette L. "Soviet Russia as Seen through the Eyes of American Policy Makers, 1933–1945: The Problems of Assessing Soviet Policy on the Eve of the Cold War." Unpublished Ph.D dissertation, Clark University, 1973.

552.   Collins, Frederick L. "G-men Go to War." *Reader's Digest,* XLI (December 1942), 89–93.

553. _____ . *The F.B.I. in Peace and War.* Rev., enl. ed. New York: Ace Books, 1962. 320p.

First published in 1943.

554. Corson, William R. *The Armies of Ignorance: The Rise of the American Intelligence Empire.* New York: Dial Press, 1977. 448p.

555. Donovan, William J. "Intelligence: Key to Defense." *Life,* XVII (September 30, 1946), 108–120.

Brief account of the O.S.S.

556. Eliscu, William. *Count Five and Die.* New York: Ballantine Books, 1959. 152p.

557. Fajans, Irving. "Ravage Repeat Ravage: A Slightly Fictionalized Story Gives an Authentic Picture of the Wartime Operations of the O.S.S. and Its Partisan Agents." *Infantry Journal,* LX (March 1947), 24–33.

558. Ford, Corey, and Alastair MacBain. "Cloak-and-Dagger: Espionage and Secret Intelligence Service of the O.S.S." *Collier's,* CXVI (October 6–27, 1945), 12–13+, 18–19+, 20+, 30+.

559. _____ . *Cloak-and-Dagger: The Secret Story of the O.S.S.* New York: Random House, 1946. 216p.

560. Grahame, Arthur. "How G-men Trap Axis Spies." *Popular Science,* CXLIII (October 1943), 49–53.

561. Haltom, John F. "National Security and Civil Liberty: (U.S.) Government Techniques Employed to Combat Subversive Activities, 1938–1953." Unpublished Ph.D. dissertation, University of Texas, 1954.

562. Hoover, J. Edgar. "Spy Trap: The Federal Bureau of Investigation." *Popular Mechanics,* LXXX (December 1943), 1–5+.

563. Hymoff, Edward. *The O.S.S. in World War II.* New York: Ballantine Books, 1972.

564. Irwin, Will, and Thomas M. Johnson. "The All-seeing I: How Our Intelligence Services Work." *Collier's,* CXI (May 8, 1943), 13+.

565. Jeffrey–Jones, Rhodri. *American Espionage: From Secret Service to C.I.A.* New York: Free Press, 1977. 276p.

Johnson, Thomas M., jt. author. *See* Irwin, Will

566. Kellis, James G. "The Development of U. S. National Intelligence, 1941–1961." Unpublished Ph.D dissertation, Georgetown University, 1963.

567. Kent, John L. "War Is Hell—And It Can Smell, Too: O.S.S. Skulduggery in World War II." *Army,* XXVII (June 1977), 47–48.

568. Langer, Walter C. *The Mind of Adolf Hitler: The Secret Wartime Report.* New York: Basic Books, 1972. 269p.

A pioneering remote medical diagnosis prepared by the OSS's Psychoanalytic Field Unit.

569. Langer, William L. "Scholarship and the Intelligence Problem." *American Philosophical Society Proceedings,* XCII (March 1948), 43–45.

OSS Research and Analysis Branch.

570. Lovell, Stanley P. "Cloak and Dagger Behind-the-Scenes." *Saturday Evening Post,* CCXXXV (March 3, 1962), 30+.

571. ———. "Deadly Gadgets of the O.S.S." *Popular Science,* CLXXXIII (July 1963), 56–59+.

572. ———. *Of Spies and Stratagems.* Englewood Cliffs, N. J.: Prentice–Hall, 1963. 191p.

Memoirs of the OSS director of Research and Development.

MacBain, Alastair, jt. author. *See* Ford, Corey

573. McLean, Donald B. *The Plumber's Kitchen: The Secret Story of American Spy Weapons.* Chicago: Nourmont Technical Publications, 1975. 282p.

574. Neumann, Robert G. "Political Intelligence and Its Relation to Military Government." In: Carl J. Friedrich, *et al.,* eds. *American Experience in Military Government in World War II.* New York: Rinehart, 1948. pp. 70–85.

575. Schwarzwalder, John. *We Caught Spies.* New York: Duell, Sloan and Pearce, 1946. 296p.

576. Smith, Richard H. *O.S.S.: The Secret History of America's First Central Intelligence Agency.* Berkeley: University of California Press, 1972. 458p.

577. Theoharis, Athan G. "The F.B.I.'s Stretching of Presidential Directives, 1936–1953." *Political Science Quarterly,* XCI (Winter 1976–1977), 649–673.

578. Tully, Andrew. *The F.B.I.'s Most Famous Cases.* New York: Morrow, 1965. 242p.

579. Turner, William W. *Hoover's F.B.I.: The Men and the Myth.* Los Angeles, Calif.: Sherbourne Press, 1970. 352p.

580. Ungar, Sanford J. *F.B.I.* Boston: Little, Brown, 1975. 682p.

581. United States. War Department. Office of Strategic Services, Assessment Staff. *The Assessment of Men.* New York: Rinehart, 1947. 541p.

582. _____ . _____ . _____ , History Project. *War Report of the O.S.S.* 2 vols. New York: Walker, 1976–1977

5. Other

a. China

583. McCormick, Donald. *The Chinese Secret Service.* By Richard Deacon, pseud. New York: Taplinger, 1974. 523p.

b. Japan

584. Coox, Alvin D. "Japanese Foreknowledge of the Soviet–German War, 1941." *Soviet Studies,* XXIII (April 1972), 554–572.

585. Seth, Ronald. *Secret Servants: A History of Japanese Espionage.* New York: Farrar, Straus, 1957. 278p.

c. France

586. Stead, Philip J. *Second Bureau.* London: Evans, 1959. 212p.

Further References

References to the work of the various secret service and police organizations may also be found in some of the materials cited in section I, subsections B, C, and D, above, as well as in sections V, VII, and VIII, subsection A, below. A large number of individuals involved with the various agencies and organizations are highlighted in subsection B of section VIII below; check the introductory national listing under "3."

IV/Military Intelligence: Land, Sea, and Air

Introduction

The works cited in the four subsections of this chapter are directly concerned with combat–tactical intelligence and the methods employed by warring nations to obtain and protect information useful in giving battle on land, at sea, and in the air.

Examples of methods by which combat–tactical intelligence was gathered range from infantry reconnaissance to aerial overflights and submarine sightings. Our references to the U. S. Army Counterintelligence Corps provide insight into how one military force operated to guard its secrets.

Much of the information gathered by purely military methods during the war was supported or amplified by that provided by secret agents, partisans, fifth columns, and such means as are presented in section III, subsection B, above. Sifted and evaluated from echelon to echelon and agency to agency and placed into the giant jigsaw puzzle of national–strategic intelligence, combat–tactical intelligence could provide an important tool not only to field commanders but to political leaders as well. The Normandy invasion, the German invasion of Russia, Pearl Harbor, the strategic bombing campaign, and even the dropping of the A-bomb can be used to demonstrate a close relationship between national–strategic and combat–tactical intelligence and their employment by military and political leaders alike.

A. General Works

587. Baldwin, Hanson W. *Great Mistakes of the War.* New York: Harper, 1950. 114p.

588. Borden, William L. *There Will Be No Time: The Revolution in Strategy.* New York: Macmillan, 1946. 225p.

589. Kirkpatrick, Lyman B., Jr. *Captains without Eyes: Intelligence Failures of World War II.* New York: Macmillan, 1969. 303p.

Case studies of "Operation Barbarossa," the Pearl Harbor attack, and the battles of Dieppe, Arnhem, and the Bulge.

590. "The Significance and Effects of Surprise in Modern War." *History, Numbers, and War*, I (Spring 1977), 3–15.

Further References

Readers will find a few additional citations relative to this subsection by checking the materials noted in section I, subsection D, and section III, subsection B, above. The results of military intelligence flow through the references in section V.

B. Military Intelligence (Land)

591. Baldwin, Hanson W. "Battlefield Intelligence." *Combat Forces*, III (February 1953), 30–41.

592. Bidwell, Bruce W. "History of the Military Intelligence Division, Department of the Army, General Staff: Part I." Unpublished paper, U.S. Army Center of Military History Library, 1954.

593. Booth, Walter B. "War by 'Other Means.'" *Army*, XXV (January 1975), 21–24.

594. Chandler, Stedman, *et al. Front-line Intelligence.* Washington, D. C.: Infantry Journal Press, 1946. 183p.

595. Churchill, Marlborough. "The Military Intelligence Division, General Staff." *Journal of the United States Artillery*, LIV (April 1970), 293–315.

596. Fletcher, J. "Intelligence: A Principle of War." *Military Review*, L (August 1970), 52–57.

597. Garthoff, Raymond L. "Prediction, Intelligence, and Reconnaissance." In: His *Soviet Military Doctrine.* Glencoe, Ill.: Free Press, 1953. pp. 265–277.

598. Heymont, Irving. *Combat Intelligence in Modern Warfare.* Harrisburg, Pa.: Stackpole Books, 1960. 244p.

599. Holst, Johan J. "Surprise, Signals, and Reaction: The Attack on Norway, April 9, 1940—Some Observations." *Cooperation and Conflict,* I (1966), 31–45.

600. Johnson, Thomas M. "The Golden Sphinx: The Army's Counterintelligence Corps." In: *Reader's Digest,* Editors of. *Secrets and Spies: Behind-the-Scenes Stories of World War II.* Pleasantville, N. Y.: Reader's Digest Association, 1964. pp. 364–368.

601. Kahn, David. *Hitler's Spies: German Military Intelligence in World War II.* New York: Macmillan, 1978. 671p.

602. Leverkuehn, Paul. *German Military Intelligence.* Translated from the German. New York: Praeger, 1954. 209p.

603. Matloff, Maurice, and Edwin M. Snell. *Strategic Planning for Coalition Warfare, 1941–1944.* United States Army in World War II: The War Department. 2 vols. Washington, D. C.: Office of the Chief of Military History, Department of the Army, 1953–1959.

604. Matsulenko, V. "Surprise: How It Is Achieved and Its Role." *Soviet Military Review,* nos. 5–6 (May–June 1972), 37–39.

605. Nelson, Otto L., Jr. *National Security and the General Staff: A Study of Organization and Administration.* Washington, D. C.: Infantry Journal Press, 1946. 608p.

606. "Oak Leaf," pseud. "A Look at G–2." *Infantry Journal,* LVIII (April 1946), 19–21.

607. Pettee, G. S. "Faults and Errors [of Military Intelligence] in World War II." *Infantry Journal,* LIX (October 1946), 27–34.

608. Pogue, Forrest C. *The European Theater of Operations: The Supreme Command.* United States Army in World War II: European Theater of Operations. Washington, D. C.: Office of the Chief of Military History, Department of the Army, 1954. 610p.

609. Powe, Marc B. "American Military Intelligence Comes of Age: A Sketch of the Man [Ralph H. Van Deman] and His Times." *Military Review,* LV (December 1975), 17–30.

610. _____ , and Edward E. Wilson. "The Evolution of American Military Intelligence." Unpublished paper, U. S. Army Intelligence Center, Ft. Huachua, Ariz., May 1973.

Snell, Edwin M., jt. author. *See* Matloff, Maurice

611. Thomas, Shipley. *S–2 in Action.* Harrisburg, Pa.: Military Service Publishing Co., 1940. 128p.

612. United States. Army. Counterintelligence School. *History and Mission of the Counterintelligence Corps in World War II.* Special text. Baltimore, Md.: CIC School, Counterintelligence Center, 1951. 83p.

613. _____ . _____ . Security Agency, Historical Section. *Origin and Development of the Army Security Agency, 1917–1945.* Cryptographic Series. Laguna Hills, Calif.: Aegean Park Press, 1978.

614. _____ . _____ . General Staff, Military Intelligence Division. *German Operational Intelligence: A Study.* Washington, D. C., 1946. 164p.

615. _____ . _____ . _____ . "Materials on the History of Military Intelligence in the United States, 1885–1944." Unpublished paper, U. S. Army Center of Military History Library, 1944.

616. _____ . Strategic Bombing Survey. *Japanese Military and Naval Intelligence (Japanese Intelligence Section G–2).* Washington, D. C., 1946.

617. Vagts, Alfred. "Diplomacy, Military Intelligence, and Espionage." In: his *Defense and Diplomacy: The Soldier and the Conduct of Foreign Relations.* New York: King's Crown Press, 1958. pp. 61–78.

618. Whitehouse, Arthur G. J. "Arch." *Espionage and Counterespionage: Adventures in Military Intelligence.* Garden City, N. Y.: Doubleday, 1964. 298p.

619. Williams, Robert W. "Moving Information: The Third [Army] Imperative—Patton Knew the Secret." *Army,* XXV (April 1975), 17–21.

Wilson, Edward E., jt. author. *See* Powe, Marc B.

Further References

Additional references relative to this subsection will be found in section I, subsection D, and section III, subsections B and C, above. Section V, subsection C, section VI, subsection A, and section VII below also contain some information. When checking the nationality of individuals listed in section VIII, subsection B, below, be sure to note those with 4:B in the parentheses following their names.

C. Naval Intelligence

620. Beesly, Patrick. *Very Special Intelligence: The Story of the* [British] *Admiralty's Operational Intelligence Center*, *1939–1945*. Garden City, N.Y.: Doubleday, 1978. 282p.

621. Campbell, Rodney. *The Luciano Project: The Secret Wartime Collaboration of the Mafia and the U. S. Navy.* New York: McGraw–Hill, 1977. 299p.

Deacon, Richard, pseud. *See* McCormick, Donald

622. Farago, Ladislas. *Tenth Fleet.* New York: Paperback Library, 1964. 319p.

623. Furer, Julius A. "Naval Intelligence, Combat Intelligence Division, [and] Tenth Fleet." In: his *Administration of the Navy Department in World War II.* Washington, D. C.: U. S. Government Printing Office, 1959. pp. 119–120, 156–162.

624. "Japanese Naval Intelligence." *ONI Review*, I (July 1946), 36–40.

625. Lonsdale–Bryans, James. *Blind Victory:* [British] *Secret Communications, Halifax–Hassell.* London and New York: Skeffington, 1951. 191p.

626. McCormick, Donald. *The Silent War: A History of Western Naval Intelligence.* By Richard Deacon, pseud. New York: Hippocrene Books, 1978. 288p.

627. McLachlan, Donald. "Naval Intelligence in the Second World War." *Journal of the Royal United Service Institution*, CXII (August 1967), 159–162.

628. Tolley, Kemp. "The Cruise of the *Lanikai*." *U. S. Naval Institute Proceedings*, XCIX (1973), 76–79.

629. ———. ———. Annapolis: U. S. Naval Institute, 1973. 356p.

630. ———. "The Strange Assignment of the *Lanikai*." *U. S. Naval Institute Proceedings*, LXXXVIII (1962), 70–83.

631. ———. "The Strange Mission of the *Lanikai*." *American Heritage*, XXIV (October 1973), 56–61, 93–95.

632. United States. Navy Department. Office of the Chief of Naval Operations, Office of Naval Intelligence. "The Office of Naval Intelligence." Unpublished paper. 4 vols. Operational Archives, U. S. Naval Historical Center, n.d.

633. ———. ———. ———, Op 32–E. *German Naval Intelligence: A Report Based on German Documents.* Washington, D. C., 1946. 84p.

634. _____ . _____ . Pacific Fleet and Pacific Ocean Area, Intelligence Section. *Cincpac–Cincpoa Weekly Intelligence.* 2 vols. [Honolulu, Hawaii], 1944–1945.

635. _____ . _____ . _____ . "A History of the Combat Intelligence Section, Staff, Commander-in-Chief, Pacific Fleet, from December 7, 1941 until September 1945." Unpublished paper, Operational Archives, U. S. Naval Historical Center, 1945. 450p.

636. _____ . _____ . _____ . "Report of Intelligence Activities in the Pacific Ocean Area." *Cincpac–Cincpoa RIA.* (October 15, 1945), 1–79.

637. _____ . _____ . Tenth Fleet. "History of the Anti-Submarine Measures Division of Tenth Fleet." Unpublished paper, Fleets File, Operational Archives, U. S. Naval Historical Center, 1945. 67p.

638. Wells, A. R. "Studies in British Naval Intelligence, 1880–1945." Unpublished Ph.D. dissertation, University of London, 1972.

Further References

Some materials in section I, subsection D, and section III, subsections B and C, above together with items in section V, subsection C, and section VI, subsection A, below will yield additional information relative to this subsection. Certain individuals highlighted in section VIII, subsection B, below were also involved in the pursuit of naval intelligence.

D. Aerial Intelligence and Reconnaissance

1. Aerial Intelligence

639. "Air Combat Intelligence." *Flying,* XXXV (October 1944), 123–124.

640. Babington–Smith, Constance. *Air Spy: The Story of Photo Intelligence in World War II.* New York: Harper, 1957. 266p. Rpr. 1975.

641. Barber, Charles H. "Some Problems of Air Intelligence." *Military Review,* XXVI (August 1946), 76–78.

642. Barnes, Derek G. *Cloud Cover: Recollections of an* [RAF] *Intelligence Officer.* London: Rich, 1943. 176p.

Brodie, Henry, jt. author. *See* Ruggles, Richard

643. Canada. Royal Canadian Air Force. Intelligence Division. *The German Air Force: An R.C.A.F. Intelligence Summary.* Ottawa, 1941. 90p.

644. Cohen, Victor H. *Development of the Intelligence Function in the United States Air Force.* Special Studies Report. Maxwell AFB, Ala.: Research Studies Institute, Air University, 1957.

645. Gregory, Jesse O. "Flak Intelligence Memories." *Coast Artillery Journal,* XCI (May–June 1948), 18–24.

U. S. Air Force intelligence on German AA positions.

646. Kauffman, George R. "Intelligence in Heavy Bombardment." *Military Review,* XXVI (November 1946), 20–28.

647. Kebric, Harry L. *Dragon Tigers.* New York: Vantage Press, 1971. 137p.

Intelligence for the U. S./Chinese Composite Wing.

648. Medhurst, C. E. H. "Air Intelligence." *Flying,* XXXI (September 1942), 141+.

649. Olson, Mancur, Jr. "The Economics of Strategic Bombing in World War II." *Air Power Historian,* IX (April 1962), 121–127.

650. _____. "The Economics of Target Selection for the Combined Bomber Offensive." *Journal of the Royal United Service Institution,* CVII (November 1962), 308–314.

651. "Picking the Target." *Popular Mechanics,* LXXXII (September 1944), 28–31+.

652. Ruggles, Richard, and Henry Brodie. "An Empirical Approach to Economic Intelligence in World War II." *Journal of the American Statistical Association* (March 1947), 72–91.

653. United States. Army Air Forces. Air Combat Intelligence School. *The Life and Times of AC–15.* New Haven, Conn.: Yale University Press, 1946. 121p.

654. Wead, Frank W. "Air Intelligence: Gathering and Disseminating All Battle Data." *Flying,* XXXII (February 1943), 163–164.

655. Whitney, Cornelius V. *Lone and Level Sand.* New York: Farrar, 1951. 314p.

AAF intelligence in North Africa and the Pacific.

2. Aerial Reconnaissance

656. Bart, H. L. "Bombing Proof." *Flying,* XXXIV (May 1944), 44–45+.

657. Birtles, Philip J. "Wooden Warbird: Photo-reconnaissance Mosquitos." *Air Classics,* XV (March 1979), 70–82.

658.   Bishop, Edward. *Mosquito: Wooden Wonder.* Ballantine's Illustrated History of the Violent Century: Weapons Book, no. 24. New York: Ballantine Books, 1971. 160p.

659.   Bowyer, Chaz. *Mosquito at War.* London: Ian Allen, 1973. 144p.

One of the most versatile aircraft of the war, the De Havilland "Mossie" was also involved in several spectacular missions in support of European resistance movements. Citations to those strikes, along with reconnaissance duties, will be found in the general Mosquito histories cited in this section. Details on individual missions are entered in the appropriate subsections of part VII:A below.

660.   ———. *Path Finders at War.* London: Ian Allen, 1977. 160p.

661.   Boyle, Robert D. "A History of Photographic Reconnaissance in North Africa, including My Experiences with the [U.S.] Third Photo Group." Unpublished Ph.D. dissertation, University of Texas, 1949.

662.   Christy, Joe. *P-38 Lightning at War.* New York: Scribner's, 1978. 143p.

Most Allied and Axis fighters were from time to time employed in the reconnaissance role; the photo-version of this Lockheed "bird" was the F–5.

663.   Cornelius, George. "Air Reconnaissance: The Great Silent Weapon." *U. S. Naval Institute Proceedings,* LXXXV (1959), 34–42.

664.   Creal, Richard E. "The History of Reconnaissance in World War II." *Tactical Air Reconnaissance Digest,* II (February 1968), 14–18.

665.   Elmhurst, Thomas. "Air Reconnaisance: The Purpose and the Value." *Journal of the Royal United Service Institution,* XCVII (February 1952), 84–86.

666.   Flaven, John E., and William J. Fletcher, comps. *The Story of the 31st Photo Reconnaissance Squadron.* Nuremberg, Germany, 1945. 94p.

Fletcher, William J., jt. compiler. *See* Flaven, John E.

667.   "The Flying Undertaker." *Air Classics,* V (December 1968), 6–14.

The photo-reconnaissance version of the P–51 Mustang.

668.   Forrest, Ian. "This Was Hitler's Spy Squadron." *RAF Flying Review,* XVI (November 1960), 17–18+.

669.   Freeman, Roger. "Focus Cats." In: his *The Mighty Eighth, Units, Men, Machines: A History of the U. S. Eighth Air Force.* Garden City, N. Y.: Doubleday, 1970. pp. 198–201.

670.   French, W. F. "Photo Eyes for Our Fighters." *Science Digest,* XV (January 1944), 57–60.

671. Futrell, Robert F. *Command of Observation Aviation: A Study in Control of Tactical Air Power.* USAF Historical Study, no. 24. Washington, D. C.: Office of Air Force History, Department of the Air Force, 1956. 44p.

672. "German Aerial Cameras Spy Out the Military Secrets of Britain." *Life,* VII (December 18, 1939), 13–17.

673. Germann, Paul O. "Argus in the Sky." *TAF Review,* II (September 1956), 14–17.

10th Tactical Reconn. Wing., U. S. 12th Air Force.

674. Goddard, George W. *Overview: A Life-long Adventure in Aerial Photography.* Garden City, N. Y.: Doubleday, 1969. 415p.

675. Hardy, Michael J. *De Havilland Mosquito.* Arco Aircraft Classics, no. 3. New York: Arco Publishers, 1977. 128p.

676. Helman, Grover. *Aerial Photography: The Story of Aerial Mapping Reconnaissance.* New York: Macmillan, 1972. 180p.

677. "High Spy: A P [hotographic] R [econnaissance] U [nit]." *Flying,* XXXIII (November 1943), 54–55.

678. Holliday, Joseph. *Mosquito: The Wooden Wonder Aircraft of World War II.* Garden City, N.Y.: Doubleday, 1970. 236p.

679. Infield, Glenn B. *Unarmed and Unafraid.* New York: Macmillan, 1970. 292p.

680. Jones, John J. "Target—Hiroshima." *Air Power Historian,* IX (April 1962), 112–116.

20th Reconn. Squadron, U. S. 20th Air Force.

681. Millington, Geoffrey. *The Unseen Eye.* London: Gibbs and Phillips, 1961. 192p.

Mondey, David, jt. author. *See* Taylor, John W. R.

682. Musgrove, Gordon. *Pathfinder Force: A History of* [RAF] *No. 8 Group.* New York: Hippocrene Books, 1976. 302p.

683. Nelson, David C. "History of the 67th T.R.W." *Tactical Air Reconnaissance Digest,* II (February and May, 1968), 22–26, 6–11.

684. Peaslee, B. J. "Air Scouts of the [U.S.] Eighth Bomber Command." *Flying,* LX (February 1957), 32–34+.

685. Pratt, Donald, "'Zero–Seven–Victor, Where Are You?' A P–38 Photo Report." *Air Classics,* VIII (May 1972), 46–53.

686. Robinson, T. F. "Our Flying Spies. *American Photography,* XXXVIII (July 1944), 18–20.

687.   Rust, Kenn C. *The Ninth Air Force in World War II.* Rev. ed. Fallbrook Calif.: Aero Publishers, 1970. 245p.

Much on aerial reconnaissance.

688.   Sharp, Cecil M. *Mosquito.* London: Faber, 1967. 494p.

689.   Shores, Christopher F. "The Reconnaissance Units." In: his *2nd Tactical Air Force* [R.A.F.] Reading, Berks., Eng.: Osprey, 1970. pp. 85–111.

690.   Sims, Charles. "Over the Fence." *Flying Review International,* XXIII (August 1968), 445–446+ .

RAF photo reconnaissance.

691.   Taylor, John W. R., and David Mondey. *Spies in the Sky.* London: Ian Allen, 1972. 128p.

692.   United States. Army Air Force. Air Intelligence School. *Handbook for Combat Air Intelligence Officers.* 2d ed. Harrisburg, Pa., 1944. 159p.

693.   _____. _____. 8th Photo Squadron. *The Diary of the 8th Photo Squadron, New Guinea.* New York: Ad Press, 1945. 217p.

694.   _____ . _____ . 17th Photo Squadron. *17th Photo Reconn Squadron, 13th U.S. Army Air Force.* Los Angeles, Calif.: Brown and de Haven, 1946. 127p.

695.   _____ . _____ . 30th Photo Squadron. *The 30th in the E.T.O.* Gottingen, Germany: Muster–Schmidt, 1945. 48p.

696.   White, William L. "They Fight with Cameras." *American Mercury,* LVII (November 1943), 537–542.

697.   Whiteley, E. A. "[Adrian] Warburton and PR from Malta, 1940–1944." *Royal Air Forces Quarterly,* XVIII (Spring 1978), 19–30.

698.   Whitehouse, Arthur G. J. "Arch." *Spies with Wings.* New York: Putnam, 1967. 156p.

Further References

Adding weight to the citations in this subsection are certain materials in section I, subsection D, and section III, subsections B and C, above. Additional items will also be found in section V, subsection A, section VI, subsection C, and section VII below. Individuals involved with this topic are often noted in subsection B of section VIII below.

V/Selected Military Campaigns and Battles Influenced by Intelligence Operations

Introduction

Many of the most important campaigns and battles of World War II were heavily influenced by the possession or lack of national–strategic or combat–tactical intelligence. Recent revelations and document de-classifications now make this point more clear than ever before. Where reliable processed information was available, success-at-arms was likely. Conversely, disaster could—and often did—result from its absence.

The references in the three subsections of this chapter describe air, sea, and land campaigns and battles where intelligence contributed to the outcome. Information, obtained from a variety of sources, was sometimes well and sometimes poorly analyzed, forecast, or employed, resulting in a body of battle literature both wide and narrow in scope. Although the titles cited here spend hundreds of pages on battle operations, most also contain discussion of those elements in the intelligence process that brought glory or despair.

Intelligence successes can be said to have occurred in such campaigns and battles as those at Kursk (1943), Midway (1942), and Normandy (1941). Intelligence failures brought disaster at Pearl Harbor (1941), at Arnhem (1944), and in the Ardennes (1944). Intelligence agencies and evaluators on both Allied and Axis sides were unable to fathom the resilience of populations to aerial bombing, campaigns well informed by those in charge of economic and technical intelligence. Even with a variety of new technical developments and the involvement of vast numbers of specially trained and irregular personnel in the intelligence-gathering process, forecasting on both the national–strategic and combat–tactical levels was shown by field achievements to be a most "iffy" affair.

A. Aerial Campaigns

1. General Works

699. Craven, Wesley F., and James L. Cate, eds. *The Army Air Forces in World War II*. 7 vols. Chicago: University of Chicago Press, 1948–1958.

700. Higham, Robin. *Air Power: A Concise History*. New York: St. Martin's Press, 1972. 282p.

701. Kenney, George C. *General Kenney Reports*. New York: Duell, Sloan, and Pearce, 1949. 594p.

702. Lyall, Gavin, ed. *The War in the Air: The Royal Air Force in World War II*. New York: Morrow, 1968. 422p.

703. Macmillan, Norman. *The Royal Air Force in the World War*. 4 vols. London: Harrap, 1942–1950.

704. Siegring, Thomas. *U.S.A.F. in World War II*. Secaucus, N.J.: Chartwell Books, 1977. 192p.

705. Wood, Anthony. *Hitler's Luftwaffe*. New York: Crescent Books, 1977. 248p.

2. The Battle of Britain, 1940

706. Ansel, Walter. *Hitler Confronts England*. Durham, N.C.: Duke University Press, 1960. 348p.

707. Bishop, Edward. *The Battle of Britain*. London: Allen and Unwin, 1960. 236p.

708. _____ . *Their Finest Hour: The Story of the Battle of Britain, 1940*. Ballantine's Illustrated History of the Violent Century. New York: Ballantine Books, 1968. 160p.

709. Clark, Ronald W. *Battle for Britain*. London: Harrap, 1965. 175p.

710. Clitheroe, Graham. *Coventry under Fire*. 2d rev. ed. Gloucester, Eng.: British Publications, 1942. 62p.

711. Collier, Basil. *The Battle of Britain*. New York: Macmillan, 1962. 187p.

712. _____ . *The Defence of the United Kingdom*. History of the Second World War: United Kingdom Military Series. London: H.M. Stationery Office, 1957. 557p.

713. Collier, Richard. *Eagle Day: The Battle of Britain, August 6–September 14, 1940*. London: Hodder and Stoughton, 1966. 316p.

Dempster, Derek, jt. author. *See* Wood, Derek

714.   Dowling, Christopher. "The Battle of Britain." In: Noble Frankland and Christopher Dowling, eds. *Decisive Battles of the Twentieth Century.* New York: McKay, 1976. pp. 114–127.

715.   Evans, N.E. "Air Intelligence and the Coventry Raid." *Journal of the Royal United Service Institution for Defence Studies,* CXXI (September 1976), 66–74.

716.   Fleming, Peter. *Operation Sea Lion.* New York: Simon and Schuster, 1957. 323p.

717.   Goldsmith–Carter, George. *The Battle of Britain.* London and New York: Mason and Lipscomb, 1974. 279p.

718.   Jullian, Marcel. *The Battle of Britain, July–September 1940.* Translated from the French. London: Cape, 1967. 295p.

719.   Longmate, Norman. *Air Raid: One Bombing of Coventry, 1940.* London: Hutchinson, 1976. 302p.

720.   McKee, Alexander. *Strike from the Sky: The Story of the Battle of Britain.* London: Souvenir Press, 1960. 288p.

721.   Mosley, Leonard. *Backs to the Wall.* New York: Random House, 1971. 430p.

722.   ———. *The Battle of Britain.* World War II Series. New York: Time–Life, Inc., 1977. 208p.

723.   Parkinson, Roger. *Summer, 1940: The Battle of Britain.* New York: McKay, 1977. 236p.

724.   Price, Alfred. *Blitz on Britain.* London: Ian Allan, 1977. 192p.

725.   Taylor, Telford. *The Breaking Wave: The German Defeat in the Summer of 1940.* New York: Simon and Schuster, 1967. 381p.

726.   Thompson, Laurence. *1940: The Year of Britain's Supreme Agony.* New York: Morrow, 1966. 256p.

727.   Townsend, Peter. *Duel of Eagles.* New York: Simon and Schuster, 1970. 480p.

728.   Wheatley, Ronald. *Operation Sea Lion: German Plans for the Invasion of England, 1939–1942.* Oxford, Eng.: At the Clarendon Press, 1958. 201p.

729.   Wood, Derek, and Derek Dempster. *The Narrow Margin: The Battle of Britain and the Rise of Air Power, 1930–1940.* Rev. ed. New York: Paperback Library, 1969. 505p.

See especially chapters V and VI.

730.   Wright, Robert. *The Man Who Won the Battle of Britain*. New York: Scribner's, 1969. 291p.

Air Chief Marshal Sir Hugh Dowding.

3. Allied/Axis Bomber and Counterbomber Operations, 1941/1945

731.   Baumback, Werner. *The Life and Death of the Luftwaffe*. Translated from the German. New York: Coward–McCann, 1960. 224p.

732.   Berenbrook, Hans D. *The Luftwaffe War Diaries*. By Cajus D. Beeker, pseud. Garden City, N.Y.: Doubleday, 1968. 399p.

733.   Birdsall, Steve. *Flying Buccaneers: The Illustrated Story of Kenney's Fifth Air Force*. Garden City, N.Y.: Doubleday, 1977. 312p.

734.   _____. *Log of the Liberators*. Garden City, N.Y.: Doubleday, 1973. 340p.

735.   Boyle, James M. "The XXI Bomber Command: A Primary Factor in the Defeat of Japan." Unpublished Ph.d. dissertation, St. Louis University, 1964.

736.   _____. _____. *Air Power Historian*, XI (April 1964), 49–53.

737.   Braham, John R. D. *Scramble*. London: Muller, 1961. 256p.

738.   Caidin, Martin. *Black Thursday*. New York: Dutton, 1960. 320p.

Schweinfurt.

739.   _____. *Flying Forts: The B-17 in World War II*. New York: Ballantine Books, 1968. 504p.

740.   Chisholm, Roderick. *Cover of Darkness*. London: Chatto and Windus, 1953. 222p.

741.   Coffey, Thomas M. *Decision over Schweinfurt: The U.S. 8th Air Force Battle for Daylight Bombing*. New York: McKay, 1977. 373p.

742.   Dugan, James, and Carroll Stewart. *Ploesti: The Great Ground–Air Battle of 1 August 1943*. New York: Random House, 1962. 407p.

743.   _____. "Ploesti: German Defenses and Allied Intelligence." *Air Power Historian*, IX (January 1962), 1–20.

Frankland, Noble, jt. author. *See* Webster, Charles

744.   Galland, Adolf. *The First and the Last*. Translated from the German. New York: Ballantine Books, 1957. 280p.

745.   _____, et al. *The Luftwaffe at War*, *1939–1945*. Edited by David Mondey. Chicago: Regnery, 1973. 247p.

746. Girbig, Werner. *Six Months to Oblivion: The Eclipse of the German Fighter Force*. Translated from the German. New York: Hippocrene Books, 1975. 140p.

747. Harris, Arthur. *Bomber Offensive*. New York: Macmillan, 1947. 288p.

748. Howard–Williams, Jeremy. *Night Intruder: A Personal Account of the Radar War between the Royal Air Force and Luftwaffe Nightfighter Forces*. North Pomfret, Vt.: David and Charles, 1976. 192p.

749. Infield, Glenn B. *Disaster at Bari*. New York: Macmillan, 1971. 301p.

750. ———. *The Poltava Affair*. New York: Macmillan, 1973. 265p.

751. Jablonski, Edward. *Double Strike: The Epic Air Raids on Regensburg-Schweinfurt, August 17, 1943*. Garden City, N.Y.: Doubleday, 1974. 271p.

752. Jackson, Robert. *Storm from the Skies: The Strategic Bombing Offensive, 1943–1945*. London: Barker, 1974. 174p.

753. Middlebrook, Martin. *The Nuremberg Raid*. New York: Morrow, 1974. 369p.

Mondey, David, editor. *See* Galland, Adolf

754. Price, Alfred. *Battle over the Reich*. New York: Scribner's, 1973. 207p.

755. ———. *The Bomber in World War II*. London: Macdonald and Jane's, 1976. 150p.

756. Rawnsley, Cecil F., and Robert Wright. *Night Fighter*. London: Collins, 1957. 383p.

757. Rust, Kenneth C. *The 12th Air Force Story in World War II*. Glendale, Calif.: Aviation Book Company, 1975. 64p.

758. ———. *The 15th Air Force in World War II*. Glendale, Calif.: Aviation Book Company, 1976. 64p.

Stewart, Carroll, jt. author. *See* Dugan, James

759. Sweetman, John. *Ploesti: Oil Strike*. Ballantine's Illustrated History of World War II. New York: Ballantine Books, 1974. 159p.

760. ———. *Schweinfurt: Disaster in the Skies*. Ballantine's Illustrated History of World War II. New York: Ballantine Books, 1971. 160p.

761. Sylva, David. "The Raid on Ploesti." *Aerospace Safety*, XXXII (June 1976), 14–17.

762.   Taylor, Geoffrey. *Nuremberg Massacre*. North Pomfret, Vt.: David and Charles, 1976. 246p.

763.   United States. Strategic Bombing Survey, European War. *The Effects of Strategic Bombing on German Morale*. Report no. 64b. 2 vols. Washington, D. C.: U. S. Government Printing Office, 1946.

764.   ————. ————, Pacific War. *The Effects of Strategic Bombing on Japanese Morale*. Report no. 14. Washington, D. C.: U. S. Government Printing Office, 1945. 262p.

765.   Verrier, Anthony. *The Bomber Offensive*. London: Batsford, 1968. 373p.

766.   Webster, Charles, and Noble Frankland. *The Strategic Air Offensive against Germany, 1939–1945*. History of the Second World War: United Kingdom Military Series. 4 vols. London: H. M. Stationery Office, 1961.

767.   Wolff, Leon. *Low-level Mission*. Garden City, N. Y.: Doubleday, 1957. 240p.

Ploesti.

Wright, Robert, jt. author. *See* Rawnsley, Cecil F.

4. "Operation Crossbow"

768.   Angell, Joseph W. "Crossbow" In: Wesley F. Craven and James L. Cate, eds. *The Army Air Forces in World War II*. 7 vols. Chicago: University of Chicago Press, 1948–1958. III, 84–106, 525–546.

769.   ————. "Guided Missiles Could Have Won." *Atlantic Monthly*, CLXXXVIII (December x951), 29–39; CLXXXIX (January 1952), 57–63.

770.   Babington–Smith, Constance. "How Photographic Detectives Solved the Secret Weapons Mystery." *Life*, XLIII (October 28, 1957), x26–127+.

771.   Collier, Basil. *The Battle of the V-weapons, 1944–1945*. New York: Morrow, 1965. 191p.

772.   Dixon, Thomas F. "Solving the V–2 Mystery in 1944 [Project Big Ben]." *Air Power Historian*, 49.

773.   Dornberger, Walter. *V–2*. Translated from the German. New York: Viking Press, 1954. 264p.

774.   Irving, David. *The Mare's Nest*. Boston: Little, Brown, 1965. 320p.

775.   McGovern, James. *Crossbow and Overcast*. New York: Morrow, 1964. 279p.

776.   Olsen, Jack. *Aphrodite: Desperate Mission.* New York: Putnam, 1970. 328p.

777.   United States. Strategic Bombing Survey, European War. *The V-weapons ("Crossbow") Campaign.* Report no. 60. Washington, D. C.: U.S. Government Printing Office, 1947. 42p.

Further References

Readers will find certain additional information relative to this subsection among the items noted in section I, subsection D, section III, subsections B and C, and section IV, subsection D, above as well as in section VI, subsection C, and section VII below. Individuals and groups noted in connection with this topic are often cited in section VIII.

B. Naval Campaigns

1. General Works

778.   Blair, Clay, Jr. *Silent Victory: The U. S. Submarine War against Japan.* Philadelphia: Lippincott, 1975. 1,071p.

779.   Dull, Paul S. *A Battle History of the Imperial Japanese Navy, 1941–1945.* Annapolis, Md.: U. S. Naval Institute, 1978. 402p.

Hummelchen, Gerhard, jt. author. *See* Rohwer, Jurgen

780.   Lundstrom, John B. *The First South Pacific Campaign:* [U.S.] *Pacific Fleet Strategy, December 1941–June 1942.* Annapolis, Md.: U. S. Naval Institute, 1976. 240p.

781.   Macintyre, Donald G. F. W. *The Battle for the Pacific.* Rev. ed. London: Hutchinson, 1975. 224p.

782.   Morison, Samuel E. *History of United States Naval Operations in World War II.* 15 vols. Boston: Little, Brown, 1947–1962.

783.   Rohwer, Jurgen, and Gerhard Hummelchen. *Chronology of the War at Sea, 1939–1945.* Translated from the German. 2 vols. New York: Arco Publishing Co., 1973–1974.

784.   Roskill, Stephen W. *The War at Sea.* History of the Second World War: United Kingdom Military Series. 3 vols. London: H. M. Stationery Office, 1954.

2. The Battle of the Atlantic

785.   Berenbrook, Hans D. *Hitler's Naval War.* By Cajus Beeker, pseud. Garden City, N.Y.: Doubleday, 1974. 400p.

786.   Buchheim, Lothar–Günther. *U-boat War.* Translated from the German. New York: Knopf, 1978.

788.   Bush, Harold. *U-boats at War.* Translated from the German. London: Putnam, 1955. 286p.

789.   Campbell, Ian M. R. "The Russian Convoys, 1941–1945." *Journal of the Royal United Service Institution,* CII (May 1946), 227–240.

790.   _____ , and Donald G. F. W. Macintyre. *The Kola Run: A Record of Arctic Convoys, 1941–1945.* London: Muller, 1958. 254p.

791.   Carse, Robert. *A Cold Corner of Hell.* Garden City, N. Y.: Doubleday, 1969. 268p.

Costello, John, jt. author. *See* Hughes, Terry

792.   Drummond, John D. *H. M. U-boat.* London: Ian Allan, 1958. 227p.

The secret capture of U–570 on August 27, 1941.

793.   Forestern Cecil S. *The Last Nine Days of the Bismarck.* Boston: Little, Brown, 1959. 138p.

794.   Frank, Wolfgang. *The Sea Wolves: The Story of the German U-boats at War.* Translated from the German. New York: Rinehart, 1955. 340p.

795.   Grenfell, Russell. *The Bismarck Episode.* New York: Macmillan, 1949. 219p.

796.   Gretton, Peter W. *Crisis Convoy: The Story of HX–231.* London: Davies, 1974. 182p.

797.   Howe, John A. "Wolfpack: Measures and Countermeasures." *Naval War College Review,* XXIII (August 1971), 1–65.

798.   Hoyt, Edwin P. *The Sea Wolves.* New York: Lancer Books, 1972. 160p.

799.   _____ . *U-boats Offshore: When Hitler Struck America.* New York: Stein & Day, 1978. 288p.

800.   Hughes, Terry, and John Costello. *The Battle of the Atlantic.* New York: Dial Press, 1977. 314p.

801.   Irving, David. *The Destruction of Convoy PQ–17.* New York: Simon and Schuster, 1969. 337p.

802.   Jones, Geoffrey P. *The Month of the Lost U-boats.* London: Kimber, 1977. 207p.

803.   Joubert de la Ferté, Philip B. *Birds and Fishes: The Story of Coastal Command.* London: Hutchinson, 1960. 224p.

804. Kennedy, Ludovic. *Pursuit: The Chase and Sinking of the Bismarck.* New York: Viking Press, 1974. 256p.

805. Kemp, Peter K. *The Escape of the Scharnhorst and Gneisnau.* Sea Battles in Close-up, no. 13. Annapolis, Md.: U. S. Naval Institute, 1975. 96p.

806. Lund, Paul, and Harry Ludlam. *Night of the U-boats.* London: Foulsham Press, 1973. 204p.

807. Macintyre, Donald G. F. W. *The Battle for the Atlantic.* Rev. ed. London: Hutchinson, 1975. 208p.

————, jt. author. *See* Campbell, Ian M. R.

808. Mason, David. *U-boat: The Secret Weapon.* Ballantine's Illustrated History of the Violent Century. New York: Ballantine Books, 1972. 160p.

809. Middlebrook, Martin. *Convoy.* New York: Morrow, 1977. 378p.

810. Morison, Samuel E. *The Atlantic Battle Won, May 1943–May 1945.* Vol. X of *The History of United States Naval Operations in the Second World War.* Boston: Little, Brown, 1956. 399p.

811. ————. *The Battle of the Atlantic, September 1939 to May 1943.* Vol. I of *The History of United States Naval Operations in the Second World War.* Boston: Little, Brown, 1947.

812. Nimitz, Chester W., *et al. Triumph in the Atlantic: The Naval Struggle against Hitler.* Englewood Cliffs, N. J.: Prentice–Hall, 1960. 188p.

813. Noli, Jean. *The Admiral's Wolf Packs.* Translated from the French. Garden City, N.Y.: Doubleday, 1974. 396p.

814. Pitt, Barrie. *The Battle of the Atlantic.* World War II Series. New York: Time-Life, Inc., 1977. 208p.

815. Price, Alfred. *Aircraft versus Submarines.* London: Kimber, 1973. 268p.

816. Rohwer, Jurgen. *The Critical Convoy Battles of March 1943.* Translated from the German. Annapolis, Md.: U.S. Naval Institute, 1977. 356p.

817. Roskill, Stephen W. "The Battle of the Atlantic." In: Noble Frankland and Christopher Dowling, eds. *Decisive Battles of the Twentieth Century.* New York: McKay, 1976. pp. 81–101.

818. ————. *The Secret Capture.* London: Collins, 1959. 161p. *U–570.*

819. Schofield, Brian B. *Loss of the Bismarck.* Sea Battles in Close-up, no. 3. Annapolis, Md.: U.S. Naval Institute, 1972. 96p.

820. _____. *The Russian Convoys.* London: Batsford, 1964. 224p.

821. Seth, Ronald S. *The Fiercest Battle: The Story of North Atlantic Convoy OSN-5, 22nd April-7th May 1943.* New York: Norton, 1962. 208p.

822. Showell, Jak P. M. *U-boats under the Swastika.* London: Ian Allan, 1973. 167 p.

823. Smith, Peter C. *Arctic Victory: The Story of Convoy PQ-18.* London: Kimber, 1975. 238p.

824. Von der Porten, Edward P. *The German Navy in World War II.* New York: Galahad Books, 1969. 274p.

825. Waters, John M., Jr. *Bloody Winter.* Princeton, N. J.: Van Nostrand, 1967. 279 p.

826. Werner, Herbert A. *The Iron Coffins.* Translated from the German. New York: Holt, 1969. 329p.

3. Pearl Harbor

827. Baker, Leonard. *Roosevelt and Pearl Harbor.* New York: Macmillan, 1970. 352p.

828. Barker, A. J. *Pearl Harbor.* Ballantine's Illustrated History of the Violent Century. New York: Ballantine Books, 1970. 160p.

829. Barnes, Harry E., *et al.* "The Mystery of Pearl Harbor." *National Review,* XVIII (December 13, 1966), 1260–1272.

830. _____. *Pearl Harbor after a Quarter of a Century.* New York: Arno Press, 1972. 132p.

831. Borg, Dorothy, *et al. Pearl Harbor as History.* New York: Columbia University Press, 1973. 801p.

832. Burtness, Paul S., and Warren U. Ober. *The Puzzle of Pearl Harbor.* Evanston, Ill.: Row, Peterson, 1962. 244p.

833. _____. "Research Methodology: The Problem of the Pearl Harbor Intelligence Reports." *Military Affairs,* XXV (Fall 1961), 132–146.

834. Coox, Alvin D. "Pearl Harbor." In: Noble Frankland and Christopher Dowling, eds. *Decisive Battles of the Twentieth Century.* New York: McKay, 1976. pp. 141–155.

835. Dupuy, Trevor N. "Pearl Harbor: Who Blundered?" *American Heritage*, XIII (February 1962), 64–81.

836. Fukudome, Shigeru. "The Hawaii Operation." *U. S. Naval Institute Proceedings*, LXXXI (1955), 1314–1331.

837. "Full Text of the Official Reports concerning the Attack on Pearl Harbor." *U. S. News*, Special Supplement, XIX (September 1, 1945), 1–86.

838. Furer, Julius A. "The Pearl Harbor Attack." In: his *Administration of the Navy Department in World War II*. Washington, D. C.: U. S. Government Printing Office, 1959. pp. 87–102.

839. Gillis, James M. "The Blame for Pearl Harbor." *Catholic World*, CLXII (October 1945), 1–7.

840. Higgins, Trumbull. "'East Wind Rain.'" *U. S. Naval Institute Proceedings*, LXXXI (1955), 1198–1205.

841. Hoehling, Adolph A. *The Week before Pearl Harbor*. New York: W.W. Norton, 1963. 238p.

842. Howard, Michael. "Military Intelligence and Surprise Attack: The 'Lessons' of Pearl Harbor." *World Politics*, XV (1963), 701–711.

843. Kimmel, Husband E. *Admiral Kimmel's Story*. Chicago: Regnery, 1955. 206p.

844. Kittridge, Tracy B. "The Muddle before Pearl Harbor." *U. S. News and World Report*, XXXVII (December 3, 1954), 52–63, 110–139.

845. Lord, Walter. "Five Missed Chances at Pearl Harbor." *Reader's Digest*, LXXI (December 1957), 42–45.

846. ———. *Day of Infamy*. New York: Holt, 1957. 233p.

847. Melosi, Martin V. "The Pearl Harbor Controversy, 1941–1946." Unpublished Ph.D. dissertation, University of Texas, 1975.

848. ———. *The Shadow of Pearl Harbor: Political Controversy over the Surprise Attack, 1941–1946*. Waco, Tex.: Texas A & M University Press, 1977. 183p.

849. Morgenstern, George. *Pearl Harbor: The Story of the Secret War*. New York: Devin–Adair, 1947. 425p.

850. Morison, Samuel E. "The Lessons of Pearl Harbor." *Saturday Evening Post*, CCXXXIV (October 28, 1961), 19–27.

851. _____ . *The Rising Sun in the Pacific, 1931–April 1942.* Vol. III of *The History of United States Naval Operations in the Second World War.* Boston: Little, Brown, 1955. 398p.

852. Morton, Louis. "Pearl Harbor in Perspective." *U. S. Naval Institute Proceedings,* LXXXI (April 1955), 461–468.

853. "New Pearl Harbor Facts: The Full Story, How the U.S. Got Japanese Secrets." *Chicago Tribune Special Supplement,* (December 7, 1966), 1–5, 10–12.

"Magic"

Ober, Warren U., jt. author. *See* Burtness, Paul S.

854. Parkinson, Roger. *The Attack on Pearl Harbor.* New York: Putnam, 1973. 128p.

855. "Pearl Harbor: The Planning Stage." *ONI Weekly Intelligence,* I (December 8, 1944), 1–22.

856. Pogue, Forrest C. "Pearl Harbor Blunders." *Look,* XXIX (December 14, 1945), 34–39.

857. Popov, Dusko. "Pearl Harbor: Did J. Edgar Hoover Blunder?" *True Magazine,* LIV (October 1973), 47, 107–114.

858. Prange, Gordon W. "Tora, Tora, Tora!" *Reader's Digest,* LXXXIII (October–November 1963), 251–258+.

859. Ramsey, Logan C. "The 'Ifs' of Pearl Harbor." *U. S. Naval Institute Proceedings,* LXXVI (1950), 364–371.

860. Samson, George. "Japan's Fatal Blunder." *International Affairs,* XXIV (October 1948), 543–554.

861. Sasaki, Okino. "Suicide Sub Attack." *Sea Classics,* V (January 1972), 36–41.

Japanese mini-subs and sea commandos at Pearl.

862. Taylor, Theodore. *Air Raid–Pearl Harbor: The Story of December 7, 1941.* New York: Crowell, 1971. 185p.

863. Theobald, Robert A. *The Final Secret of Pearl Harbor: The Washington Contribution to the Japanese Attack.* New York: Devin–Adair, 1954. 202p.

864. Toland, John. "Death Watch in the Pacific." *Look,* XXV (September 12, 1961), 86–88+.

865. Trefousse, Hans L., ed. *What Happened to Pearl Harbor? Documents Pertaining to the Japanese Attack of December 7, 1941 and Its Background.* New York: Twayne, 1958. 324p.

866. Tsunoda, Jun, and Kazutomi Uchida. "The Pearl Harbor Attack: Admiral Yamamoto's Fundamental Concept." *Naval War College Review,* XXXI (Fall 1978), 83–88.

Uchida, Kazutomi, jt. author. *See* Tsunoda, Jun

867. United States. Congress. Joint Select Committee. *Hearings on the Pearl Harbor Attack.* 39 vols. Washington, D. C.: U. S. Government Printing Office, 1946.

868. _____ . _____ . _____ . *Report.* Washington, D. C.: U. S. Government Printing Office, 1946. 604p.

869. _____ . Navy Department. Court of Inquiry. *Narrative Statement of Evidence at the Navy Pearl Harbor Investigation.* 3 vols. Washington, D. C., 1945.

870. Ward, Robert E. "The Inside Story of the [Japanese] Pearl Harbor Plan." *U. S. Naval Institute Proceedings,* LXXVII (1951), 1270–1283; LXXVIII (1952), 435–438.

871. Wilkinson, J. Burke. "Sneak Craft Attack in the Pacific." *U. S. Naval Institute Proceedings,* LXXIII (1947), 279–287.

872. Wohlstetter, Roberta. *Cuba and Pearl Harbor: Hindsight and Foresight.* RAND Memorandum RM–4328–ISA. Santa Monica, Calif.: Rand Corporation, 1965. 41p.

873. _____ . *Pearl Harbor: Warning and Decision.* Stanford, Calif.: Stanford University Press, 1962. 426p.

874. _____ . "What Really Happened at Pearl Harbor." *U. S. News and World Report,* LXI (December 12, 1966), 46–47.

4. Midway

875. Barker, A. J. *Midway: The Turning Point.* Ballantine's Illustrated History of the Violent Century. New York: Ballantine Books, 1971. 160p.

876. Fuchida, Mitsuo, and Masatake Okumiya. *Midway, the Battle That Doomed Japan: The Japanese Navy's Story.* Annapolis, Md.: U. S. Naval Institute, 1955. 266p.

877. _____ . "Prelude to Midway." *U. S. Naval Institute Proceedings,* LXXXI (1955), 505–513.

878. Lord, Walter. *Incredible Victory.* New York: Harper & Row, 1967. 331p.

879. _____ . "Midway." *Look,* XXXI (August 8, 22, 1967), 32–38+, 32–36+.

880. Mercer, Charles. *Miracle at Midway.* New York: Putnam, 1977. 160p.

881. Morison, Samuel E. *Coral Sea, Midway, and Submarine Actions, May 1942–August 1942.* Vol. IV of *The History of United States Naval Operations in the Second World War.* Boston: Little, Brown, 1955. 296p.

Okumiya, Masatake, jt. author. *See* Fuchida, Mitsuo

882. Olsmith, Edwin S., Jr. "Midway Revisited." *Signal,* XXXI (November–December 1976), 36–39.

883. Potter, Elmer B. "Admiral [Chester W.] Nimitz and the Battle of Midway." *U. S. Naval Institute Proceedings,* CII (July 1976), 60–68.

884. Prange, Gordon W. "Miracle at Midway." *Reader's Digest,* CI (November 1972), 255–262+.

885. Simkins, Peter. "Midway." In: Noble Frankland and Christopher Dowling, eds. *Decisive Battles of the Twentieth Century.* New York: McKay, 1976. pp. 171–188.

886. Smith, Ward. *Midway: Turning Point in the Pacific.* New York: Crowell, 1966. 174p.

887. Tuleja, Thaddeus V. *Climax at Midway.* New York: W. W. Norton, 1960. 248p.

888. United States. Army. Far East Command. *Midway Operation (May–June 1942).* Japanese Operational Monograph Series, no. 93. Tokyo, Japan: Military History Section, Special Staff, GHQ, Far East Command, 1952. 91p.

889. Werstein, Irving. *The Battle of Midway.* New York: Crowell, 1961. 145p.

Further References

Certain additional information readers may find relative to this subsection can be found among the items cited in section I, subsection D, section III, subsections B and C, and section IV, subsection C, above as well as in section VI, subsection C, and section VII below. Biographies of groups and individuals are often contained in section VIII.

C. *Land Campaigns*

1. General Works

890.   Canada. Department of National Defense. *The Canadian Army at War.* 3 vols. Ottawa: King's Printer, 1945–1946.

891.   Eisenhower, Dwight D. *Crusade in Europe.* Garden City, N. Y.: Doubleday, 1948. 559p.

892.   _____ . *The Papers of Dwight David Eisenhower: The War Years.* 5 vols. Baltimore, Md.: Johns Hopkins University Press, 1970.

893.   Germany. Oberkommando der Wehrmacht. *Hitler Directs His War: The Secret Records of His Daily Military Conferences.* New York: Oxford University Press, 1951. 187p.

894.   Liddell Hart, Basil H. *The German Generals Talk.* New York: Morrow, 1948. 308p.

895.   Parkinson, Roger. *Blood, Toil, Tears, and Sweat: The War History from Dunkirk to Alamein, Based on the War Cabinet Papers of 1940–1942.* New York: McKay, 1973. 538p.

896.   _____ . *A Day's March Nearer Home: The War History from Alamein to V–E Day, Based on the War Cabinet Papers of 1942–1945.* New York: McKay, 1974. 551p.

897.   _____ . *Peace for Our Time: Munich to Dunkirk—The Inside Story.* New York: McKay, 1971. 411p.

898.   Rooney, Andrew A. *The Fortunes of War.* Boston: Little, Brown, 1962. 240p.

Case studies of Stalingrad, Tarawa, Normandy, and the Bulge.

899.   United States. Marine Corps, Historical Branch. *History of United States Marine Corps Operations in World War II.* 5 vols. Washington, D. C.: U. S. Government Printing Office, 1958–1968.

2. Mediterranean Theater

a. General Works

900.   Ansel, Walter. *Hitler and the Middle Sea.* Durham, N.C.: Duke University Press, 1972. 496p.

901.   Clark, Mark W. *Calculated Risk.* New York: Harper, 1950. 500p.

902.   DeBelot, Raymond. *The Struggle for the Mediterranean, 1939–1945.* Princeton, N. J.: Princeton University Press, 1951. 287p.

903. Kesselring, Albert. *Kesselring: A Soldier's Report.* Translated from the German. New York: Morrow, 1954. 381p.

904. Macintyre, Donald G. F. W. *The Battle for the Mediterranean.* New York: W. W. Norton, 1965. 216p.

905. Marder, Arthur J. *"Operation Menace": The Dakar Expedition and the Dudley North Affair.* Oxford and New York: Oxford University Press, 1976. 289p.

906. Morison, Samuel E. "Elba Interlude, June 1944." *Military Affairs,* XXI (Fall 1957), 182–187.

907. Playfair, Ian S. O. *The Mediterranean and the Middle East.* History of the Second World War: United Kingdom Military Series. 4 vols.+. London: H. M. Stationery Office, 1954–.

b. North Africa

908. Cantril, Hadley. "Evaluating the Probable Reactions to the Landing in North Africa in 1942: A Case Study [in Military Intelligence]." *Public Opinion Quarterly,* XXIX (Fall 1965), 400–410.

909. Coster, Donald Q. "We Were Expecting You at Dakar." In: *Reader's Digest,* Editors of. *Secrets and Spies: Behind-the-Scenes Stories of World War II.* Pleasantville, N. Y.: Reader's Digest Association, 1964. pp. 230–235.

An OSS deception plan.

910. Funk, Arthur L. *The Politics of Torch: The Allied Landings and the Algiers Putsch, 1942.* Lawrence: University Press of Kansas, 1974. 322p.

911. Gosset, René. *Conspiracy in Algiers, 1942.* Translated from the French. New York: *The Nation,* 1945. 248p.

912. Howe, George F. *Northwest Africa: Seizing the Initiative in the West.* United States Army in World War II: Mediterranean Theater of Operations. Washington, D. C.: Office of the Chief of Military History, Department of the Army, 1957. 748p.

913. Jackson, William G. F. *The Battle for North Africa, 1940–1943.* New York: Mason/Charter, 1975. 393p.

914. Langer, William L. *Our Vichy Gamble.* New York: Knopf, 1947. 412p.

915. L'Herminier, Jean. *Casablanca: The Secret Mission of a Famous Submarine.* Translated from the French. London: Muller, 1953. 243p.

H.M.S. *Seraph* delivers Mark Clark in 1942.

916.   Painton, Frederick C. "[General Clark's] Secret Mission to North Africa." In: Harriet McClay and Helen Judson, eds. *Story Essays.* Rev. ed. New York: Holt, 1947. pp. 434–445.

917.   _____. "Secret Mission to North Africa." In: *Reader's Digest*, Editors of. *Secrets and Spies: Behind-the-Scenes Stories of World War II.* Pleasantville, N. Y.: Reader's Digest Association, 1964. pp. 216–225.

918.   Parkinson, Roger. *The War in the Desert.* London: Hart–Davis, 1976. 200p.

919.   Phillips, Cecil E. L. *Alamein.* Boston: Little, Brown, 1962. 434p.

920.   Tompkins, Peter. *The Murder of Admiral* [Jean] *Darlan: A Study in Conspiracy.* New York: Simon and Schuster, 1965. 287p.

921.   Tute, Warren. *The Deadly Stroke.* New York: Coward–McCann, 1973. 221p.

Mers-el-Kebir, 1940.

922.   _____. *The North African War.* London: Sidgwick, 1976. 220p.

c. Sicily and Italy

923.   Adleman, Robert H., and George Walton. *Rome Fell Today.* Boston: Little, Brown, 1968. 336p.

924.   Blumenson, Martin. *Salerno to Cassino.* United States Army in World War II: Mediterranean Theater of Operations. Washington, D.C.: Office of the Chief of Military History, Department of the Army, 1969. 491p.

925.   _____. *Sicily: Whose Victory?* Ballantine's Illustrated History of the Violent Century. New York: Ballantine Books, 1969. 160p.

926.   Bohmler, Rudolf. *Monte Cassino.* Translated from the German. London: Cassell, 1964. 314p.

927.   Chandler, Harriette L. "Another View of 'Operation Crossword.'" *Military Affairs*, XLII (April 1978), 68–75.

The "secret surrender" of Italy in 1945. Compare with Dulles, no. 930, below.

928.   Colvin, Ian G. *The Unknown Courier.* London: Kimber, 1953. 208p.

"The Man Who Never Was."

929.   Connell, Charles. *Monte Cassino: The Historic Battle.* London: Elek, 1963. 206p.

930. Dulles, Allen W. *The Secret Surrender.* New York: Harper & Row, 1966. 268p.

Garland, Albert N., jt. author. *See* Smyth, Howard M.

931. Graham, Dominick. *Cassino.* Ballantine's Illustrated History of the Violent Century. New York: Ballantine Books, 1970. 159p.

932. Kurzman, Dan. *The Race for Rome.* Garden City, N. Y.: Doubleday, 1975. 488p.

933. Leighton, Richard M. "The Planning for Sicily." *U. S. Naval Institute Proceedings,* LXXX (1962), 90–101.

934. Lewis, Norman. *Naples '44.* New York: Pantheon, 1979. 224p.

Memories of a British intelligence officer in the city.

935. Linklater, Eric R. R. *The Campaign in Italy.* The Second World War, 1939–1945: A Popular Military History. London: H. M. Stationery Office, 1951. 480p.

936. Majdalany, Fred. *The Battle of Cassino.* Boston: Houghton, Mifflin, 1957. 309p.

937. Montagu, Ewen E. S. "The Corpse That Hoaxed the Axis." *Reader's Digest,* LXIII (November 1953), 19–23.

938. _____. *The Man Who Never Was.* London: Evans, 1953. 144p.

939. Pack, Stanley W. G. *"Operation Husky": The Allied Invasion of Sicily.* New York: Hippocrene Books, 1977. 186p.

940. Pond, Hugh. *Sicily.* London: Kimber, 1962. 224p.

941. Robbins, Charles. "The Nazis Loved Monte Cassino." *Saturday Evening Post,* CCXVIII (January 19, 1946), 36–37+.

Sitzia, Elena A., jt. author. *See* Smith, Bradley F.

942. Smith, Bradley F., and Elena Agarossi Sitzia. *Operational Sunrise: The Secret Surrender.* New York: Basic Books, 1979. 248p.

943. Smith, E. D. *The Battle of Cassino.* New York: Scribner's, 1976. 192p.

944. _____. "Why Was the Monastery at Cassino Bombed?" *Army Quarterly,* XCVIII (July 1969), 220–224.

945. Smyth, Howard M., and Albert N. Garland. *Sicily and the Surrender of Italy.* United States Army in World War II: Mediterranean Theater of Operations. Washington, D. C.: Office of the Chief of Military History, Department of the Army, 1965. 609p.

946.   Von Plehwe, Fredrich–Karl. *The End of an Alliance: Rome's Defection from the Axis in 1943*. Translated from the German. London and New York: Oxford University Press, 1971. 161p.

Walton, George, jt. author. *See* Adleman, Robert H.

3. The Eastern Front

a. General Works

947.   Anders, Wladyslaw. *Hitler's Defeat in Russia*. Chicago: Regnery, 1953. 267p.

948.   Bethell, Nicholas W. B. *Russia Besieged*. World War II Series. New York: Time–Life, Inc., 1977. 208p.

Carrell, Paul, pseud. *See* Schmidt, Paul K.

949.   Clark, Alan. *Barbarossa: The Russian–German Conflict, 1941–1945*. New York: Morrow, 1965. 522p.

950.   Grechko, Andrei A. *Battle for the Caucasus*. Translated from the Russian. Moscow: Progress Publishers, 1971. 366p.

951.   Guderian, Heinz. *Panzer Leader*. Translated from the German. New York: Dutton, 1952. 528p.

952.   Higgins, Trumbull. *Hitler and Russia: The Third Reich in a Two-front War*. New York: Macmillan, 1966. 310p.

953.   Mrazkova, Damela, and Vladimir Remes. *The Russian War, 1941–1945*. Introduction by Harrison Salisbury. Preface and Notes by Alan J. P. Taylor. New York: Dutton, 1977. 152p.

954.   Minasyan, M. M., ed. *The Great Patriotic War of the Soviet Union*. Translated from the Russian. Moscow: Progress Publishers, 1974. 469p.

The official Russian history, untranslated, is *History of the Great Patriotic War of the Soviet Union*, which was published in 6 volumes by the Military History Publishing House of the Ministry of Defense of the U.S.S.R. in 1961–1965.

Remes, Vladimir, jt. author. *See* Mrazkova, Damela

955.   Schmidt, Paul K. *Hitler Moves East, 1941–1943*. By Paul Carrell, pseud. Boston: Little, Brown, 1965. 640p.

956.   _____. *Scorched Earth: The Russian–German War, 1943–1944*. By Paul Carrell, pseud. Boston: Little, Brown, 1970. 556p.

957.   Seaton, Albert. *The Russo–German War, 1941–1945*. New York: Praeger, 1971. 628p.

958. Shtemenko, Sergei M. *The Soviet General Staff at War*, *1941–1945*. 2d ed. Moscow: Progress Publishers, 1975. 389p.

959. United States. Military Academy, Department of Military Arts and Engineering. *Operations on the Russian Front*. 3 vols. in 1. West Point, N. Y., 1945–1946.

960. Von Manstein, Erich. *Lost Victories*. Translated from the German. Chicago: Regnery, 1958. 574p.

961. Werth, Alexander. *Russia at War*, *1941–1945*. New York: Dutton, 1964. 1,100p.

962. Ziemke, Earl F. *Stalingrad to Berlin: The German Defeat in the East*. Army Historical Series. Washington, D. C.: Office of the Chief of Military History, Department of the Army, 1968. 549p.

963. Zubkov, I., ed. *The Second World War*. Translated from the Russian. Moscow: Progress Publishers, n.d. 560p.

b. "Barbarossa"–Moscow

964. Blau, George E. *The German Campaign in Russia: Planning and Operations*, *1940–1942*. Department of the Army Pamphlets. Washington, D. C.: Office of the Chief of Military History, Department of the Army, 1955. 197p.

965. Cecil, Robert. *Hitler's Decision to Invade Russia*, *1941*. London: Davis, Poynter, 1975. 192p.

966. Erickson, John. *The Road to Stalingrad: Stalin's War with Germany* [1940–1941]. New York: Harper & Row, 1975. 595p.

967. Hilger, Gustav, and Alfred G. Meyer. *The Incompatible Allies: A Memoir–History of German–Soviet Relations, 1918–1941*. New York: Macmillan, 1953.

968. Jukes, Geoffrey. *The Defense of Moscow*. Ballantine's Illustrated History of the Violent Century. New York: Ballantine Books, 1970. 160p.

969. Keegan, John. *Barbarossa: Invasion of Russia*, *1941*. Ballantine's Illustrated History of the Violent Century. New York: Ballantine Books, 1971. 160p.

970. Leach, Barry R. *German Strategy against Russia*, *1939–1941*. Oxford, Eng.: At the Clarendon Press, 1973. 308p.

Meyer, Alfred G., jt. author. *See* Hilger, Gustav

971. Petrov, Vladimir. *"June 22, 1941": Soviet Historians and the German Invasion, Including a Complete Translation of Aleksandr M. Nekrich's "1941, 22 Iyunia."* Columbia: University of South Carolina Press, 1968. 322p.

972.   Sas, Anthony. "The Invasion of Russia." *Military Review,* LI (June 1971), 38–46.

973.   Sella, Amnon. "'Barbarossa': Surprise Attack and Communication." *Journal of Contemporary History,* (July 1978), 555–583.

974.   Seth, Ronald S. *"Operation Barbarossa."* London: Blond, 1964. 191p.

975.   Turney, Alfred W. *Disaster at Moscow:* [Fedor] *Von Bock's Campaigns, 1941–1942.* Albuquerque: University of New Mexico Press, 1970. 228p.

976.   Whaley, Barton. *Codeword BARBAROSSA.* Cambridge, Mass.: M.I.T. Press, 1973. 376p.

977.   _____. "Operation Barbarossa: A Case Study of Soviet Strategic Information Processing before the German Invasion." Unpublished Ph.d. dissertation, Massachusetts Institute of Technology, 1969.

c. Stalingrad

978.   Craig, William. *Enemy at the Gates: The Battle of Stalingrad.* New York: Reader's Digest Press; dist. by Dutton, 1973. 466p.

979.   Kerr, Walter B. *The Secret of Stalingrad.* Garden City, N. Y.: Doubleday, 1978. 274p.

980.   Werth, Alexander. *The Year of Stalingrad.* New York: Knopf, 1947. 480p.

d. Kursk

981.   Caidin, Martin. *The Tigers Are Burning.* New York: Hawthorn Books, 1974. 243p.

982.   Chant, Christopher. *Kursk.* London: Almark, 1975. 48p.

983.   Christyakov, I. "The Victory at Kursk." *Soviet Military Review,* no. 7 (July 1978), 42–45.

984.   Erickson, John. "Kursk." In: Noble Frankland and Christopher Dowling, eds. *Decisive Battles of the Twentieth Century.* New York: McKay, 1976. pp. 222–238.

985.   Jukes, Geoffrey. *Kursk, the Clash of Armor.* Ballantine's Illustrated History of the Violent Century. New York: Ballantine Books, 1969. 160p.

986.   Koltunov, G. A. "Kursk." In: Bernard Fitsimons, ed. *Tanks and Weapons of World War II.* New York: Beekman House, 1973. pp. 81–97.

987. "The Kursk Battle—30 Years." *Soviet Military Review,* no. 6 (June 1973), 2–39.

988. Parrish, Michael. "The Battle of Kursk." *Army Quarterly,* XCIX (October 1969), 39–51.

989. Rokossovsky, Sovetskogo S. K. "The Kursk Battle, July 5–August 23, 1943." *Soviet Military Review,* nos. 7–8 (July–August 1968), 2–7, 30–36.

990. Zhukov, Georgi K. "The Battle of Kursk, 1943." *Military Review,* XLIX (August 1969), 82–96.

4. Northwest Europe

a. General Works

991. Ellis, L. F. *Victory in the West.* History of the Second World War: United Kingdom Military Series. 2 vols. London: H. M. Stationery Office, 1962–1968.

992. Koch, Oscar W., and R. G. Hays. *G–2: Intelligence for Patton.* Philadelphia: Published for *The Army Times* by Whitmore Publishing Co., 1972. 167p.

993. Toland, John. *The Last 100 Days.* New York: Random House, 1966. 694p.

b. Normandy

994. Belfield, Eversley M. G., and Hubert Essame. *The Battle for Normandy.* Philadelphia: Dufour, 1965. 239p.

995. Blumenson, Martin. "Normandy, 1944." In: Noble Frankland and Christopher Dowling, eds. *Decisive Battles of the Twentieth Century.* New York: McKay, 1976. pp. 265–276.

Carrell, Paul, pseud. *See* Schmidt, Paul K.

996. Essame, Hubert. *Normandy Bridgehead.* Ballantine's Illustrated History of the Violent Century. New York: Ballantine Books, 1971. 160p.

————, jt. author. *See* Belfield, Eversley M. G.

997. Harrison, Gordon A. *Cross-channel Attack.* United States Army in World War II: European Theater of Operations. Washington, D. C.: Office of the Chief of Military History, Department of the Army, 1951. 519p.

998. Howarth, David A. *D–Day, the Sixth of June 1944.* New York: McGraw–Hill, 1959. 255p.

999.   Ingersoll, Ralph M. *Top Secret*. New York: Harcourt, 1946. 343p.

1000.   Jackson, William G. F. *"Overlord": Normandy, 1944*. London: Davis–Poynter, 1978. 250p.

1001.   Michie, Allan A. *The Invasion of Europe: The Story behind D–Day*. New York: Dodd, Mead, 1965. 203p.

1002.   Morgan, Frederick E. *Overture to Overlord*. Garden City, N. Y.: Doubleday, 1950. 296p.

1003.   Pogue, Forrest C. "Final Preparations for the Invasion." In: his *The Supreme Command*. U. S. Army in World War II: European Theater of Operations. Washington, D. C.: Office of the Chief of Military History, Department of the Army, 1954. pp. 158–171.

1004.   Ryan, Cornelius. *The Longest Day, June 6, 1944*. New York: Simon and Schuster, 1959. 350p.

1005.   Schmidt, Paul K. *Invasion—They're Coming! The German Account of the Allied Landings and the 80 Days' Battle for France*. By Paul Carrell, pseud. Translated from the German. New York: Dutton, 1963. 288p.

1006.   Speidel, Hans. *Invasion 1944: Rommel and the Normandy Campaign*. Translated from the German. Chicago: Regnery, 1950. 176p.

1007.   Thompson, P. W. *D–Day: Spearhead of Invasion*. Ballantine's Illustrated History of the Violent Century. New York: Ballantine Books, 1968. 160p.

1008.   Turner, John F. *Invasion '44: The First Full Story of D–Day in Normandy*. New York: Putnam, 1959. 253p.

1009.   Wilt, Alan F. *The Atlantic Wall: Hitler's Defenses in the West, 1941–1944*. Ames: Iowa State University Press, 1975. 244p.

c. Arnhem

1010.   Bauer, Cornelius. *The Battle of Arnhem*. Translated from the Dutch. New York: Stein & Day, 1967. 254p.

1011.   Farrer–Hockley, Anthony. *Airborne Carpet: "Operation Market–Garden."* Ballantine's Illustrated History of the Violent Century. New York: Ballantine Books, 1972. 160p.

1012.   Haslam, E. B. "A Bridge Too Far." *Royal Air Forces Quarterly*, XVIII (Spring 1978), 86–92.

1013.   Hibbert, Christopher. *The Battle of Arnhem*. London: Batsford, 1962. 224p.

1014.   MacDonald, Charles B. "The Decision to Launch 'Operation Market–Garden.'" In: Kent R. Greenfield, ed. *Command Decisions.* Washington, D. C.: Office of the Chief of Military History, Department of the Army, 1960. pp. 429–442.

1015.   Ryan, Cornelius. *A Bridge Too Far.* New York: Simon and Schuster, 1974. 670p.

1016.   Thompson, W. F. K. "'Operation Market Garden.'" In: Philip de St. Croix, ed. *Airborne Operations: An Illustrated Encyclopedia of the Great Battles of Airborne Forces.* New York: Crescent Press, 1978. pp. 106–128.

1017.   Tugwell, M. A. J. "Arnhem: The Ten Germs of Failure." *Journal of the Royal United Service Institution,* CXIV (December 1969), 61–66.

1018.   Urquhart, Robert E. *Arnhem.* London: Cassell, 1958. 239p.

1019.   Whiting, Charles. *A Bridge at Arnhem.* London: Futura, 1974. 264p.

d. The Ardennes

1020.   Cole, Hugh M. *The Ardennes: Battle of the Bulge.* United States Army in World War II: European Theater of Operations. Washington, D. C.: Office of the Chief of Military History, Department of the Army, 1965. 720p.

1021.   Davis, Franklin M. *Breakthrough: The Epic Story of the Battle of the Bulge.* Derby, Conn.: Monarch Books, 1961. 159p.

1022.   Eisenhower, John S. D. *The Bitter Woods: The Dramatic Story, Told at All Echelons from Supreme Command to Squad Leader , of the Crisis That Shook the Western Coalition: Hitler's Surprise Ardennes Offensive.* New York: Putnam, 1969. 506p.

1023.   Elstob, Peter. *Hitler's Last Offensive: The Full Story of the Battle of the Bulge.* New York: Macmillan, 1971. 413p.

1024.   Merriam, Robert E. *Dark December: The Full Account of the Battle of the Bulge.* Chicago: Ziff–Davis, 1947. 234p.

1025.   Nobecourt, Jacques. *Hitler's Last Gamble: The Battle of the Bulge.* Translated from the French. New York: Schocken, 1967. 302p.

1026.   Parrish, Thomas D. *The Bulge.* Cleveland, Ohio: World Publishers, 1966. 47p.

1027.   Rosengarten, Adolph G., Jr. "The Bulge: A Glimpse of Combat Intelligence." *Military Review,* XLI (June 1961), 29–33.

1028.   Sears, Stephen W. *The Battle of the Bulge.* New York: American Heritage Press; dist. by Harper & Row, 1969. 153p.

1029.   Strawson, John. *The Battle for the Ardennes.* New York: Scribner's, 1972. 212p.

1030.   Toland, John. *The Battle of the Bulge.* New York: Random House, 1966. 178p.

1031.   Von Luttichau, Charles V. P. "The German Counteroffensive in the Ardennes." In: Kent R. Greenfield, ed. *Command Decisions.* Washington, D. C.: Office of the Chief of Military History, Department of the Army, 1960. pp. 443–461.

5. The Pacific

a. General Works

1032.   Belote, J. H., and William M. *Typhoon of Steel: The Battle for Okinawa.* New York: Harper & Row, 1970.

1033.   Dorn, Frank. *The Sino–Japanese War, 1937–1941.* New York: Macmillan, 1974.

1034.   Long–hsuen, Hsu. *History of the Sino–Japanese War, 1937–1945.* Translated from the Chinese. Taiwan: Chung Wu Publishing Co., 1971. 642p.

1035.   MacArthur, Douglas. *Reminiscences.* New York: McGraw–Hill, 1964. 439p.

1036.   _____. *A Soldier Speaks: Public Papers.* New York: Praeger, 1965. 367p.

1037.   Newcomb, Richard F. *Iwo Jima.* New York: Holt, 1971.

1038.   Russell, Michael. *Iwo Jima.* Ballantine's Illustrated History of the Violent Century. New York: Ballantine Books, 1974. 160p.

1039.   Supreme Commander for the Allied Powers. *Reports of General MacArthur, Prepared by His Staff.* 2 vols. in 4. Washington, D. C.: U. S. Government Printing Office, 1966.

1040.   Tuchman, Barbara W. *Stilwell and the American Experience in China, 1911–1945.* New York: Macmillan, 1970.

1041.   United States. Army. Far East Command, Military Intelligence Section. *A Brief History of the G–2 Section, GHQ, Southwest Pacific Area and Affiliated Units.* 10 vols. Tokyo, 1948.

1042.   _____ . _____ . _____ . *Operations of the [U.S.] Counterintelligence Corps in the Southwest Pacific Area.* Tokyo, 1948. Unpaged.

b. Tarawa

1043. Bailey, S. Thomas. *Tarawa.* Derby, Conn.: Monarch Books, 1962. 155p.

1044. Baldwin, Hanson W. "The Bloody Epic That Was Tarawa." *New York Times Magazine,* (Novbmeer 16–23, 1958), 19–21+, 19+.

1045. Hoyt, Edwin P. *Storm over the Gilberts: War in the Central Pacific, 1943.* New York: Van Nostrand, 1978. 175p.

1046. McKiernan, Patrick. "Tarawa: The Tide That Failed." *U. S. Naval Institute Proceedings,* LXXXVIII (1962), 38–50.

1047. Russ, Martin. *Line of Departure: Tarawa.* Garden City, N. Y.: Doubleday, 1975.

1048. Shaw, Henry I., Jr. *Tarawa: A Legend Is Born.* Ballantine's Illustrated History of the Violent Century. New York: Ballantine Books, 1970. 160p.

1049. Sherrod, Robert L. *Tarawa: The Story of a Battle.* Fredricksburg, Tex.: Admiral Nimitz Foundation, 1973. 206p.

1050. Steinberg, Rafael. "The Tarawa Killing Ground." In: his *Island Fighting.* New York: Time–Life, Inc., 1978. pp. 120–152.

1051. Werstein, Irving. *Tarawa: A Battle Report.* New York: Crowell, 1965. 146p.

Further References

Additional information relative to this subsection can be found in certain of the citations in section I, subsection D, section III, subsections B and C, and section IV, subsection B, above as well as in section VI, subsection A, and section VII below. Appropriate biographical material may also be found in both subsections of section VIII.

VI/Special Forces Military Units

Introduction

The sources in this section all concentrate on those special units of regular military forces established for the purpose of conducting secret and dangerous hit-and-run operations, both overt and covert. Often with unusual training, support, and aims, these groups provided valuable service to their masters. Their employment could—and did— bring military success (usually limited), which could boost morale at home and stiffen the resolve of allies abroad. Occasionally their adventures would result in the production of useful combat–tactical intelligence or positive contributions in the "psywar" arena.

Our emphasis here, as in section III, subsection C, above is primarily on the organizational aspects of special forces military units as a whole. Operational and biographical information, however, is contained in almost every one of the references.

A. Land

1052.   Adleman, Robert H. *The Devil's Brigade.* Philadelphia: Chilton, 1966. 259p.

U. S.–Canadian 1st Special Service Force.

1053.   Altieri, James J. *Darby's Rangers: An Illustrated Portrayal of the Original* [U.S. 1st Ranger Battalion]*Rangers, World War II, in Training and Combat.* Durham, N. C.: Seeman Printery, 1945. 151p.

1054.   _____. *The* [U.S. 4th Ranger Battalion] *Spearheaders.* Indianapolis: Bobbs–Merrill, 1960. 318p.

1055.   Arnold, Richard. *The True Book about the Commandos.* London: Muller, 1954. 144p.

1056.   Austin, Alexander B. *We* [Commandos] *Landed at Dawn.* New York: Harcourt, Brace, 1943. 217p.

1057.   Baer, Alfred E. *"D-for-Dog": The Story of a* [U.S.] *Ranger Company.* Memphis, Tenn., 1946. 119p.

1058.   Baker, Alan. *Merrill's* [U.S. 5307th Provisional Regiment] *Marauders.* Ballantine's Illustrated History of the Violent Century. New York: Ballantine Books, 1972. 159p.

1059.   Bellah, James W. "The Long Range Penetration Groups." *Infantry Journal,* LX (October 1948), 45–47.

The British–Indian "Chindits."

1060.   Blankfort, Michael. *The Big Yankee: A Biography of Evans Carlson.* Boston: Little, Brown, 1947. 380p.

1061.   Burchett, W. G. *Wingate's Phantom Army.* London: Muller, 1946. 195p.

1062.   Burham, Robert D. *The First Special Service Force: A War History of the North Americans, 1942–1944.* Elite Unit Series. Bennington, Vt.: Battery Press, 1978. 376p.

1063.   Calvert, Michael. *Chindits: Long Range Penetration Groups.* Ballantine's Illustrated History of the Violent Century. New York: Ballantine Books, 1973. 160p.

1064.   Carter, Hodding. *The Commandos of World War II.* New York: Random House, 1966. 168p.

1065.   "Commandos Are Tough." *Popular Mechanics,* LXXVIII (October 1942), 8–11.

1066.   Cook, Graeme. *Commandos in Action.* New York: Taplinger, 1974. 175p.

1067.   Cowles, Virginia S. *The Phantom Major: The Story of David Sterling and the S*[pecial]*A*[ir]*S*[ervice]*Regiment.* New York: Harper, 1958. 320p.

1068.   Crichton–Stuart, Michael. *G–Patrol.* London: Kimber, 1958. 206p.

The British Long Range Desert Group.

1069.   Durdin, F. Tillman. "The Roughest and the Toughest: [Evans] Carlson's Raiders." *New York Times Magazine,* (November 8, 1942), 13+.

1070.   Drysdale, D. B. "Special Forces." *Marine Corps Gazette,* XXXVIII (June 1954), 47–53.

Royal Marine Commandos and U. S. Marine Raiders.

1071.   Durnford–Slater, John. *Commando.* London: Kimber, 1953. 222p.

1072.   Falls, Cyril. "Commandos and Their Raids." *Illustrated London News,* CC (May 2, 1942), 516–517.

1073.   _____ . "Record of the Commandos." *Illustrated London News,* CCVIII (April 13, 1946), 398.

1074.   Farran, Roy A. "Operation Tombola." London: Collins, 1960. 256p.

The British SAS.

1075.   Fergusson, Bernard. *The Watery Maze: The Story of Combined Operations.* London: Collins, 1961. 445p.

1076.   Forty, George. *Desert Rats at War.* London: Ian Allan, 1975. 192p.

1077.   Great Britain. Amphibious Warfare Headquarters. *History of the Combined Operations Organization, 1940–1945.* London: H. M. Stationery Office, 1956. 199p.

1078.   _____ . Office of War Information. *Combined Operations: The Official Story of the Commandos.* New York: Macmillan, 1943. 155p.

1079.   Griffith, Samuel B., II. "Correy's Boys." *Marine Corps Gazette,* XXXVI (March 1952), *passim.*

U. S. 1st Marine Raider Battalion.

1080.   Harrison, Derrick I. *These Men Are Dangerous: The Special Air Service at War.* London: Cassell, 1957. 240p.

1081.   Henderson, Ralph E. "Jump into Adventure: The American–Kachin Rangers." *Reader's Digest,* XLVI (June 1945), 43–51.

1082.   Hollis, Leslie C. *One* [Royal] *Marine's Tale.* London: Deutsch, 1956. 192p.

1083.   Horan, H. E. "Combined Operations." *Journal of the Royal United Service Institution,* XCVIII (February 1953), 55–65.

1084.   Hubbard, Lucien. "Colonel Carlson and His Gung-ho Raiders." *Reader's Digest,* XLIII (December 1943), 63–68.

1085.   Hunter, Charles N. *Galahad.* San Antonio, Tex.: Naylor, 1963. 233p.

Merrill's Marauders.

1086.   Judge, C. B. "Commandos and Their Methods." *U. S. Naval Institute Proceedings,* LXX (1944), 842–852.

1087.   Keyes, Roger J. B. *Amphibious Warfare and Combined Operations.* The Lee Knowles Lectures, 1943. Cambridge, Eng.: At the University Press, 1943. 101p.

1088.   King, Michael J. "William Orlando Darby: A Military Biography." Unpublished Ph.D. dissertation, Northern Illinois University, 1977.

1089.   Ladd, James. *Commandos and Rangers of World War II.* New York: St. Martin's Press, 1978. 288p.

1090.   Landsborough, Gordon. *Tobruk Commando.* London: Cassell, 1956. 216p.

1091.   Larsen, Colin R. *Pacific Commandos: New Zealanders and Fijians in Action, a History of Southern Independent Commando and First Commando Fiji Guerrillas.* Wellington, New Zealand: Reed, 1946. 161p.

1092.   Lebra, Joyce C. *Japanese-trained Armies in Southeast Asia: Independence and Volunteer Forces in World War II.* New York: Columbia University Press, 1977. 226p.

1093.   Lepotier, Adolph. *Raiders from the Sea.* Translated from the French. London: Kimber, 1954. 200p.

1094.   Locke, Peter. "Hard-hitting Commandos." *New York Times Magazine,* (April 5, 1942), 6–7+.

1095.   Lockhart, Robert H. B. *The Marines Were There: The Story of the Royal Marines in the Second World War.* London: Putnam, 1950. 229p.

1096.   McDougall, Murdock C. *Swiftly They Struck: The Story of No. 4 Commando.* London: Odham's Press, 1954. 208p.

1097.   Marrinan, Patrick. *Colonel Paddy.* Dungannon, No. Ireland, 1968. 207p.

The British SAS.

1098.   Mills–Roberts, Derek. *Clash-by-Night: A Commando Chronicle.* London: Kimber, 1956. 204p.

1099.   Mason, Herbert M., Jr. *The Commandos.* New York: Duell, Sloan and Pearce, 1966. 154p.

1100.   Moulton, James L. *Haste to the Battle: A Marine Commando at War.* London: Cassell, 1963. 210p.

1101.   Newman, H. T. "The Functions of the Royal Marines in Peace and War." *Journal of the Royal United Service Institution,* C (February 1944), 21–32.

1102.   Ogburn, Charlton, Jr. *The Marauders.* New York: Harper, 1956. 305p.

1103.   Owen, David L. *The Desert My Dwelling Place.* London: Cassell, 1957. 271p.

The British Long Range Desert Group.

1104.   Pope, Vernon. "Russian Commandos." *Collier's,* CXII (July 24, 1943), 22–23.

1105.   Powers, William M. "Almost beyond Human Endurance." *U. S. Naval Institute Proceedings,* CIII (December 1977), 60–69.

Commandos.

1106.   Regan, James F. "'No Greater Love': [U. S.] Marine Raiders in the South Pacific." *American Magazine,* CXXXIX (June 1945), 17+.

1107.   "The Royal Marines." *Army Quarterly,* (January, April 1944), 176–183, 51–55.

1108.   Saber, Clifford. *Desert Rat Sketch Book.* New York: Sketchbook, 1959. 187p.

1109.   Samain, Brian. *Commando Men: The Story of a Royal Marine Commando in North West Europe.* London: White Lion, 1976. 188p.

1110.   Saunders, Hilary St. G. *The Green Beret: The Story of the Commandos.* London: Joseph, 1949. 320p.

1111.   Shaw, William B. K. *Long Range Desert Group: The Story of Its Work in Libya, 1940–1943.* London: Collins, 1945. 192p.

1112.   Spencer, James. *The Awkward* [Royal] *Marine.* London: Longmans, Green, 1948. 251p.

1113. Stokoe, E. G. *Lower the Ramps: The Story of the 43rd R. M. Commando.* London: Brown, Watson, 1955. 158p.

1114. Swinson, Arthur. *The Raiders: Desert Strike Force.* Ballantine's Illustrated History of the Violent Century. New York: Ballantine Books, 1968. 160p.

The British Long Range Desert Group.

1115. Thomas, Bruce. "Commandos." *Harper's Magazine,* CLXXXIV (March 1943), 438–440.

1116. Thompson, James A. *Only the Sun Remembers.* London: Dakers, 1950. 276p.

Commandos.

1117. Truby, J. David. "'Crazy' Jack Churchill." *Military Journal,* II (Winter 1978–1979), 36–37, 50.

British commando leader.

1118. United States. Navy Department. Pacific Fleet and Pacific Ocean Area. *Japanese Mobile Raiding Units.* Cincpac–Cincpoa Bulletin 90–44. Honolulu, 1944.

1119. ———. War Department. Military Intelligence Division. *Merrill's Marauders (February–May 1944).* American Forces in Action Series. Washington, D. C.: U. S. Government Printing Office, 1945. 117p. Rpr. 1978.

1120. Updegraph, Charles L., Jr. *U. S. Marine Corps Special Units of World War II.* Historical Reference Pamphlet. Washington, D. C.: Historical Division, H. Q., U. S. Marine Corps, 1972. 105p. Rpr. 1977.

1121. Warner, Philip. *The Special Air Service.* London: Kimber, 1971. 285p.

1122. Young, Peter. *Commando.* Ballantine's Illustrated History of the Violent Century. New York: Ballantine Books, 1969. 160p.

1123. ———. *Storm from the Sea.* London: Kimber, 1958. 221p.

Further References

Readers will find additional citations relative to this subsection in section I, subsection D, section IV, subsection B, and section V, subsection C above as well as in section VII, subsections A, B, and C, below. Biographical material may also be found in section VIII, subsection B, especially the biographies of Dudley Clarke, Roger Keyes, and Otto Skorzeny.

B. Sea

Adamson, Hans C., jt. author. *See* Dissette, Edward

1124.   Agar, Augustus. *Baltic Episode: A Classic of Secret Service in Russian Waters.* London: Hodder and Stoughton, 1963. 252p.

Beeker, Cajus D., pseud. *See* Berenbrook, Hans D.

Benson, James, jt. author. *See* Warren, Charles E. T.

1125.   Berenbrook, Hans D. *The K-Men: The Story of German Frogmen and Midget Submarines.* By Cajus D. Beeker, pseud. London: Kimber, 1955. 202p.

1126.   Berry, Erick. *Underwater Warriors: The Story of the American Frogmen.* New York: McKay, 1967. 152p.

1127.   Best, Herbert. *The Webfoot Warriors: The Story of U.D.T., the U. S. Navy's Underwater Demolition Team.* New York: John Day, 1962. 187p.

1128.   Borghese, Iunio V. *The Sea Devils.* Translated from the Italian. Chicago: Regnery, 1954. 261p.

1129.   ———. "The Trojan Horse of Alexandria." Translated from the Italian. *American Neptune,* XXVII (July 1967), 185–201.

1130.   Brou, Willy. *The War beneath the Sea.* Translated from the German. London: Muller, 1958. 239p.

German K-men.

1131.   Cocchia, Aldo. *The Hunters and the Hunted.* Translated from the Italian. Annapolis, Md.: U. S. Naval Institute, 1958. 179p.

1132.   Cook, Graeme. *Small Boat Raiders.* London: Hart–Davis, 1977. 131p.

1133.   Dissette, Edward, and Hans C. Adamson. *Guerrilla Submarines.* New York: Ballantine Books, 1972. 238p.

1134.   Durand de la Penne, Luigi. "Frogmen Attack: The Italian Assault on the British Fleet at Alexandria." *Atlantic,* CXCVII (May 1956), 50–55.

1135.   ———. "The Italian Attack on the Alexandria Naval Base." *U.S. Naval Institute Proceedings,* LXXXII (1956), 125–135.

1136.   Fane, Francis D., and Donald Moore. *The Naked Warriors.* New York: Appleton–Century–Crofts, 1956. 308p.

1137. _____ . _____ . *U. S. Naval Institute Proceedings*, LXXXII (1956), 913–922.

USN frogmen.

1138. Fehler, Johann H. *Dynamite for Hire: The Story of Hein Fehler.* Translated from the German. London: Laurie, 1956. 264p.

1139. Fell, William R. *The Sea Our Shield.* London: Cassell, 1966. 232p.

British mini-subs known as "X-craft."

1140. Fraser, Ian. *Frogmen, V.C.* London: Angus and Robertson, 1957. 224p.

1141. "Frog Men." *Popular Science*, CXLVII (December 1945), 121–124.

1142. Gibson, Charles. *The Ship with Five Names.* London and New York: Abelard–Schuman, 1965. 153p.

A German steamer used for secret missions.

1143. Gleeson, James, and Thomas J. Waldron. *Midget Submarines.* Ballantine's Illustrated History of the Violent Century. New York: Ballantine Books, 1975. 160p.

1144. _____ . *Now It Can Be Told.* London: Elek Books, 1954. 188p.

1145. Hampshire, A. Cecil. "Night Run to Sweden: The Story of a Secret Wartime Operation." *The Trident,* (October 1956), 309–312.

1146. _____ . *The Secret Navies.* London: Kimber, 1978. 272p.

1147. Howarth, David A. *Across to Norway.* New York: Sloane, 1952. 286p.

British–Norwegian small boat service in aid of the Norwegian resistance.

1148. Hutton, Bernard J. *Frogman Spy: The Incredible Case of Commander* [Lionel K.] *Crabbe.* New York: McDowell, Obolensky, 1960. 180p.

1149. "Italy's Underwater Giant Killers." *Sea Classics,* III (March 1970), 32+.

1150. Jewell, Norman L. A. *Secret Mission Submarine [H.M.S. Seraph].* Chicago: Ziff–Davis, 1945. 159p.

1151. Jullian, Marcel. *H.M.S. Fidelity.* Translated from the French. New York: W. W. Norton, 1958. 223p.

A French steamer used as a British spy ship.

1152.   Lodwick, John. *The Filibusterers: The Story of the Special Boat Service.* London: Methuen, 1947. 188p.

1153.   Manus, Max. *Underwater Saboteur.* Translated from the Norwegian. London: Kimber, 1953. 239p.

Moore, Donald, jt. author. *See* Fane, Francis D.

Pearson, Michael, jt. author. *See* Strutton, Bill

1154.   Phillips, Cecil E. L. *Cockleshell Heroes.* London: Heinemann, 1958. 208p.

1155.   Ratcliff, J. D. "Italy's Gallant Frogmen." *Reader's Digest,* LXXIII (August 1958), 188–192.

1156.   Robertson, Terence. *The Ship [H.M.S. Seraph] with Two Captains.* New York: Dutton, 1957. 256p.

1157.   Say, Harold B. "They Hit the Beach in Swim Trunks." *Saturday Evening Post,* CCXVIII (October 13, 1945), 14–15+.

1158.   Shaw, E. V. "Tough Tender." *Blackwood's Magazine,* CCLVIII (August 1945), 140–144.

R. N. small boat service.

1159.   Stewart, A. J. "Those Mysterious [Japanese] Midgets." *U. S. Naval Institute Proceedings,* C (April, December 1974), 69–76, 54–63.

1160.   Stitt, George. "Human Torpedoes: The [Italian] Attack on the British Battleships *Queen Elizabeth* and *Valiant* in Alexandria Harbor, December 1941." *Blackwood's Magazine,* CCLVIII (September 1945), 178–182.

1161.   Strutton, Bill, and Michael Pearson. *The Secret Invaders.* London: Hodder and Stoughton, 1958. 287p.

The British Combined Operations Pilotage Parties.

1162.   Thomson, David W. "Swimmers and Divers in War." *U. S. Naval Institute Proceedings,* LXVIII (1942), 682–685.

1163.   United States. Navy Department. Office of the Chief of Naval Operations, Amphibious Forces, Underwater Demolition Teams. "Histories." Unpublished papers, 21 vols. Shore Establishment File, Operational Archives, U. S. Navy Historical Center, 1945.

1164.   _____ . _____ . _____ . "History of Commander U.D.T. and U.D.F., Amphibious Forces, Pacific Fleet." Unpublished paper, Shore Establishment File, Operational Archives, U. S. Navy Historical Center, 1945. 6p.

1165. Waldron, Thomas J., and James Gleeson. *The Frogmen: The Story of Wartime Underwater Operations.* London: Evans, 1950. 191p.

1166. Warren, Charles E. T., and James Benson. *The Midget Raiders.* New York: Sloane, 1954. 256p.

1167. Wilkinson, J. Burke. *By Sea and by Stealth: Accounts of Surprise Attack by Sea during World War II.* New York: Coward–McCann, 1956. 218p.

1168. Wright, Bruce S. *The Frogmen of Burma.* London and Toronto: Clarke, Irwin, 1968. 152p.

1169. Yakota, Yutaka. *The Kaiten Weapon.* Translated from the Japanese. New York: Ballantine Books, 1962. 256p.

Further References

Certain additional references valuable in pursuit of this subsection can be found in section I, subsection D, section IV, subsection D, and section V, subsection B, above as well as in section VII, subsections A, B, and C, below. Biographical material in section VIII is very limited on this topic.

C. Air

1170. "Air Commando Fleet Shuttles Supplies for the China Drive on the Japs." *Aviation News,* I (November 29, 1943), 7–8.

1171. Bellah, James W. "The Air Commando Tradition." *Air Force and Space Digest,* XLVI (February 1963), 69–79.

1172. _____ . "The Password Was 'Mandalay'" *Reader's Digest,* XLV (September 1944), 33–36.

1173. Bright, John G. "From a Flying Tiger." *Atlantic,* CLXX (October 1942), 42–48.

1174. Chivers, Sydney P. "The Flying Tigers." *Air Classics,* VIII (February 1972), 50–63.

1175. _____ . _____ : *A Pictorial History of the American Volunteer Group.* Canoga Park, Calif.: Challenge Publications, 1965. 50p.

1176. Chennault, Anna. *Chennault and the Flying Tigers.* New York: Taplinger, 1963. 298p.

1177.   Chennault, Claire L. *The Way of a Fighter.* New York: Putnam, 1949. 329p.

1178.   Clemens, William. "Chennault and His Flying Tigers." *Reader's Digest,* XL (June 1942), 81–85.

1179.   ———. "How Chennault Kills Japs." *Collier's,* CX (July 4, 1942), 16+.

1180.   "The Flying Tigers in Burma." *Life,* XII (March 30, 1942), 27–33.

1181.   Ford, Corey. "[Philip G.] Cochran's Commandos." *Collier's,* XCIV (August 26, 1944), 20+.

1182.   Grinnel, Roy. "The Christmas Day Battle That Began a Legend." *Popular Mechanics,* CXLIV (December 1975), 45–47+.

   AVG.

1183.   Heiferman, Ronald. *Claire Chennault.* Ballantine's Illustrated History of the Violent Century: War Leader Book. New York: Ballantine Books, 1970. 160p.

1184.   ———. *The Flying Tigers.* Ballantine's Illustrated History of the Violent Century. New York: Ballantine Books, 1971. 160p.

1185.   Hibel, Franklin. "Chennault: From Maverick to Marvel." *Air Force Magazine,* LVII (November 1974), 90–94.

1186.   Holloway, Bruce K. "The Flying Tigers." *Air Force and Space Digest,* L (November 1967), 96–100.

1187.   Hotz, Robert B. *With General Chennault: The Story of the Flying Tigers.* New York: Coward–McCann, 1943. 276p.

1188.   McCann, John A. "Air Power and 'the Man'" *Air Power Historian,* VI (April 1959), 108–124.

   U. S. 1st Air Commando support for Wingate's Chindits.

1189.   Mitchelmore, G. "The 'First' First Air Commandos." *Airman,* XIV (February 1970), 63+.

1190.   Moser, Donald. "The Flamboyant Tigers: A Picture Essay." In: his *China–Burma–India.* World War II Series. New York: Time–Life, Inc., 1978. pp. 68–78.

1191.   Nalty, Bernard C. *Tigers over Asia.* New York: Elsevier–Dutton, 1978. 182p.

1192.   Page, Robert C. *Air Commando Doc.* New York: Ackerman, 1945. 186p.

1193.   Peragallo, James L. "Chennault, Guerrilla of the Air." *Aerospace Historian,* XX (March 1973), 1–6.

1194.   Schaller, Michael. "American Air Strategy in China, 1939–1941: The Origins of Clandestine Air Warfare." *American Quarterly,* XXVIII (Spring 1976), 3–19.

1195.   Sciutti, W. J. "The First Air Commando Group, August 1943– May 1944." *American Aviation Historical Society Journal,* XIII (Fall 1968), 178–185.

1196.   Scott, Robert L. *Boring a Hole in the Sky.* New York: Random House, 1961. 292p.

1197.   _____. *Flying Tiger: Chennault of China.* Garden City, N. Y.: Doubleday, 1959. 285p.

1198.   _____. *God Is My Copilot.* New York: Scribner's 1943. 277p.

1199.   "The Tiger Legend." *Air Classics,* III (March 1967), 46–56.

1200.   "The Tiger Warriors." *Air Classics,* IV (November 1967), 36–44.

1201.   Toland, John. *The Flying Tigers.* New York: Random House, 1963. 170p.

1202.   Walker, Wayne T. "The Flying Tigers." *World War II Magazine,* II (April 1973), 32–42.

1203.   Whelan, Russell. *The Flying Tigers: The Story of an American Volunteer Group.* New York: Viking Press, 1942. 224p.

Further References

Limited material relative to this subsection appears in the various citations found in section I, subsection D, section IV, subsection D, and section V, subsection A, above as well as in section VII, subsections B and C, below.

VII/Secret Operations: Resistance Movements, Special Forces, Intelligence Agents, and Paramilitary Units

Introduction

In our previous sections and subsections on secret agencies and special forces (section III, subsection C, and section VI), our emphasis, despite spillover operational and biographical data, was on the treatment of those groups as whole organizations. The purpose of this chapter, the largest in this guide, is to present the operational side of those entities. Here you will find references that deal not only with the exploits of spies and commandos, but with guerrilla partisans and collaborators as well. Careful reading of many of these titles will also demonstrate the destruction-effectiveness of certain secret groups as well as the relationship between field operations and the intelligence process.

Wherever Axis forces were in occupation, resistance movements came into existence as a form of opposition. In a few cases, mainly in Asia, guerrilla bands already fighting the local or colonial powers turned their attention "for the duration" to dealing with the invader. The degree of activity, cohesiveness, and enthusiasm of these groups varied by locality, as did their overall war contribution. In Europe, some partisans, such as those in Russia or Yugoslavia, were quite aggressive and became quite formidable military opponents. Others, like those in Holland, Norway, or France, were often penetrated by the enemy and sometimes slow to show or prove their mettle. In the Far East, irregulars were active with varying degrees of success in Asia and some of the Pacific islands, most notably the Solomons and the Philippines. In certain cases, in both Europe and Asia, participants changed sides. For example, some Russians and Western Europeans fought for the Germans and bands of Indo-Chinese aided the Japanese.

In Europe, Asia, and the western hemisphere, operatives from the intelligence agencies of both Axis and Allied nations were very active in pursuit of various goals. Employing both technical and nontechnical means, Axis agents sought both national–strategic and combat–tactical intelligence in Allied nations while counterintelligence personnel, with some considerable success on occasion, blocked western efforts at penetration. In addition to the information objective, agents of Allied intelligence bureaus supported and stiffened local resistance movements with varying good and bad fortune. Specially trained men and women, often nationals of the countries to be aided, were placed behind the enemy lines to gather information, eliminate opposition leaders and personnel, spread rumors and engage in other "psywar" activities, and to assume leadership or advisory posts in partisan units. In the Americas, Allied and Axis agents and agencies sought to influence the political positions of several nations at different times while some, notably the Soviets, sought secrets held by "friends." German intrigues, unlike the Russian ones, were generally well met by the counterintelligence and "psywar" forces of the American allies.

Meanwhile, both Allied and Axis nations trained and employed special forces military units of different sizes and composition to obtain limited military-political goals. In China, for example, U. S. Navy and Australian commando personnel actively assisted the Chinese resistance while American mercenaries flew for Chiang Kai-shek for a time as the "Flying Tigers." In Europe, British commandos and Special Air Service troops, among others, waged apparently ceaseless "combined forces" attacks on Axis targets. Many of the Commonwealth forces contained large contingents of exile soldiers. On the Continent, German special troops under Otto Skorzeny rescued Mussolini in 1943, scared American GIs during the Battle of the Bulge, and attempted to keep Hungary in the war when her defeat was in sight. In the Pacific, U.S., Australian, and Japanese marine raiders, coast watchers, and local defense forces (e.g., in Fiji) harried outposts and brought home bundles of captured enemy documents to aid the combat–technical intelligence lads. At sea, both Allied and Axis fleets employed miniature submarines and special boat units to great advantage.

Operations by intelligence, resistance, and special forces military personnel were, indeed, many and varied. With recent declassifications and continuing revelations, more accounts can be expected in the years ahead.

A. General Works

1204.   Asprey, Robert, *War in the Shadows: The Guerrilla in History.* Garden City, N. Y.: Doubleday, 1975. 1,662p.

1205.   Bailey, Ronald H. *Partisans and Guerrillas.* World War II Series. New York: Time–Life, Inc., 1978. 208p.

Barret, K. W., jt. author. *See* Nurick, Lester

1206.   Blacker, Irwin, ed. *Irregulars, Partisans, and Guerrillas.* New York: Simon and Schuster, 1954. 487p.

1207.   Dole, D. M. "Leaders and Guerrillas." *Infantry Journal,* LIII (July 1943), 60–62.

1208.   Dupuy, Trevor. N. *Asian and Axis Resistance Movements.* New York: Watts, 1965. 88p.

1209.   Ellis, John A. *A Short History of Guerrilla Warfare.* New York: St. Martin's Press, 1976. 220p.

1210.   Harris, Albert E. "Partisan Operations." *Military Review,* XXX (August 1950), 10–20.

1211.   Harvey, A. D. "Wartime Resistance in Peacetime Perspective." *Contemporary Review,* CCXXXIII (July 1978), 21–28.

1212.   Johnson, Brian D. G. *The Secret War: Based on the B.B.C. Television Series.* London: B.B.C. Publications, 1978. 352p.

1213.   Kriedel, Hellmuth. "Agents and Propaganda in Partisan Warfare." *Military Review,* XXXIX (November 1959), 102–105.

1214.   Laqueur, Walter. *Guerrilla: A Historical and Critical Study.* Boston: Little, Brown, 1976. 462p.

1215.   _____ , ed. *The Guerrilla Reader: A Historical Anthology.* Philadelphia: Temple University Press, 1977. 246p.

1216.   Metcalf, George T. "Offensive Partisan Warfare." *Military Review,* XXXII (April 1952), 53–61.

1217.   Miksche, Ferdinand O. *Secret Forces: The Technique of Underground Movements.* London: Faber and Faber, 1951. 181p.

1218.   Nurick, Lester, and R. W. Barrett. "The Legality of Guerrilla Forces under the Laws of War." *American Journal of International Law,* XL (July 1946), 563–583.

1219.   Praeger, Arthur, and Emily Praeger. *World War II Resistance Stories.* Triumph Series. New York: Franklin Watts, 1979.

1220. Rayleigh, Steven. "Wasps of War: Guerrilla Fighters Paving the Way to the Eventual Defeat of Hitler and Hirohito." *Saturday Evening Post,* CCXIV (April 25, 1942), 9–10+.

1221. United States. Department of the Air Force. Aerospace Studies Institute, Concepts Division. *The Role of Air Power in Guerrilla Warfare, World War II.* Maxwell Air Force Base, Ala.: Air University, 1962. 264p.

1222. Waldenstrom, Stig. "Resistance Movements." *Military Review.* XXXII (May 1952), 73–78.

Further References

Readers will find other general information in section I, subsections B, C, and D, above as well as in section VII, subsection A, below.

B. Europe

1. General Works

1223. Brown, MacAlister. "The Third Reich's Mobilization of the German Fifth Column in Eastern Europe." *Journal of Central European Affairs,* XIX (July 1959), 128–148.

1224. Buckley, Christopher. *Norway, the Commandos, Dieppe.* The Second World War, 1939–1945: A Popular Military History. London: H. M. Stationery Office, 1951. 276p.

1225. Cech, Jan. *Death Stalks the Forest.* London: Drummond, 1943. 75p.

1226. Conference on Britain and the European Resistance, 1939–1945, Oxford, 1962. *Proceedings.* Oxford, Eng.: St. Antony's College [1964?]. Various paging.

Cookridge, E. H., pseud. *See* Spiro, Edward

1227. Cowan, Lore. *Children of the Resistance: The Young Ones Who Defied the Nazi Terror.* London: Frewin, 1968. 191p.

1228. Dupuy, Trevor N. *European Resistance Movements.* New York: Watts, 1965. 88p.

1229. Embry, Basil. *Mission Completed.* New York: Praeger, 1958. 350p.

1230. Foot, Michael R. D. *Resistance: European Resistance to Nazism, 1940–1945.* New York: McGraw–Hill, 1977. 346p.

1231. Garlinski, Josef. *Hitler's Last Weapons: The Underground War against the V–1 and V–2.* London: Friedman, 1978. 244p.

1232. Hawes, Stephen, and Ralph White, eds. *Resistance in Europe, 1939–1945: Based on the Proceedings of a Symposium Held at the University of Salford, March 1973.* London: Allen Lane, 1975. 235p.

1233. Heilbrunn, Otto. *Partisan Warfare.* New York: Praeger, 1962. 199p.

1234. _____. *Warfare in the Enemy's Rear.* New York: Praeger, 1963. 231p.

1235. Hodges, L. M. "Flying Secret Agents To and From Enemy Country." *Royal Air Forces Quarterly,* II (Spring 1963), 13–16.

1236. Howard, Patrick, ed. *Special Operations.* London: Routledge and Kegan Paul, 1955. 239p.

1237. International Conference on the History of the Resistance Movements, First, Liège, 1958. *European Resistance Movements, 1939–1945: Proceedings.* London and New York: Pergamon Press, 1960. 410p.

1238. _____, Second, Milan, 1961. *European Resistance Movements, 1939–1945: Proceedings.* New York and London: Macmillan, 1964. 663p.

1239. _____, Third, Karlovy Vary. *Papers.* 13 parts. Karlovy Vary, 1963. Various paging.

1240. _____, Fourth, Vienna. *Papers.* Vienna, Austria, 1965. Various paging.

1241. Johnson, Stowers. *Agents Extraordinary.* London: Hale, 1975. 192p.

British SOE agents in Europe.

1242. Kirschen, Gilbert S. *Six Friends Arrive Tonight.* London: Nicholson and Watson, 1949. 160p.

1243. Kraus, René. *Europe in Revolt.* New York: Macmillan, 1942. 563p.

1244. Langelaan, George. *Knights of the Floating Silk.* Garden City, N. Y.: Doubleday, 1959. 284p.

1245. Levi, Maxine. *The Communists and the Liberation of Europe.* New York: New Century Publishers, 1945. 63p.

1246. Macksey, Kenneth J. *The Partisans of Europe in the Second World War.* New York: Stein & Day, 1975. 271p.

1247.   Malinowski, W. R. "The Pattern of Underground Resistance." *Annals of the American Academy of Political and Social Sciences*, CCXXXII (March 1944), 126–133.

1248.   Medhurst, C. E. H. "Secret Service of the Air." *Science Digest*, XII (November 1942), 1–4.

1249.   Michel, Henri. *The Shadow War: European Resistance, 1939–1945.* Translated from the French. New York: Harper & Row, 1972. 416p.

1250.   Michie, Allan A. "Scarlet Pimpernels of the Air: The Special Air Squadrons ["Moon Squadrons"] Which Ferried Agents and Dropped Supplies to the Resistance Forces in Europe." *Reader's Digest*, XLVII (August 1954), 73–76.

1251.   Miller, J. W., Jr. "Forest Fighting on the Eastern Front in World War II." *Geographic Review*, LXII (April 1972), 186–202.

1252.   Morris, J. A. "What You Can Believe about the Underground." *Saturday Evening Post*, CCXVI (September 18, 1943), 17+.

1253.   Moss, William S. *A War of Shadows.* London and New York: Boardman, 1952. 240p.

Munson, Kenneth, jt. author. *See* Taylor, John W. R.

1254.   Neave, Airey. *Saturday Night at MI9: A History of Underground Escape Lines in North-west Europe in 1940–1945, by a Leading Organizer of MI9.* London: Hodder and Stoughton, 1969. 327p.

1255.   Orbaan, Albert. *Duel in the Shadows: True Accounts of Anti-Nazi Underground Warfare during World War II.* Garden City, N. Y.: Doubleday, 1965. 229p.

1256.   Osman, William H., ed. *Pigeons in World War II.* London: Racing Pigeon Association, 1951. 146p.

1257.   Piekalkiewicz, Janusz. *Secret Agents, Spies, and Saboteurs: Famous Undercover Missions of World War II.* Translated from the German. New York: Morrow, 1974. 528p.

1258.   _____ . *Total Espionage.* New York: Putnam, 1941. 318p.

1259.   Riess, Curt. *Underground Europe.* New York: Dial Press, 1942. 325p.

1260.   Sanderson, James D. *Behind Enemy Lines.* Princeton, N. J.: Van Nostrand, 1959. 322p.

1261.   Seth, Ronald S. *The Noble Saboteurs.* New York: Hawthorn Books, 1966. 188p.

1262. _____ . *Undaunted: The Story of the Resistance in Western Europe.* New York: Philosophical Library, 1956. 327p.

1263. *Sixth Column: Inside the Nazi-occupied Countries.* Chicago: Alliance Press, 1942. 313p.

1264. Spiro, Edward. *Set Europe Ablaze.* By E. H. Cookridge, pseud. New York: Crowell, 1967. 410p.

Work of the British SOE

1265. _____ . *They Came from the Sky.* By E. H. Cookridge, pseud. New York: Crowell, 1967. 257p.

1266. Stafford, David A. T. "Britain Looks at Europe, 1940: Some Origins of S[pecial] O[perations] E[xecutive]." *Canadian Journal of History*, X (August 1975), 231–248.

1267. _____ . "The Detonator Concept: British Strategy, S.O.E., and European Resistance after the Fall of France." *Journal of Contemporary History*, X (April 1975), 185–217.

1268. _____ . "Upstairs/Downstairs: British Foreign Policy and Special Operations in Europe, 1940–1945." *Journal of European Studies*, V (March 1975), 55–61.

1269. Syrkin, Marie. "Parachutists from Palestine: A Chapter in the European Resistance Movement." *Commentary*, I (May 1946), 30–38.

1270. Taylor, John W. R., and Kenneth Munson. "The Moon Men." In: their *History of Aviation.* New York: Crown Publishers, 1976. pp. 316–320.

1271. Thorne, Charles B. *St. George and the Octopus.* London: Love, 1945. 158p.

British aid to the European resistance movements.

1272. Tickell, Jerrard. *Moon Squadron.* Garden City, N. Y.: Doubleday, 1958. 204p.

1273. United States. War Department. Office of Strategic Services, Research and Analysis Branch. *Germany and Its Occupied Territories during World War II.* Part IV of *O.S.S./State Department Intelligence and Research Reports.* 22 reels, 35mm microfilm. Washington, D. C.: University Publications of America, 1976–1977.

1274. Wachsman, Z. H. *Trailblazers for Invasion.* New York: Ungar, 1943. 284p.

1275. Warren, Harris G. "Air Support for the Underground." In: Wesley F. Craven and James L. Cate, eds. *The Army Air Forces in World War II.* 7 vols. Chicago: University of Chicago Press, 1948–1958. III, 493–524.

1276. _____. *Special Operations: A.A.F. Aid to European Resistance Movements, 1943–1945.* USAF Historical Study, no. 121. Washington, D. C.: H. Q., U. S. Army Air Force, 1947. 259p.

White, Ralph, jt. editor. *See* Hawes, Stephen

1277. Whiting, Charles. *The War in the Shadows.* New York: Ballantine Books, 1973. 268p.

1278. Wilmot, Chester. *The Struggle for Europe.* New York: Harper, 1952. 766p.

1279. Woodhouse, Christopher M. "Prolegomena to a Study of Resistance." *19th Century,* CXLIV (November 1948), 269–276; CXLIX (February 1949), 86–93.

1280. Woodman, Dorothy. *Europe Rises! The Story of Resistance in Occupied Europe.* London: Gollancz, 1943. 154p.

2. Northern Europe

a. United Kingdom and Ireland

1281. Blake, John W. *Northern Ireland in the Second World War.* Belfast, N.I.: H.M. Stationery Office, 1956. 535p.

1282. Carter, Carolle H. *The Shamrock and the Swastika: German Espionage in Ireland in World War II.* Palo Alto, Calif.: Pacific Books, 1977. 287p.

1283. Coituriend, V. V. *Isolated Island: A History and Personal Reminiscences of the German Occupation of the Island of Guernsey, June 1940–May 1945.* Guernsey: Guernsey *Star*, 1948. 334p.

1284. Falla, Frank W. *The Silent War.* London: Frewin, 1967. 172p.

1285. Fargo, Ladislas. *The Game of the Foxes: The Untold Story of German Espionage in the United States and Great Britain during World War II.* New York: McKay, 1972. 696p.

1286. Firmin, Stanley. *They Came to Spy.* London: Hutchinson, 1947. 156p.

1287. Maugham, Reginald C. F. *Jersey under the Jackboot.* London: W. H. Allen, 1946. 158p.

1288. Stephan, Enno. *Spies in Ireland.* Translated from the German. Harrisburg, Pa.: Stackpole Books, 1965. 311p.

1289. Toms, Carel. *Hitler's Fortress Islands*. London: New English Library, 1967. 160p.

1290. Wood, Alan, and Mary Wood. *Islands in Danger: The Story of the German Occupation of the Channel Islands, 1940–1945*. London: Evans, 1955. 255p.

b. France

(*1*) RESISTANCE AND INTELLIGENCE AGENTS

1291. Aron, Robert. *DeGaulle before Paris: The Liberation of France, June–August 1944*. London: Putnam, 1963. 312p.

1292. _____. *The Vichy Regime, 1940–1944*. New York: Macmillan, 1958. 536p.

1293. Bergier, Jacques. *Secret Weapons—Secret Agents*. Translated from the French. London: Hurst and Blackett, 1956. 184p.

1294. Bird, Michael J. *The Secret Battalion*. New York: Holt, Rinehart and Winston, 1964. 189p.

1295. Blumenson, Martin. "The Early French Resistance in Paris." *Naval War College Review*, XXX (Summer 1977), 64–72.

1296. _____. *The Vilde Affair: Beginnings of the French Resistance*. Boston: Houghton, Mifflin, 1977. 287p.

1297. Booth, Walter B. *Mission Marcel Proust*. Philadelphia: Dorrance, 1972. 168p.

1298. Buckmaster, Maurice J. *Specially Employed: The Story of British Aid to French Patriots of the Resistance*. London: Batchworth, 1952. 200p.

1299. _____. *They Fought Alone: The Story of British Agents in France*. New York: W. W. Norton, 1958. 255p.

1300. Case, L. M. "The Marquis Republic of Verrors." *Infantry Journal*, LX (April 1947), 29–37.

1301. Chambard, Claude. *The Marquis: A History of the French Resistance Movement*. Translated from the French. Indianapolis: Bobbs–Merrill, 1976. 237p.

1302. Clark, Blake. "The Phantom Army." In: *Reader's Digest*, Editors of. *Secrets and Spies: Behind-the-Scenes Stories of World War II*. Pleasantville, N. Y.: Reader's Digest Association, 1964. pp. 384–390.

1303. _____. "The Spark Plugs of France's Secret Army: Americans and British Who Parachuted into France to Help Organize the Resistance." *Reader's Digest*, XLVI (April 1945), 95–98.

1304.   Collier, Richard. *Ten Thousand Eyes*. New York: Dutton, 1958. 320p.

1305.   Collins, Larry, and Dominique Lapierre. *Is Paris Burning?* New York: Simon and Schuster, 1965. 376p.

1306.   _____. "The Story behind the Liberation of Paris a Quarter Century Ago." *New York Times Magazine*, (September 7, 1969), 46–47+.

1307.   Dank, Milton. *The French against the French: Collaboration and Resistance*. Philadelphia: Lippincott, 1974. 365p.

1308.   De La Gorce, Paul M. *The French Army: A Military–Political History*. Translated from the French. New York: Braziller, 1963. 568p.

1309.   De Rochemont, Richard. "The French Underground." *Life*, XIII (August 24, 1942), 86–88+.

1310.   De Vomecourt, Philippe. *An Army of Amateurs*. Translated from the French. Garden City, N. Y.: Doubleday, 1961. 307p.

1311.   Dunoyer, Alphonse. "We Blind the Wehrmacht: The Marquis Is Doing a Tremendous Job." *Collier's*, CXIV (April 19, 1944), 20–21+.

1312.   Ehrlich, Blake. *Resistance: France, 1940–1945*. Boston: Little, Brown, 1965. 278p.

1313.   Ernst, Otto. "Memories of the Resistance in France." *Contemporary Review*, CLXXI (February 1947), 97–103.

1314.   Foot, Michael R. D. *S.O.E. in France: An Account of the World of the British Special Operations Executive in France, 1940–1944*. London: H. M. Stationery Office, 1966. 550p.

1315.   Fourcade, Marie M. *Noah's Ark*. Translated from the French. New York: Dutton, 1974. 377p.

1316.   Frenay, Henri. *The Night Will End*. Translated from the French. New York: McGraw–Hill, 1975. 469p.

1317.   Frohock, W. M. "The Years of Shame." *Massachusetts Review*, XVI (Autumn 1975), 789–797.

1318.   Fuller, Jean O. *Double Webs: Light on the Secret Agents' War in France*. New York: Putnam, 1958. 256p.

1319.   _____. *The German Penetration of S.O.E.: France, 1941–1944*. London: Kimber, 1975. 192p.

1320.   Funk, Arthur L. "American Contacts with the Resistance in France, 1940–1943." *Military Affairs*, XXXIV (February 1970), 15–21.

1321.   Girard, André. "The French Underground Fights." *Reader's Digest*, XLIV (May 1944), 107–112.

1322.   Haarer, Alec E. *A Cold-blooded Business*. London: Staples Press, 1958. 208p.

1323.   Hadsel, F. L. "Some Sources on the Resistance Movement in France during the Nazi Occupation." *Journal of Modern History*, XVIII (December 1946), 333–340.

1324.   Harrison, Gordon A. "The French Resistance." In: his *Cross-channel Attack*. United States Army in World War II: European Theater of Operations. Washington, D. C.: Office of the Chief of Military History, Department of the Army, 1951. pp. 198–207.

1325.   Heinzen, Ralph. "I Visit the French Underground." *Saturday Evening Post*, CCXVI (June 10, 1944), 28–29+.

1326.   Hofstadter, Dan. "Memories of Resistance: The French Return to the Years of War." *Dissent*, XXII (Summer 1975), 261–268.

1327.   Hume, Steven. "'Operation Marie Louise.'" *Blackwood's Magazine*, CCLIX (May 1946), 341–350.

1328.   Instone, Gordon. *Freedom the Spur*. London: Burke, 1953. 256p.

1329.   Johnston, Robert H. "The Great Patriotic War and the Russian Exiles in France." *Russian Review*, XXXV (July 1976), 303–321.

1330.   Jucker, Ninetta. *Curfew in Paris: A Record of the German Occupation*. London: Hogarth, 1960. 206p.

1331.   Kedward, Harry R. *Resistance in Vichy France: A Study of Ideas and Motivation in the Southern Zone, 1940–1942*. London and New York: Oxford University Press, 1978. 311p.

1332.   Kennard, Coleridge A. F. *Gestapo—France, 1943–1945*. London: Grant, Richards, 1947. 208p.

1333.   Knapton, E. J. "France Awaits the Decisive Hour: The Committee of National Liberation Joins the French Underground." *Current History*, V (December 1943), 320–326.

1334.   Knight, Frida. *French Resistance, 1940 to 1944*. New York: Beekman House, 1972. 242p.

1335.   Lanius, Charles. "Underground Escape Route from France." *Saturday Evening Post*, CCXVI (January 15, 1944), 20–21+.

Lapierre, Dominique, jt. author. *See* Collins, Larry

1336. Lay, Beirne, Jr. "Down in Flames, Out by Underground." *Saturday Evening Post,* CCXVIII (July 28, August 4–11, 1945), 24–25+, 22–23+, 20+.

1337. _____. *I've Had It: The Survival of a* [U. S. 407th] *Bomb Group Commander.* Hew York: Harper, 1945. 141p.

1338. Liebling, Abbot J. *The Republic of Silence.* New York: Harcourt, Brace, 1947. 522p.

1339. Littlejohn, David. *The Patriotic Traitors: The History of Collaboration in German-occupied Europe, 1940–1945.* Garden City, N. Y.: Doubleday, 1972. 391p.

1340. Marchand, Lucienne. "Women of the Marquis." *Free World,* X (September 1945), 62–64.

1341. Marshall, Samuel L. A., *et al.* "French Forces of the Interior." Unpublished paper, French Resistance Unit, Foreign Military Studies Program, Historical Division, U. S. Army Europe, 1945. 1,500p.

1342. Maublanc, René. "French Teachers in the Resistance Movement." *Science and Society,* XI (January 1947), 38–52.

1343. Mounier, Emmanual. "Resistance." *Commonweal,* XLII (May 25, 1945), 136–138.

1344. _____. "Structures of Liberation." *Commonweal,* XLII (May 18, 1945), 112–114.

1345. Muggeridge, Malcolm. "Beyond the Marquis Fringe." *New Statesman and Nation,* LXX (December 10, 1965), 919–920.

1346. "'Ne Obliviscaris': The Resistance of France to the Nazi Overlord." *Blackwood's Magazine,* CCLVIII (September 1945), 205–216.

1347. Norden, Peter. *Madame Kitty: A True Story.* Translated from the French. New York: Abelard–Schuman, 1973. 223p.

1348. Novick, Peter. *The Resistance versus Vichy: The Purge of Collaborators in Liberated France.* New York: Columbia University Press, 1968. 245p.

1349. Pearson, Michael. *The Tears of Glory.* Garden City, N.Y.: Doubleday, 1979.

The battle of Verrors.

1350. Perrault, Gilles. *The Secret of D–Day.* Boston: Little, Brown, 1965. 249p.

1351. Pickles, D. M. "The Political Situation in France." *Political Quarterly,* XVI (April 1945), 93–105.

1352.   Pogue, Forrest C. "Relations with the French, June–September 1944." In: his *The Supreme Command.* United States Army in World War II: European Theater of Operations. Washington, D. C.: Office of the Chief of Military History, Department of the Army, 1954. pp. 231–244.

1353.   Pollock, John. "France's Home War." *Quarterly Review,* CCLXXXII (July 1944), 353–369.

1354.   Raisky, Abraham. "We Fought Back in France: A Chapter in Resistance History." *Commentary,* I (February 1946), 60–65.

1355.   Rieber, Alfred. *Stalin and the French Communist Party, 1941– 1947.* New York: Columbia University Press, 1962. 395p.

1356.   Roy, Claude. *Eight Days That Freed Paris.* London: Pilot, 1945. 95p.

1357.   "Saboteur," pseud. "By Submarine to [the French] Underground." *Blackwood's Magazine,* CCLX (October 1946), 275–288.

1358.   _____. "The R.A.F. and the French Resistance." *Blackwood's Magazine,* CCLIX (September 1946), 185–192.

1359.   Shaw, Irving. "Morts pour la Patrie." *New Yorker,* XXI (August 25, 1945), 36–44.

The liberation of Paris.

1360.   Shiber, Etta. "Paris Underground." *Reader's Digest,* XLIII (October 1943), 119–144.

1361.   Simon, Matila. *The Battle of the Louvre: The Struggle to Save French Art in World War II.* New York: Hawthorn, 1971. 214p.

1362.   Simon, Paul. *One Enemy Only—the Invader: A Record of French Resistance.* London: Hodder and Stoughton, 1942. 167p.

1363.   Steinfels, Peter. "Mystery of Resistance." *Commonweal,* XCVI (April 14, 1972), 135+.

1364.   Sweets, John F. "The Mouvements Unis de la Résistance (M.U.R.): A Study of the Noncommunist Resistance Movements in France, 1940–1944." Unpublished Ph.D. dissertation, Duke University, 1972.

1365.   _____. *The Politics of Resistance in France, 1940–1944: A History of the Mouvements Unis de la Résistance.* Dekalb: Northern Illinois University Press, 1976. 267p.

1366.   Tchok, Ivan M. *The First to Resist.* London: New Europe Publishing Co., 1945. 64p.

1367. "They [Civilians] Took to the Marquis." *Free World,* VIII (August 1944), 134–138.

1368. Thornton, Willis. *The Liberation of Paris.* New York: Harcourt, Brace, 1962. 231p.

1369. Wahl, Anthony N. "De Gaulle and the Resistance: The Rise of Reform Politics in France." Unpublished Ph.D. dissertation, Harvard University, 1956.

1370. Walter, Gerald. *Paris under Occupation.* New York: Orion Press, 1960. 209p.

1371. Werth, Alexander. *France, 1940–1955.* New York: Holt, 1956. 764p.

1372. Wilhelm, Maria. *For the Glory of France: The Story of the French Resistance.* New York: Julian Messner, 1968. 192p.

1373. Willard, Germaine. "Traditions of the [French] Resistance Live On." *World Marxist Review,* XVIII (May 1975), 29–36.

1374. Williams, Orio. "Aspects of the Marquis." *National Review,* CXXV (August 1945), 166–171.

1375. Wright, Gordon. "Reflections on the French Resistance, 1940–1944." *Political Science Quarterly,* LXXVII (September 1962), 336–349.

(2) SPECIAL FORCES

1376. Austin, Alexander B. *We Landed at Dawn: The Story of the Dieppe Raid.* New York: Harcourt, 1943. 217p.

1377. Botting, Douglas. "Britain's Shock Troops." In: his *The Second Front.* World War II Series. New York: Time–Life, Inc., 1978. pp. 162–172.

1378. Chant, S. W. "The Raid on St. Nazaire." *Reader's Digest,* XLV (July 1944), 13–17.

1379. Crookenden, Napier. *Dropzone Normandy.* New York: Scribner's, 1976. 304p.

Much on the British SAS and commandos.

1380. Dempster, Guy. *Commando Raid at Dawn.* London: Lutterworth Press, 1943. 192p.

1381. Forbes, Charles M. "The Attack on St. Nazaire, 1942 [Official Report of April 13, 1942]." Supplement 38086, *London Gazette,* October 2, 1947.

1382.   Horan, H. E. "'Operation Chariot': The Raid on St. Nazaire, 27th–28th March 1942." *Journal of the Royal United Service Institution,* CVI (November 1961), 561–566.

1383.   Hughes–Hallet, J. "The Dieppe Raid [Official Report of August 30, 1942]." Supplement 38045, *London Gazette,* August 14, 1947.

1384.   Leasor, James. *Green Beach.* New York: Morrow, 1975. 292p.

The technical intelligence aspects of Dieppe.

1385.   Maguire, Eric. *Dieppe, August 19.* London: Cape, 1963. 205p.

1386.   Mason, David. *The Raid on St. Nazaire.* Ballantine's Illustrated History of the Violent Century. New York: Ballantine Books, 1970. 157p.

1387.   Menard, David. "A Commando Raider's Story: An Interview." *Yale Review,* New Series XXXII (March 1943), 440–450

Dieppe.

1388.   Millar, George R. *The Burneval Raid: Flashpoint in the Radar War.* Garden City, N. Y.: Doubleday, 1975. 221p.

1389.   Moore, W. R. "Rehearsal at Dieppe." *National Geographic Magazine,* LXXXII (October 1942), 495–502.

1390.   Mordal, Jacques. *Dieppe: The Dawn of Decision.* London: Souvenir Press, 1963. 285p.

1391.   Mountbatten, Louis. "'Operation Jubilee': The Place of the Dieppe Raid in History." *Journal of the Royal United Service Institution for Defence Studies,* CXIX (March 1974), 25–30.

1392.   Reyburn, Wallace. *Dawn Landing.* London: Brown, Watson, 1958. 160p.

Dieppe.

1393.   Reynolds, Quentin. *Dress Rehearsal: The Story of Dieppe.* New York: Random House, 1943. 278p.

1394.   Robertson, Terence. *The Shame and the Glory: Dieppe.* London: Hutchinson, 1963. 508p.

1395.   Roskill, Stephen W. "The Dieppe Raid and the Question of German Foreknowledge." *Journal of the Royal United Service Institution,* CIX (1964), 27–31.

1396.   Ryder, Robert E. D. *The Attack on St. Nazaire, 28th March 1942.* London: Murray, 1947. 118p.

1397.   Schreiner, Charles W. "The Dieppe Raid: Its Origins, Aims, and Results." *Naval War College Review,* XXV (May–June 1973), 83–98.

1398.   Stacey, Charles P. "Dieppe, 19 August 1942." *Canadian Geographic Journal,* XXVII (August 1943), 47–63.

1399.   Thompson, Reginald W. *At Whatever Cost: The Story of the Dieppe Raid.* New York: Coward–McCann, 1957. 215p.

c. Holland and Belgium

1400.   Best, Sigismund P. *The Venlo Incident.* London and New York: Hutchinson, 1951. 260p.

1401.   Bruins–Slot, J. A. H. I. S. "[Dutch] Resistance during the German Occupation." *Annals of the American Academy of Political and Social Science,* CCXLV (May 1946), 144–148.

1402.   Davidson, F. H. N. "My Mission to Belgium, 1940." *Journal of the Royal United Service Institution for Defence Studies,* CXIV (December 1969), 80–82.

1403.   De Graaf, Klaas. *Desperate Carnival.* Translated from the Dutch. London: Muller, 1953. 288p.

1404.   De Jong, Louis. *Holland Fights the Nazis.* London: Drummond, 1941. 138p.

1405.   Doneux, Jacques. *They Arrived by Moonlight.* London: Odhams Press, 1957. 230p.

SOE agents dropped into Belgium.

1406.   Eloy, Victor. *The Fight in the Forest.* Translated from the French. London: Hale, 1949. 192p.

Belgian resistance.

1407.   Embry, Basil. "D–Day: Mosquitos Foil the Gestapo." In: Stanley M. Ulanoff, ed. *Bombs Away!* Garden City, N. Y.: Doubleday, 1971. pp. 277–298.

1408.   _____ . "The Raid on Shell House." In: Gavin Lyall, ed. *War in the Air: The Royal Air Forces in World War II.* New York: Morrow, 1969. pp. 360–363.

"Operation Jericho."

1409.   Fisher, George. "Jailbreak Jericho." *Coronet,* XLIX (January 1961), 118–122.

1410.   Ganier–Raymond, Philippe. *The Tangled Web.* Translated from the French. New York: Pantheon, 1968. 203p.

Dutch resistance.

1411.   Goris, Jan A. *Belgium in Bondage.* New York: Fischer, 1943. 259p.

1412.   ———— . *Strangers Should Not Whisper.* New York: Fischer, 1945. 260p.

1413.   ———— , ed. *Belgium under Occupation.* New York: Moutus Press for the Belgian Government Information Center, 1947. 240p.

1414.   Hackett, John W. *I Was a Stranger.* Boston: Houghton, Mifflin, 1978. 219p.

Dutch underground.

1415.   Huizinga, J. H. "Holland's Illegality: The Resistance Movement." *Fortnightly,* CLXIV (September 1945), 169–175.

1416.   Maass, Walter B. *The Netherlands at War, 1940–1945.* New York: Abelard–Schuman, 1970. 264p.

1417.   Martens, Allard. *The Silent War: Glimpses of the Dutch Underground and Views of the Battle of Arnhem.* London: Hodder and Stoughton, 1961. 318p.

1418.   Motz, Roger. *Belgium Unvanquished.* New York: Transatlantic, 1942. 135p.

1419.   Moulton, James L. *The Battle for Antwerp.* New York: Hippocrene Books, 1978. 208p.

As seen by the C.O. of the British 4th Commandos.

1420.   Neave, Airey. *The Little Cyclone.* London: Hodder and Stoughton, 1954. 189p.

Belgium.

1421.   ———— . *They Have Their Exits.* Boston: Little, Brown, 1953. 275p.

1422.   Pointon, Patrick. "They Blasted Amiens Jail." *Roundel,* VI (December 1954), 21–24.

1423.   Posthumus, H. W., ed. *The Netherlands during German Occupation.* New York: American Academy of Political and Social Science, 1946. 231p.

1424.   Rigby, Françoise L. *In Defiance.* London: Elek, 1960. 224p.

Belgian underground.

1425.   Van Woerdan, Peter. *In the Secret Place: A Story of the Dutch Underground.* Wheaton, Ill.: Van Kampen Press, 1954. 64p.

1426.   ———— . *The Dutch under German Occupation, 1940–1945.* Stanford, Calif.: Stanford University Press, 1963. 338p.

1427. Warmbrunn, Walter. "The Netherlands under German Occupation, 1940–1945." Unpublished Pd.D. dissertation, Stanford University, 1955.

1428. Warrack, Graeme. *Travel by Dark after Arnhem.* London: Harvill, 1963. 256p.

d. Norway and Denmark

    (1) RESISTANCE AND INTELLIGENCE AGENTS

1429. Andersen, William D. "The German Armed Forces in Denmark, 1940–1943: A Study in Occupation Policy." Unpublished Ph.D. dissertation, University of Kansas, 1972.

1430. Baden–Powell, Dorothy. *Pimpernel Gold: How Norway Foiled the Nazis.* New York: St. Martin's Press, 1978. 207p.

1431. Balchen, Bernt. "Our Secret Way in Scandinavia." *Collier's,* CXVII (March 9–16, 1946), 14–15+, 72+.

    Norwegian underground.

1432. Bennett, Jeremy. *British Broadcasting and the Danish Resistance Movement, 1940–1945: A Study of the Wartime Broadcasts of the B.B.C. Danish Service.* Cambridge, Eng.: Cambridge University Press, 1966. 266p.

1433. Brandt, Willy. *In Exile: Essays, Reflections, and Letters, 1933–1947.* Translated from the German. London: Wolff, 1971. 264p.

1434. Brock, Theodore. *The Mountains Wait.* London: Joseph, 1943. 191p.

1435. "The Campaign [of Sabotage] against the Germans." *American–Scandinavian Review,* XXXIII (March 1944), 69–72.

1436. Derry, Kingston. *The Campaign in Norway.* History of the Second World War: United Kingdom Military Series. London: H. M. Stationery Office, 1952. 289p.

1437. Flender, Harold. *Rescue in Denmark.* New York: Simon and Schuster, 1963. 281p.

1438. Gomsrud, A. A., ed. "The Rebirth of a Nation: The Extraordinary Story of Norway's Underground." *Free World,* X (October 1945), 64–70.

1439. Graham, Burton. "'Operation Carthage.'" In: his *The Pictorial History of Air Battles.* Indianapolis: Bobbs–Merrill, 1974. pp. 84–91.

    RAF raid on Copenhagen's Gestapo H. Q.

1440. Haestrup, Jorgen. "From Occupied to Allied: The Danish Resistance Movement, 1940–1945." *Military Journal,* I (March, August 1977), 34–36, 32–36.

1441. Halck, Jorgen. *Strictly Confidential.* Translated from the Danish. London: Cape, 1961. 175p.

1442. Havas, Laslo. *The Long Jump.* Translated from the Norwegian. London: Spearman, 1967. 256p.

1443. Hovelsen, Leif. *Out of the Evil Night.* Translated from the Norwegian. London: Blandford, 1959. 160p.

1444. Howarth, David A. *We Die Alone.* New York: Macmillan, 1955. 231p.

1445. Johnson, Amanda. *Norway: Her Invasion and Occupation.* New York: Nordisk Tidende, 1948. 372p.

1446. Lampe, David. *The Danish Resistance.* New York: Ballantine Books, 1960. 179p.

1447. _____ . *The Savage Canary.* London: Cassell, 1957. 236p.

1448. Liversidge, Douglas. *The Third Front: The Strange Story of the Secret War in the Arctic.* London: Souvenir Press, 1960. 219p.

1449. Madsen, K. B. "Fighting Denmark: A Resumé." *American–Scandinavian Review,* XXXIII (December 1945), 328–336.

1450. Mentz, Ernst, ed. *Five Years: The Occupation of Denmark in Pictures.* New York: Bonnier, 1946. 230p.

1451. Munthe, Malcolm. *Sweet Is War.* London: Duckworth, 1954. 185p.

Nökleby, Berit, jt. author. *See* Riste, Olav

1452. Norway. Royal Norwegian Government Information Office. *The Gestapo at Work in Norway.* London, 1942. 38p.

1453. Nytrup, Per. *An Outline of the German Occupation of Denmark, 1940–1945.* Translated from the Danish. Copenhagen: Published by the Museum of the Danish Resistance Movement, Danish National Museum, 1968. 48p.

1454. Outze, Borge, ed. *Denmark during the German Occupation.* Chicago: Scandinavian Publishing Co., 1946. 155p.

1455. Petrow, Richard. *The Bitter Years: The Invasion and Occupation of Denmark and Norway, April 1940–May 1945.* New York: Morrow, 1974. 403p.

1456. Reilly, David R. *The Sixth Floor.* London: Frewin, 1969. 224p. "Operation Carthage."

1457. Riste, Olav, and Berit Nökleby. *Norway, 1940–1945: The Resistance Movement.* Translated from the Norwegian. Tanum's Tokens of Norway. Oslow, Norway: Tanum, 1970. 92p.

1458. Singer, Kurt D. *Duel for the Northland: The War of Enemy Agents in Scandinavia.* New York: McBride, 1943. 212p.

1459. Tauras, K. V. *Guerrilla Warfare on the Amber Coast.* New York: Voyages Press, 1962. 110p.

1460. Thomas, John O. *The Giant-killers: The Story of the Danish Resistance Movement, 1940–1945.* New York: Taplinger, 1976. 320p.

1461. Tilman, Harold W. *When Men and Mountains Meet.* Cambridge, Eng.: Cambridge University Press, 1946. 232p.

1462. Toksvig, Signe K. "Denmark's Resistance." *Atlantic,* ALXX (August 1942), 66–72.

1463. *Triumph in Disaster: Denmark's Fight Against Germany.* London: H. M. Stationery Office, 1945. 64p.

1464. Vigness, Paul C. *The German Occupation of Norway.* New York: Vantage Press, 1970. 285p.

1465. Voorhis, Jerry L. "Germany and Denmark, 1940–1943." *Scandinavian Studies,* XLIV (Spring 1972), 171–185.

1466. Walker, Roy. *A People Who Loved Peace: The Norwegian Struggle against Nazism.* London: Gollancz, 1946. 111p.

1467. Warbey, William. *Look to Norway.* London: Secker and Warburg, 1945. 242p.

1468. Werstein, Irving. *That Denmark Might Live: The Saga of the Danish Resistance in World War II.* New York: Macrae Smith, 1967. 143p.

1469. Wright, Myrtle. *Norwegian Diary, 1940–1945.* London: Friends Peace and International Relations Committee, 1974. 255p.

(*2*) Special Forces

1470. Barry, C. B. "The Attack on the *Tirpitz* by Midget Submarines on 22 September 1943 [Official Report of November 8, 1943]." Supplement 38204, *London Gazette,* February 11, 1948.

1471. Brennecke, Hans J. *The Tirpitz: The Drama of the "Lone Queen of the North."* Translated from the German. London: Hale, 1963. 187p.

1472. "British Commandos Raid Hitler's Europe: The Adventure at Vagsöy." *Life,* XII (January 26, 1942), 17–21.

1473. "The British Turn the Tables on the Nazis with a Sudden Raid on the [Lofoten] Islands Off Norway." *Life,* X (March 31, 1941), 31–35.

1474. Brown, David. *Tirpitz: The Floating Fortress.* Annapolis, Md.: U.S. Naval Institute, 1977. 160p.

1475. Devins, Joseph H., Jr. *The Vaagso Raid.* Philadelphia: Chilton, 1967. 222p.

1476. Drummond, John D. *But for These Men: How Eleven Commandos Saved Western Civilization.* London: Allen, 1962. 205p.

1477. Frere–Cook, Gervis. *The Attacks on the Tirpitz.* Sea Battles in Close-up, no. 8. Annapolis, Md.: U. S. Naval Institute, 1973. 112p.

1478. Gallagher, Thomas M. *Assault in Norway: Sabotaging the Nazi Nuclear Bomb.* New York: Harcourt, Brace, 1975. 234p.

1479. _____. "These Brave Men: The Sabotage of the Vemork Plant." *Reader's Digest,* CVII (October 1975), 215–220+.

1480. _____. *The X-craft Raid* [on *Tirpitz*]. New York: Harcourt, Brace, 1971. 170p.

1481. Haukelid, Knut. *Skis against the Atom.* Translated from the Norwegian. New York: Ryerson, 1954. 201p.

1482. Horan, H. E. "'Operation Archery.'" *U. S. Naval Institute Proceedings,* LXXXVII (1961), 70–75.

The Vaagso raid.

1483. Hutchinson, R. C. "Excursion to Norway: A Commando in Action." *Atlantic,* CLXX (July 1942), 7–13.

Vaagso.

1484. "The Lofoten Raid." *Illustrated London News,* CC (January 17, 1942), 84–85.

1485. Mikes, George. *The Epic of Lofoten.* London: Hutchinson, 1941. 79p.

1486. Phillips, Cecil E. L. *The Greatest Raid of All: An Account of the Famous World War II Commando Raid against Ships of the German Navy.* Boston: Little, Brown, 1960. 270p.

1487. Place, Godfrey. "The Midget Attack on the *Tirpitz*." In: John Winton, ed. *The War at Sea: The British Navy in World War II.* New York: Morrow, 1967. pp. 288–295.

1488. "Raid on the Lofotens." *Illustrated London News,* CXCVIII (March 15, 1941), 333–335, 338–341.

1489. Sanderson, James D. "The A-bomb That Never Was." In: his *Behind Enemy Lines.* New York: Van Nostrand, 1959. pp. 138–157.

1490. Schofield, Stephen. "'Musketoon'—*Commando Raid: Glomfjord, 1942.*" London: Cape, 1964. 156p.

1491. Sondern, Frederick. "Eleven against the Nazi A-bomb." *Reader's Digest,* XLIX (November 1946), 25–30.

1492. Sonsteby, Gunnar F. T. *Report from No. 24.* Translated from the Norwegian. New York: L. Stuart, 1965. 192p.

1493. Tovey, John C. "Raid on Military and Economic Objectives in the Lofoten Islands [Official Report of April 3, 1941]." Supplement 38331, *London Gazette,* June 23, 1948.

1494. _____. "Raid on Military and Economic Objectives in the Vicinity of Vaagso Island [Official Report of January 7, 1942]." Supplement 38342, *London Gazette,* July 5, 1948.

1495. Wilkinson, J. Burke. "A *Tirpitz* Tale." *U. S. Naval Institute Proceedings,* LXXX (1954), 374–383.

1496. Woodward, David. *The Tirpitz.* New York: W. W. Norton, 1953. 223p.

e. The Greater Reich: Germany, Austria, and Czechoslovakia

1497. Almond, Gabriel A. "The German Resistance Movement." *Current History,* X (May–June 1946), 409–419, 519–527.

1498. _____, ed. *The Struggle for Democracy in Germany.* New York: Russell and Russell, 1965. 345p.

_____, jt. author. *See* Kraus, Wolfgang

1499. Bayles, William D. *Seven Were Hanged: An Authentic Account of the Student Revolt in Munich University.* London: Gollancz, 1945. 80p.

1500. Blond, Georges. *The Death of Hitler's Germany.* Translated from the French. New York: Macmillan, 1954. 302p.

1501. _____. "The Plot to Kill Hitler." In: *Reader's Digest,* Editors of. *The Reader's Digest Illustrated History of World War II.* Pleasantville, N. Y.: Reader's Digest Association, 1969. pp. 376–386.

1502. Brandt, Karl. "German Resistance, an American Perspective: An Address, July 20, 1965." *Vital Speeches,* XXXI (September 15, 1965), 713–717.

1503.   Bullock, Alan. *Hitler: A Study in Tyranny.* Rev. ed. New York: Harper & Row, 1962. 848p.

1504.   Carlson, Verner R. "Operation Walkure." *U. S. Naval Institute Proceedings,* LXXXVI (June 1960), 75–82; LXXXVII (March 1961), 108–111.

The July 20, 1944 bomb plot against Hitler.

1505.   *Czechoslovakia Fights Back.* New York: American Council on Public Affairs, 1943. 210p.

1506.   Deutsch, Harold C. *The Conspiracy against Hitler in the Twilight War.* Minneapolis: University of Minnesota Press, 1968. 394p.

1507.   Donohoe, James. *Hitler's Conservative Opponents in Bavaria, 1939–1945: A Study of Catholic, Monarchist, and Separatist Anti–Nazi Activities.* Leiden, Belgium: Brill, 1961. 348p.

1508.   _____. "The Munich Student Revolt." *Pacific Spectator,* IV (January 1950), 49–59.

1509.   Duff, Shiela G. *German Protectorate: The Czechs under Nazi Rule.* New York: Macmillan, 1942. 304p.

1510.   Dulles, Allen W. *Germany's Underground.* New York: Macmillan, 1947. 207p. Rpr. 1978.

1511.   Elias, Andrew. "The Slovak Uprising of 1944." Unpublished Ph.D. dissertation, New York University, 1963.

1512.   FitzGibbon, Constantine. *20 July.* New York: W. W. Norton, 1956. 285p.

1513.   Ford, F. L. "The Twentieth of July in the History of the German Resistance." *American Historical Review,* LI (July 1946), 609–626.

1514.   Fraenkel, Heinrich. *The German People versus Hitler.* London: Allen and Unwin, 1940. 370p.

1515.   _____. *The Other Germany.* London: Drummond, 1942. 144p.

_____, jt. author. *See* Manvell, Roger

1516.   Gallin, Mary. *Ethical and Religious Factors in the German Resistance to Hitler.* Washington, D. C.: Press of the Catholic University of America, 1955. 231p.

1517.   Gisevius, Hans B. *To the Bitter End.* Translated from the German. Boston: Houghton, Mifflin, 1947. 632p.

1518. Gollwitzer, Helmut, *et al.*, eds. *Dying We Live: The Final Messages and Records of the* [German] *Resistance.* Translated from the German. New York: Pantheon Books, 1956. 285p.

1519. Goerlitz, Walter. *The German General Staff.* Translated from the German. London: Hollis and Carter, 1953. 508p.

Much on July 20.

1520. Hoffmann, Peter. *The History of the German Resistance, 1933–1945.* Translated from the German. Cambridge, Mass.: M.I.T. Press, 1977. 847p.

1521. Holland, Caroline. "The Foreign Contacts Made by the German Opposition to Hitler." Unpublished Ph.D. dissertation, University of Pennsylvania, 1967.

1522. Huss, Pierre. "The Plot against Hitler." *Cosmopolitan Magazine,* XL (July 1946), *passim.*

1523. Hutak, Jakub B. *With Blood and with Iron: The Lidice Story.* London: Hale, 1957. 160p.

1524. Irving, David. *The German Atomic Bomb: The History of Nuclear Research in Nazi Germany.* New York: Simon and Schuster, 1967. 329p.

Much on Allied countermeasures.

1525. Jansen, Jon B., and Stefan Weyl. "Spy at Work: The Underground Movement in Germany." *Atlantic Monthly,* LXXI (February 1943), 71–77.

1526. Kempner, Robert M. W. *Blueprint of the Nazi Underground—Past and Future Subversive Activities.* Pullman: Research Studies of the State College of Washington, 1945.

1527. Kraus, Wolfgang, and Gabriel A. Almond. "Resistance and Repression under the Nazis." In: Gabriel A. Almond, ed. *The Struggle For Democracy in Germany.* Chapel Hill: University of North Carolina Press, 1949. pp. 33–63.

1528. Leber, Annedore, comp. *Conscience in Revolt: Sixty-four Stories of Resistance in Germany, 1933–1945.* Translated from the German. London: Vallentine, 1957. 270p.

1529. Leuner, Heinz D. *When Compassion Was a Crime: Germany's Silent Heroes, 1933–1945.* Translated from the German. London: Wolff, 1966. 164p.

Liddell–Hart, Basil H., ed. *See* Rommel, Erwin

1530. Luza, Radomir. "The Communist Party in Czechoslovakia and the Czech Resistance, 1939–1945." *Slavic Review,* XXVIII (December 1969), 561–576.

———, jt. author. *See* Mamatez, Victor S.

1531. MacDonald, Charles B. "The Myth of the Redoubt." In: his *The Last Offensive.* United States Army in World War II: European Theater of Operations. Washington, D. C.: Office of the Chief of Military History, Department of the Army, 1972. pp. 407–443.

1532. Mackworth, Cecily. *Czechoslovakia Fights Back.* New York: Transatlantic, 1944. 117p.

1533. Mamatez, Victor S., and Radomir Luza. *A History of the Czechoslovak Republic, 1918–1948.* Princeton, N. J.: Princeton University Press, 1973. 534p.

1534. Manvell, Roger. *The Conspirators: 20th July 1944.* Ballantine's Illustrated History of the Violent Century. New York: Ballantine Books, 1971. 160p.

1535. ———, and Heinrich Fraenkel. *The Canaris Conspiracy: The Secret Resistance to Hitler in the German Army.* New York: McKay, 1969. 267p.

1536. ———. *The Men Who Tried to Kill Hitler.* New York: Coward–McCann, 1964. 272p.

1537. Mason, Herbert M., Jr. *To Kill the Devil: The Attempts on the Life of Adolph Hitler.* New York: W. W. Norton, 1978. 280p.

1538. Mastny, Vojtech. *The Czechs under Nazi Rule: The Failure of National Resistance, 1939–1942.* New York: Columbia University Press, 1971. 274p.

1539. Minott, Rodney G. *The Fortress That Never Was: The Myth of the Nazi Alpine Redoubt.* London: Longmans, Green, 1965. 208p.

1540. Mulholland, Virginia. "The Plots to Assassinate Hitler, 1938–1944." *Strategy and Tactics,* (November–December 1976), 4–15.

1541. O'Donnell, James P. *The Bunker: The History of the Reich Chancellery Group.* New York: Harper, 1978. 512p.

1542. Pachter, H. M. "The Legend of the 20th of July." *Social Research,* XXIX (Spring, Winter 1962), 109–115, 481–488.

1543. Persico, Joseph E. "The Fearless Yanks Who Spied on Hitler." *Parade,* (February 11, 1979), 6–9.

1544. _____ . *Piercing the Reich: The Penetration of Nazi Germany by American Secret Agents in World War II.* New York: Viking Press, 1979. 350p.

1545. "The Plot That Almost Changed History: The July 20, 1944 Plot against Hitler." *U. S. News and World Report,* LVII (July 27, 1964), 52–53.

1546. Prittie, Terence C. F. *Germans against Hitler.* Boston: Little, Brown, 1964. 291p.

1547. Rommel, Erwin. *The Rommel Papers.* Edited by Basil H. Liddell Hart. Translated from the German. New York: Harcourt, 1953. 545p.

1548. Rothfels, Hans. *The German Opposition to Hitler: An Appraisal.* Hinsdale, Ill.: Regnery, 1948. 166p.

1549. _____ . "German Resistance in Its International Aspects." *International Affairs,* XXXIV (October 1958), 477–489.

1550. Royce, Hans, ed. *Germans against Hitler, July 20, 1944.* Translated from the German. 4th ed. Bonn: Press and Information Office of the Federal German Republic, 1964. 360p.

1551. Scholl, Inge. *Students against Tyranny: The Resistance of the White Rose Munich, 1942–1943.* Middletown, Conn.: Wesleyan University Press, 1970. 160p.

1552. Schramm, Wilhelm. *Conspiracy among Generals.* Translated from the German. New York: Scribner's 1957. 215p.

1553. Steiner, Eugen. *The Slovak Dilemma.* Cambridge and New York: Cambridge University Press, 1973.

1554. Theimer, Walter. "The Bomb in the Brief Case: A Conspiracy That Failed." *Harper's Magazine,* CXCIII (October 1946), 377–384.

1555. Tilt, Notburga. *The Strongest Weapon.* Harrisburg, Pa.: Stackpole Books, 1972. 227p.

Austrian resistance.

1556. Toma, P. A. "Soviet Strategy in the Slovak Uprising of 1944." *Journal of Central European Affairs,* XIX (October 1959), 290–298.

1557. Vyvyan, Michael. "The German 'Opposition' and Nazi Morale." *Cambridge Journal,* II (December 1948), *passim.*

1558. Waddington, P. A. J. "The Coup d'État: An Application of a Systems Framework." *Political Studies,* XXII (September 1974), 299–310.

July 20.

1559. Werner, Alfred. "The Junker Plot to Kill Hitler: The Dying Gesture of a Class." *Commentary,* IV (July 1947), 36–42.

Weyl, Stefan, jt. author. *See* Jansen, Jon B.

1560. Wheeler–Bennett, John W. "July 20, 1944." In: his *The Nemesis of Power: The German Army in Politics, 1918–1945.* New York: St. Martin's Press, 1964. pp. 635–694.

1561. Whiting, Charles. *Hitler's Werewolves: The Story of the Nazi Resistance Movement, 1944–1945.* New York: Stein & Day, 1972. 208p.

1562. _____ . *Spymasters: The True Story of Anglo–American Intelligence Operations within Nazi Germany, 1939–1945.* New York: Saturday Review Press, 1976. 240p.

1563. Zahn, Gordon. *German Catholics and Hitler's War.* London and New York: Sheed and Ward, 1963. 232p.

1564. Zassenhaus, Hiltgunt M. *Walls: Resisting the Third Reich.* Translated from the German. Boston: Beacon Press, 1974. 248p.

1565. Zeller, Eberhard. *The Flame of Freedom: The German Struggle against Hitler.* Translated from the German. Coral Gables, Fla.: University of Miami Press, 1969. 471p.

3. Southern Europe

a. Italy

1566. Barlow, Dorothy. "Twentieth Century Resistance History, with Particular Reference to Italy in Late 1943." Unpublished Ph.D. dissertation, University of Manchester (Eng.), 1972.

1567. Battaglia, Roberto. *The Story of the Italian Resistance.* Translated from the Italian. London: Odhams Press, 1957. 287p.

1568. Bellini, Mario. "Garibaldi's Return: The Partisan Movement in Italy." *Nation,* CLVII (September 16, 1944), 324–325.

1569. _____ . "Italian Partisans." *Nation,* CLX (March 3, 1945), 249–250.

1570. Cameron, J. E. "Prisoner-snatching in Italy: A Rescue Party for British Prisoners." *Blackwood's Magazine,* CCLIX (February 1946), 109–114.

1571. Collier, Richard. *Duce! The Rise and Fall of Benito Mussolini.* London: Collins, 1971. 447p.

Killed by partisans in 1945.

1572. Dabrowski, Roman. *Mussolini: Twilight and Fall.* London: Heinemann, 1956. 248p.

1573.   Deakin, Frederick W. *The Brutal Friendship: Mussolini, Hitler, and the Fall of Italian Fascism.* London: Weidenfeld and Nicolson, 1962. 896p.

1574.   _____. *The Last Days of Mussolini.* Rev. ed. London: Penguin Books, 1966. 378p.

1575.   Derry, Samuel I. *Rome Escape Line: The Story of the British Organization in Rome for Assisting Escaped Prisoners-of-War, 1943–1944.* London: Harrap, 1960. 239p.

1576.   Detzell, Charles F. "Italian Anti–Fascist Resistance in Retrospect." *Journal of Modern History,* XLVII (March 1975), 66–96.

1577.   _____. *Mussolini's Enemies: The Italian Anti–Fascist Resistance.* Princeton, N. J.: Princeton University Press, 1961. 620p.

1578.   Farran, Roy A. *"Operation Tombola."* London: Collins, 1960. 256p.

1579.   Ford, Corey. "Our German Wehrmacht Is Being Stopped by a Shadow." *American Heritage,* XXI (February 1970), 44–46+.

1580.   "Foreign Agent," pseud. "Nazi-ruled Italy Hates This War: 'Foreign Agent' Reports on the Activities of the Anti–Fascist Underground." *Life,* XII (February 9, 1942), 94–101.

1581.   "K," pseud. *Agent in Italy.* Garden City, N. Y.: Doubleday, 1942. 331p.

1582.   Krivitsky, Aleksandr S. "Two Sketches." *Soviet Literature,* no. 5 (May 1974), 109–120+.

1583.   Lett, Gordon. *Rossano: An Adventure of the Italian Resistance.* London: Hodder and Stoughton, 1955. 223p.

1584.   Luzzatto, Riccardo. *The Unknown War in Italy.* Translated from the Italian. London: New Europe Publishing Co., 1946. 135p.

1585.   Macksey, Kenneth J. *Kesselring: The Making of the Luftwaffe.* New York: McKay, 1979. 262p.

Title somewhat misleading. The general and the Italian partisans are emphasized.

1586.   Maugeri, Franco. *From the Ashes of Disgrace.* Translated from the Italian. New York: Reynal and Hitchcock, 1948. 376p.

1587.   Meneghello, Luigi. *Outlaws.* Translated from the Italian. New York: Harcourt, Brace, 1968. 272p.

1588.   Smith, Charles W. "SS General Karl Wolff and the Surrender of the German Troops in Italy, 1945." Unpublished Ph.D. dissertation, University of Southern Mississippi, 1970.

1589. Smyth, Howard M. *Secrets of the Fascist Era: How Uncle Sam Obtained Some of the Top-level Documents of Mussolini's Period.* Carbondale: Southern Illinois University Press, 1975. 305p.

1590. "Spies in Surplices: The Failure of Nazi Espionage in Rome." *Time,* XCV (January 19, 1970), 29.

1591. Toland, John. "Twilight of a Tyrant." *Look,* XXIX (May 18, 1965), 38–40+.

1592. Wallace, Robert. "Friends among the Foe: A Picture Essay." In: his *The Italian Campaign.* World War II Series. New York: Time–Life, Inc., 1978. pp. 86–118.

1593. Whittle, Peter. *One Afternoon at Mezzegra: Mussolini's Death and Burial.* New York: Manor Books, 1973. 129p.

b. The Balkans and Mediterranean: General Works

1594. Auty, Phyllis, and Richard Clogg, eds. *British Policy towards Wartime Resistance in Yugoslavia and Greece.* New York: Published in Association with the School of Slovonic and East European Studies, University of London, by Harper & Row, 1975. 308p.

1595. Cardif, Maurice. *Achilles and the Tortoise: An Eastern Aegean Exploit.* By John Lincoln, pseud. London: Heinemann, 1958. 256p.

Clogg, Richard, jt. ed. *See* Auty, Phyllis

1596. Havas, Laslo. *Hitler's Plot to Kill the Big Three.* Translated from the Hungarian. Rev. ed. New York: Cowles Book Co., 1969. 280p.

1597. Higgins, Trumbull. *Winston Churchill and the Second Front, 1940–1943.* London and New York: Oxford University Press, 1957. 281p.

1598. Hirszowicz, Lukasz. *The Third Reich and the Arab–East.* London: Routledge and Kegan Paul, 1966. 403p.

1599. Jamieson, Edward. *Balkans Fight for Freedom.* London: Laurence, 1942. 70p.

1600. Johnson, Stowers. *Agents Extraordinary.* London: Hale, 1975. 192p.

Lincoln, John, pseud. *See* Cardif, Maurice

1601. MacCloskey, Monro. *Secret Air Missions.* New York: Richard Rosen Press, 1966. 159p.

Work of the U. S. 885th B.S. (H).

1602. Michie, Allan A. "Get Rommel Dead or Alive: The Harassing Exploit of the Commandos in Libya." *Reader's Digest,* XLI (September 1942), 111–112.

1603. Mure, David. *Practice to Deceive.* London: Kimber, 1977. 264p. Ultra and "double cross" in the Balkans and Middle East.

1604. Murphy, Robert. *Diplomat among Warriors.* Garden City, N. Y.: Doubleday, 1964. 470p.

1605. Neville, Ralph. *Survey by Starlight: A True Story of* ["Coppist" Commando] *Reconnaissance Work in the Mediterranean.* London: Hodder and Stoughton, 1949. 206p.

1606. O'Doherty, John K. "The Balkan Air Force." *Airman,* VIII (November 1964), 28–32.

1607. Smith, Peter C., and Edwir Walker. *War in the Aegean.* London: Kimber, 1974. 304p.

1608. United States. Army. Historical Division. *German Anti-guerrilla Operations in the Balkans, 1941–1944: Historical Study.* D. A. Pam. 20–243. Washington, D. C.: Department of the Army, 1954. 82p.

1609. _____. War Department. Office of Strategic Services, Research and Analysis Branch. *The Middle East.* Part VIII of *O.S.S./State Department Intelligence and Research Reports.* 3 reels, 35mm microfilm. Washington, D. C.: University Publications of America, 1976–1977.

Walker, Edwir, jt. author. *See* Smith, Peter C.

1610. Waugh, Evelyn. "The Commando Raid on Bardia." *Life,* XI (November 17, 1941), 63–66+.

c. Albania

1611. Amery, Julian. *Sons of the Eagles: A Study in Guerrilla War.* London: Macmillan, 1948. 354p.

1612. Burdick, Charles A. "'Operation Cyclamen': Germany and Albania, 1940–1941." *Journal of Central European Affairs,* XIX (April 1959), 23–31.

1613. Costa, Nicholas J. "Invasion—Action and Reaction: Albania, a Case Study." *Eastern European Quarterly,* X (Spring 1976), 53–63.

1614. Davies, Edmund P. *Illyrian Venture: The Story of the British Military Mission to Enemy-occupied Albania.* London: Bodley Head, 1952. 246p.

d. Greece

1615. Argyropoulo, Kaity. *From Peace to Chaos: A Forgotten Story.* New York: Vantage Press, 1975. 195p.

1616. Averoff–Tossizza, Evangelos. *By Fire and Axe: The Communist Party and the Civil War in Greece, 1944–1947.* Translated from the Greek. New Rochelle, N. Y.: Caratzas Brothers, 1978. 438p.

Baille–Grohman, Harold, jt. author. *See* Heckstall–Smith, Anthony

1617. Byford–Jones, W. *The Greek Trilogy: Resistance–Liberation–Revolution.* London and New York: Hutchinson, 1945. 270p.

1618. Condit, D. M. *A Case Study in Guerrilla Warfare: Greece during World War II.* Washington, D. C.: Special Warfare Research Division, American University, 1961. 338p.

1619. Eudes, Dominique. *The Kapetanios: Partisans and Civil War in Greece, 1943–1949.* Translated from the French. New York: Monthly Review Press, 1972. 381p.

1620. Heckstall–Smith, Anthony, and Harold Baille–Grohman. *Greek Tragedy.* London: Blond, 1961. 240p.

1621. Iatrides, John O. *Revolt in Athens: The Greek Communists' "Second Round," 1944–1945.* Princeton, N. J.: Princeton University Press, 1972. 340p.

1622. Jecchinis, Chris. *Beyond Olympus: The Thrilling Story of the "Train–Busters" in Nazi-occupied Greece.* London: Harrap, 1960. 218p.

1623. Jordan, William. *Conquest without Victory.* London: Hodder and Stoughton, 1969. 256p.

1624. Ladas, Alexis. "Father Eugene and the Intelligence Services." *Harper's Magazine,* CCXVI (March 1958), 72–77.

1625. McNeill, William H. *The Greek Dilemma: The War and Aftermath.* Philadelphia: Lippincott, 1947. 291p.

1626. Matthews, Kenneth. *Memoirs of a Mountain War: Greece, 1944–1947.* London: Longmans, Green, 1972. 284p.

1627. Mitgang, Herbert. "All Greeks Were Heroes." *Nation,* CCXXVII (August 5, 1978), 108–111.

1628. Myers, Edmund C. W. *Greek Entanglement.* London: Hart–Davis, 1955. 290p.

1629. Paneth, Philip. *The Glory That Is Greece.* London: Alliance Press, 1945. 138p.

1630. Pezas, Mikia. *The Price of Liberty.* New York: Washburn, 1945. 261p.

1631. St. John, Robert. *From the Land of Silent People.* London: Hamilton, 1955. 318p.

1632. Saraphes, Stephanos G. *The Greek Resistance Army: The Story of E.L.A.S.* Translated from the Greek. London: Birch Books, 1951. 324p.

1633. Spencer, Floyd A. *War and Postwar Greece: An Analysis Based on Greek Writings.* Washington, D. C.: European Affairs Division, Library of Congress, 1952. 175p.

1634. Stavrianos, Leften S. "The Greek National Liberation Front (E.A.M.): A Study in Resistance Organization and Administration." *Journal of Modern History,* XXIV (March 1952), 42–55.

1635. Thomas, Walter B. *Dare To Be Free.* London: Wingate, 1951. 256p.

1636. Tsatsos, Jeanne. *The Sword's Fierce Edge: A Journal of the Occupation of Greece, 1941–1944.* Nashville, Tenn.: Vanderbilt University Press, 1969. 131p.

1637. Woodhouse, Christopher M. *Apple of Discord: A Survey of Recent Greek Politics in Their International Setting.* London: Hutchinson, 1948. 320p.

1638. _____. *The Struggle for Greece, 1941–1949.* London: Hart–Davis, 1977. 324p.

1639. Zotos, Stephanos. *Greece: The Struggle for Freedom.* Translated from the Greek. New York: Crowell, 1967. 194p.

e. Yugoslavia

1640. Armstrong, Hamilton F. *Tito and Goliath.* London: Gollancz, 1951. 318p.

Arnold, Elliott, jt. author. *See* Thruelson, Richard

1641. Bagnall, Florence N. *Let My People Go!* Salt Lake City, Utah: Publisher's Press, 1968. 253p.

1642. Barker, Elizabeth. "Fresh Sidelights on British Policy in Yugoslavia, 1942–1943." *Slavonic and East European Review,* LIV (October 1971), 572–585.

1643. Bicanic, Rudolf. "The Effects of War on Rural Yugoslavia." *Geographic Journal,* CIII (January–February 1944), 30–49.

1644. "The Bloody Balkans: Chetniks and Partisans Score against the Germans and Each Other." *Newsweek,* XXII (November 8, 1943), 22–23.

1645.   Brown, Alec. *Mihailovich and Yugoslav Resistance.* London: Lane, 1943. 90p.

1646.   Brozovich, Josip. "The Yugoslav Peoples Fight to Live." By "Tito," pseud. *Free World,* VII (June 1944), 491–509.

1647.   Calder–Marshall, Arthur. *Watershed.* London: Contact, 1947. 216p.

1648.   Chassin, L. M. "The Liberation of Belgrade." *Military Review,* XXVIII (July 1948), 87–92.

1649.   Clissold, Stephen. *Whirlwind: An Account of Marshal Tito's Rise to Power.* New York and London: Philosophical Library, 1949. 245p.

1650.   Colakovic, Rodoljub. *Winning Freedom.* Translated from the Yugoslav. London: Lincolns–Praeger, 1962. 430p.

1651.   Committee for a Fair Trial for Draja Mihailovich. *Patriot or Traitor: The Case of General Mihailovich.* Introductory essay by David Martin. Stanford, Calif.: Hoover Institution Press, 1979. 450p.

Report, with new material, orginally compiled in 1946.

1652.   Davidson, Basil. *Partisan Picture.* New York: Universal Distributors, 1945. 351p.

1653.   Deakin, Frederick W. *The Embattled Mountain.* London and New York: Oxford University Press, 1971. 284p.

1654.   Dedijer, Vladimer. *Tito Speaks.* London: Weidenfeld and Nicolson, 1953. 472p.

1655.   _____. *With Tito through the War: A Partisan Diary, 1941–1944.* London: Hamilton, 1951. 403p.

1656.   Denich, Bette S. "Sources of Leadership in the Yugoslav Revolution: A Local-level Study." *Comparative Studies in Society and History,* XVIII (January 1976), 64–84.

1657.   Djilas, Milovan. *Wartime.* Translated from the Yugoslav. New York: Harcourt, Brace, 1977. 470p.

1658.   _____. "Wartime: Memories of Yugoslavia." *Dissent,* XXIV (Spring 1977), 174–180.

1659.   Donlagic, Ahmet, *et al. Yugoslavia in the Second World War.* Translated from the Yugoslav. Belgrade, 1967. 261p.

1660.   *General Milhailovich, the World's Verdict: A Selection of Articles on the First Resistance Leader in Europe Published in the World Press.* Gloucester, Eng.: Bellows, 1947. 223p.

1661. Gervasi, Frank. "Tito." *Collier's,* CXIII (February 19, 1944), 18–19+.

1662. Hoffman, George W., and Fred W. Neal. "World War II." In: their *Yugoslavia and the New Communism.* New York: 20th Century Fund, 1962. pp. 69–81.

1663. Huot, Louis. *Guns for Tito.* New York: Fischer, 1945. 273p.

1664. Jones, W. *Twelve Months with Tito's Partisans.* Bedford, Eng.: Bedford Books, 1946. 128p.

1665. Jukic, Ilija. *The Fall of Yugoslavia.* Translated from the Yugoslav. New York: Harcourt, Brace, 1974. 315p.

1666. Kapetanovic, Nikola. *Tito and His Partisans: What Really Happened in Yugoslavia from 1941–1945.* Translated from the Yugoslav. Belgrade: Jugoslovenska Knjiga, [195?] 50p.

Kucan, Viktor, jt. author. *See* Moraca, Peros

1667. Lawrence, Christie N. *Irregular Adventure.* London: Faber and Faber, 1947. 276p.

1668. *The Liberation Struggle of the Yugoslav Peoples, 1941–1945.* Translated from the Yugoslav. Belgrade, 1961. 146p.

1669. Ljubljana. Znanstveni Institut. *Allied Airmen and Prisoners-of-War Rescued by the Slovene Partisans: Compiled from the Records of the Headquarters of Slovenia.* Translated from the Yugoslav. Ljubljana, 1946. 88p.

1670. Maclean, Fitzroy. *The Battle of Neretva.* London: Panther, 1970. 144p.

1671. _____. *Escape to Adventure.* Boston: Little, Brown, 1950. 419p.

1672. Martin, David. *Ally Betrayed: The Uncensored Story of Tito and Mihailovich.* New York: Prentice–Mall, 1946. 372p.

1673. Mihajlov, Mihajlo. "The Mihailovich Tragedy: Disentangling History." *New Leader,* V (February 3, 1975), 7–11.

1674. Milazzo, Matteo J. *The Chetnik Movement and the Yugoslav Resistance.* Baltimore, Md.: Johns Hopkins University Press, 1975. 208p.

1675. _____. "The Cmetnik Movement in Yugoslavia, 1941–1945." Unpublished Ph.D. dissertation, University of Michigan, 1971.

1676. Montagu, Ivor. "Tito and Mihailovich: Fact and Myth." *Labour Monthly,* XXVI (January 1944), 16–21.

1677. Moraca, Pero, and Viktor Kucan. *The War and Revolution of the Peoples of Yugoslavia, 1941–1945.* New York: Vanous, 1964. 206p.

Neal, Fred W., jt author. *See* Hoffman, George W.

1678. Neil, Roy S. *Once Only.* London: Cape, 1947. 285p.

1679. Padev, Michael. *Marshal Tito.* London: Muller, 1944. 129p.

1680. Peniakoff, Vladimir. *Private Army.* London: Cape, 1950. 512p.

1681. Pribichevich, Stoyan. "Fratricide in Yugoslavia: Partisan–Mihailovich Schism Widens into a Split among Allies." *Fortune,* XXVII (June 1943), 148–153+.

1682. Roberts, Walter R. *Tito, Mihailovich, and the Allies, 1941–1945.* New Brunswick, N. J.: Rutgers University Press, 1973. 406p.

1683. Rootham, Jasper. *Miss Fire: The Chronicle of a British Mission to Mihailovich, 1943–1944.* London: Chatto and Windus, 1946. 224p.

1684. Sanftleben, A. E. "Yugoslav Incidents." *Blackwood's Magazine,* CCLVI (October 1944), 284–286.

1685. Sava, George. *The Chetniks.* London: Faber and Faber, 1942. 260p.

1686. Seitz, Albert. *Mihailovich: Hoax or Hero?* Columbus, Ohio: Leigh House, 1953. 143p.

Memories of an OSS officer.

1687. Stafford, David A. T. "S.O.E. and British Involvement in the Belgrade Coup d'État of March 1941." *Slavic Review,* XXXVI (September 1977), 399–419.

1688. Strutton, Bill. *Island of Terrible Friends.* New York: W. W. Norton, 1962. 192p.

1689. Sudjic, Milivoj J. *Yugoslavia in Arms.* London: Drummond, 1942. 128p.

1690. Thayer, Charles. *Hands across the Caviar.* London: Joseph, 1953. 222p.

1691. Thayer, M. V. "Ruth Mitchell, American Chetnik." *American Mercury,* LVI (January 1943), 16–23.

1692. Thruelsen, Richard, and Elliott Arnold. "Sweethearts of Tito: Partisan Women Work for Yugoslavia." *Saturday Evening Post,* CCXVII (November 4, 1944), 36+.

"Tito," pseud. *See* Brozovich, Josip

1693. Tomasevich, Jozo. *War and Revolution in Yugoslavia, 1941–1945.* 3 vols. Stanford, Calif.: Stanford University Press, 1975.

1694. Turner, P. S. "Tito's Army." *Journal of the Royal United Service Institution for Defence Studies,* CXVI (September 1971), 63–66.

1695. United Committee of South–Slavs in London: *The Epic of Yugoslavia, 1941–1945.* London, 1945. 96p.

1696. Yovitchitch, Lena A. *Within Close Frontiers: A Woman in Wartime Yugoslavia.* London: Chambers, 1956. 253p.

1697. Yugoslav People's Army. Military–Historical Institute. *Historical Atlas of the Liberation War of the Peoples of Yugoslavia, 1941–1945.* Belgrade, n.d. 120p.

4. Eastern Europe

a. Poland and Hungary

1698. Barkai, Meyer. *The Fighting Ghettos.* Philadelphia: Lippincott, 1962. 407p.

1699. Bartoszewski, Wladyslaw. "The Ghetto Rising, 1943." *Polish Perspectives,* XXI (April 1978), 16–25.

1700. _____. *Righteous among Nations: How Poles Helped the Jews, 1939–1945.* London: Earlscourt, 1969. 834p.

1701. _____, and Zofia Lewinowna. *The Samarians: Heroes of the Holocaust.* New York: Twayne, 1970. 442p.

1702. Berg, Mary. *Warsaw Ghetto: A Diary.* New York: Fischer, 1945. 253p.

1703. Bethell, Nicholas W. *The War Hitler Won: The Fall of Poland, September 1939.* New York: Holt, 1973. 472p.

1704. Bielecki, Tadeusz, and Leszek Szymanski. *Warsaw Aflame: The 1939–1945 Years.* Los Angeles, Calif.: Polamerica Press, 1973. 188p.

1705. Boldizsar, Ivan. *The Other Hungary.* Translated from the Hungarian. Budapest, 1946. 71p.

1706. Bor–Komorowski, Tadeusz. *The Secret Army.* Translated from the Polish. London: Gollancz, 1950. 407p.

1707. Brand, Joel. *Desperate Mission.* Translated from the Hungarian. New York: Criterion Books, 1958. 310p.

1708.   Bruce, George. *The Warsaw Uprising, 1 August–2 October 1944.* London: Hart–Davis, 1972. 224p.

1709.   Budish, Jacob M., ed. *Warsaw Ghetto Uprising, April 19th, Tenth Anniversary.* New York: United Committee to Commemorate the Tenth Anniversary of the Warsaw Ghetto, 1953. 75p.

1710.   Bytniewska, Irena. *Silent Is the Vistula: The Story of the Warsaw Uprising.* Translated from the Polish. New York: Longmans, Green, 1946. 275p.

1711.   Ciechanowski, Jan M. *Defeat in Victory.* Garden City, N. Y.: Doubleday, 1947. 397p.

1712.   _____ . "The Political and Ideological Background of the Warsaw Rising, 1944." Unpublished Ph.D. dissertation, University of London, 1968.

1713.   _____ . *The Warsaw Rising of 1944.* London and New York: Cambridge University Press, 1974. 332p.

1714.   Creel, George, ed. "Revenge in Poland." *Collier's,* CXII (October 30–November 6, 1943), 11+, 20+.

1715.   Cyprian, Tadeusz, and Jerry Sawicki. *Nazi Rule in Poland, 1939–1945.* Translated from the Polish. London: Collet's, 1961. 262p.

1716.   Deschner, Günther. *Warsaw Rising.* Ballantine's Illustrated History of the Violent Century. New York: Ballantine Books, 1972. 160p.

1717.   Friedman, Philip, ed. *Martyrs and Fighters: The Epic of the Warsaw Ghetto.* New York: Praeger, 1954. 325p.

1718.   Garlinski, Josef. *Poland, S.O.E., and the Allies.* Translated from the Polish. London: Ian Allan, 1969. 248p.

1719.   _____ . "The Polish Underground State, 1939–1945." *Journal of Contemporary History,* X (April 1975), 219–259.

1720.   Goldszmit, Henryk. *Ghetto Diary.* New York: Schocken Books, 1978. 191p.

Gorecki, J., pseud. *See* Kaminski, Aleksander

1721.   Gross, Jan T. *Polish Society under German Occupation: The General–Gouvernement, 1939–1944.* Princeton, N. J.: Princeton University Press, 1979. 325p.

1722.   Grunszpan, Roman. *The Uprising of the Death Box of Warsaw.* New York: Vantage Press, 1978. 222p.

1723.   Hammersmith, Jack L. "The U. S. Office of War Information and the Polish Question, 1943–1945." *Polish Review,* I (1974), 67–76.

1724.   Kaminski, Aleksander. *Stones for the Rampart: The Story of Two Lads in the Polish Underground Movement.* By J. Gorecki, pseud. Translated from the Polish. London: Polish Boy Scouts' and Girl Guides' Association, 1945. 68p.

1725.   Karski, Jean. *The Story of a Secret State.* Boston: Houghton, Mifflin, 1944. 391p.

1726.   Katz, Alfred. *Poland's Ghettos at War.* New York: Twayne, 1970. 175p.

1727.   Kermish, J. "The [Warsaw] Ghetto's Two-front Struggle." *Yad Vashem Bulletin,* no. 13 (October 1963), 12+.

1728.   Kleczkowski, Stefan. "Warsaw Rising, August 1944." *Contemporary Review,* CCXI (August 1967), 82–84.

1729.   Korbonski, Stefan. *Fighting Warsaw: The Story of the Polish Underground State, 1939–1945.* Translated from the Polish. New York: Funk and Wagnalls, 1968. 495p.

1730.   _____. *The Polish Underground State: A Guide to the Underground, 1939–1945.* Translated from the Polish. New York: *East European Quarterly;* dist. by Columbia University Press, 1978. 268p.

1731.   Kurzman, Dan. *The Bravest Battle: The 28 days of the Warsaw Ghetto Uprising.* New York: Putnam, 1976. 386p.

1732.   Levin, Nora. "The Warsaw Ghetto Uprising." In: her *The Holocaust: The Destruction of European Jewry, 1933–1945.* New York: Crowell, 1968. pp. 317–361.

Lewinowna, Zofia, jt. author. *See* Bartoszewski, Wladyslaw

1733.   Lipschutz, Norman. *Victory through Darkness and Despair.* New York: Vantage Press, 1960. 123p.

1734.   London. Instytut Historyczmy imienia Generala Sikorskiego. *Documents on Polish–Soviet Relations, 1939–1945.* 2 vols. London: Heinemann, 1961–1967.

1735.   Lubetkin, Zivia. "Warsaw: The January 1943 Uprising." In: Meyer Barkai, ed. *The Fighting Ghettos.* Philadelphia: Lippincott, 1962. pp. 19–28.

1736.   Lukas, Richard C. "The Big Three and the Warsaw Uprising." *Military Affairs,* XXXIV (October 1975), 129–136.

1737. _____. "The R. A. F. and the Warsaw Uprising." *Aerospace Historian*, XXII (December 1975), 188–194.

1738. McFarland, Marvin W. "Air Power and the Warsaw Uprising." *Air Power Historian*, III (October 1956), 186–194.

1739. Maks, Leon. *Russia by the Back Door*. Translated from the Polish. London and New York: Sheed and Ward, 1954. 264p.

1740. Poland. Polskie Sily Zbrojne Armia Krajowa. *The Unseen and Silent: Adventures from the Underground Movement, Narrated by Paratroops of the Polish Home Army*. London and New York: Sheed and Ward, 1959. 350p.

1741. Ringelblum, Emmanual. *Notes from the Warsaw Ghetto*. New York: McGraw–Hill, 1958. 369p.

1742. _____. *Polish–Jewish Relations during the Second World War*. New York: Fertig, 1976. 330p.

Through the 1943 Warsaw revolt.

1743. Samuels, Gertrude. *Mottele: A Partisan Odyssey*. New York: Harper & Row, 1976. 179p.

Sawicki, Jerry, jt. author. *See* Cyprian, Tadeusz

1744. Sobieski, Zygmunt. "Reminiscences from Lwow, 1939–1946." *Journal of Central European Affairs*, VI (January 1947), 351–374.

1745. Strong, A. L. "Bor's Uprising." *Atlantic Monthly*, CLVI (December 1945), 80–85.

1746. Stypulkowski, Zbigniew F. *Invitation to Moscow*. New York: Walker, 1963. 359p.

1747. Szkoda, W. E. "Soviet Tactics against the Polish Resistance in World War II." *Military Review*, XLIV (September 1964), 88–93.

Szymanski, Leszeh, jt. author. *See* Bielecki, Tadeusz

1748. Taub, Walter. "Warsaw Tragedy." *Collier's*, CXV (March 17, 1945), 17+.

1749. Tenenbaum, Joseph. *Underground: The Story of a People*. New York: Philosophical Library, 1952. 532p.

1750. "They'll Never Find Us Alive: An Eye-witness Story from the Polish Underground." *Free World*, VI (November 1943), 470–472.

1751. Tihany, L. C. "The Hungarian Resistance Movement." *American Slavic Review*, VI (May 1947), 172–174.

1752. Tushnet, Leonard. *To Die with Honor: The Uprising of the Jews in the Warsaw Ghetto.* New York: Citadel Press, 1965. 128p.

1753. Umiastowski, Roman. *Poland, Russia, and Great Britain, 1941–1945: A Study of Evidence.* London: Hollis and Carter, 1946. 544p.

1754. United States. Congress. Senate. Committee on the Judiciary, Subcommittee to Investigate the Administration of the Internal Security Act and Other Internal Security Laws. *The Warsaw Insurrection: The Communist Version versus the Facts.* 91st Cong., 1st sess. Washington, D. C.: U.S. Government Printing Office, 1969. 18p.

1755. Wdowinski, David. *And We Are Not Saved.* New York: Philosophical Library, 1963. 124p.

1756. Werstein, Irving. *The Uprising of the Warsaw Ghetto, November 1940 to May 1943.* New York: W. W. Norton, 1968. 157p.

1757. Woytak, Richard. "On the Border of War and Peace: The Role of Intelligence and the Frontier in Polish Foreign Policy, 1938–1939." Unpublished Ph.D. dissertation, University of California at Santa Barbara, 1976.

1758. ———. ———. New York: Columbia University Press, 1979. 168p.

1759. Zagorski, Waclaw. *Seventy Days.* Translated from the Polish. London: Muller, 1957. 267p.

1760. Zamoyski, Adam. "Underground Factory: Poland in 1939–1945." *History Today,* XXIV (December 1974), 868–873.

1761. Zuckerman, Yitzhak. "From the Warsaw Ghetto." *Commentary,* LX (December 1975), 62–69.

1762. Zylberberg, Michael. *A Warsaw Diary, 1939–1945.* Translated from the Polish. London: Vallentine, Mitchell and Co., 1969. 220p.

b. Soviet Union

1763. Agapov, Boris N. *After the Battle: Stalingrad Sketches and Notes of a Guerrilla Fighter.* Translated from the Russian. London and New York: Hutchinson, 1943. 78p.

1764. Anderson, James K. "Unknown Soldiers of an Unknown [Ukrainian People's] Army." *Army,* XVIII (May 1968), 62–67.

1765. "Armies of the Forest." *Time,* XLII (November 20, 1943), 25–26.

1766. Armstrong, John A. *Ukrainian Nationalism.* 2d ed. New York: Columbia University Press, 1963. 361p.

1767. _____ , ed. *Soviet Partisans in World War II*. Madison: University of Wisconsin Press, 1964. 792p.

1768. Artemiev, Vyacheslav P. "Soviet Volunteers in the German Army." *Military Review*, XLVII (November 1967), 56–64.

1769. "Attack on a Partisan Headquarters: German Anti–Partisan Operations in Russia." *Infantry*, LIII (May–June 1963), 29–32.

1770. *Avengers: Reminiscences of Soviet Members of the Resistance Movement.* Translated from the Russian. Moscow: Progress Publishers, 1965. 278p.

1771. *Behind the Front Lines: Being an Account of the Military Activities, Exploits, Adventures, and Day-to-day Life of the Soviet Guerrillas Operating behind German Lines from the Finnish–Karelian Front to the Crimea.* Translated from the Russian. London and New York: Hutchinson, 1945. 160p.

1772. Bethell, Nicholas. "The People Strike Back: A Picture Essay." In: his *Russia Besieged*. World War II Series. New York: Time–Life, Inc., 1978. pp. 88–114.

1773. Bourdow, Joseph A. "Big War Guerrillas and Counter–Guerrillas." *Army*, XIII (August 1962), 66–69.

1774. Brand, Emmanuel. "The Forest Ablaze: A Jewish Partisan Group in the [Soviet] Kovpak Division." *Yad Vashem Bulletin*, no. 2 (December 1957), 16+.

1775. Buss, Phillip H., and Andrew Mollow. *Hitler's Germanic Legions: An Illustrated History of Western European Legions with the SS* [in Russia], *1941–1943*. New York: Beekman House, 1978. 160p.

1776. Chubatyi, Nicholas D. "The Ukrainian Underground." *Ukrainian Quarterly*, II (Winter 1946), 154–166.

1777. Cooper, Matthew. *The Nazi War against Soviet Partisans, 1941–1944*. New York: Stein & Day, 1979.

1778. Dallin, Alexander. "German Policy and the Occupation of the Soviet Union, 1941–1944." Unpublished Ph.D. dissertation, Columbia University, 1953.

1779. _____ . *German Rule in Russia, 1941–1945: A Study of Occupation Policies.* New York: St. Martin's Press, 1957. 695p.

1780. _____ . *The Kaminsky Brigade, 1941–1944: A Case Study of German Military Exploitation of Soviet Dissatisfaction.* Cambridge, Mass.: Russian Research Center, Harvard University, 1956. 122p.

1781. _____ . "Soviet Reaction to Vlasov." *World Politics,* VIII (April 1956), 307–322.

1782. Daumantas, Juozas. *Fighters for Freedom: Lithuanian Partisans vs. the U.S.S.R.* [1944–1947]. Translated from the Lithuanian. Woodhave, N.Y.: Manylands Books, 1975. 254p.

1783. Dixon, Cecil A., and Otto Heilbrunn. *Communist Guerrilla Warfare.* New York: Praeger, 1954. 229p.

1784. Drum, Karl. *Air Power and Russian Partisan Warfare.* Translated from the German. USAF Historical Studies. Maxwell Air Force Base, Ala.: Research Studies Institute, Air University, 1962. 63p.

1785. Dupont, Pierre. "Behind Enemy Lines in White Russia." *Free World,* VII (February 1944), 166–169.

1786. Erickson, John. *The Soviet High Command: A Political–Military History, 1918–1941.* New York: St. Martin's Press, 1962. 889p.

1787. Fedorov, Aleksei F. *The Underground Committee Carries On.* Translated from the Russian. Moscow: Foreign Languages Publishing House, 1952. 517p.

1788. Feehan, Sean. "Russian Guerrillas." *Military Review,* XXIV (September 1944), 108–109.

1789. Fischer, George. *Soviet Opposition to Stalin: A Case Study in World War II.* Cambridge, Mass.: Harvard University Press, 1952. 230p. Rpr. 1970.

1790. _____ . "[Andrei A.] Vlasov and Hitler." *Journal of Modern History,* XXIII (March 1951), 58–71.

1791. "The Forest Camp: German Antipartisan Operations in Russia." *Infantry,* LIII (March–April 1963), 19–21.

1792. Gallagher, Matthew P. *The Soviet History of World War II: Myths, Memories, and Realities.* New York: Praeger, 1963. 205p.

1793. Garthoff, Raymond G. "Soviet Employment of Partisan Forces." In: his *Soviet Military Doctrine.* Glencoe, Ill.: Free Press, 1953. pp. 391–411.

1794. Gordon, Gary H. "Soviet Partisan Warfare, 1941–1944: The German Perspective." Unpublished Ph.D. dissertation, University of Iowa, 1972.

Heilbrunn, Otto, jt. author. *See* Dixon, Cecil A.

1795. Heiman, Leo. "Guerrilla Warfare: An analysis." *Military Review,* XLIII (July 1963), 26–36.

1796.   Howell, Edgar M. *The Soviet Partisan Movement, 1941–1944.* D.A. Pam. 20–244. Washington, D. C.: Department of the Army, 1956. 217p.

1797.   Hurley, James A. "Soviet Air Support to Insurgents." *Marine Corps Gazette,* XLVII (January 1963), 13–14.

1798.   Ignatov, Petr K. *Partisans of the Kuban.* Translated from the Russian. London and New York: Hutchinson, 1945. 212p.

1799.   Kamenetsky, Ihor. *Hitler's Occupation of the Ukraine, 1941–1944: A Study of Totalitarian Imperialism.* Translated from the Russian. Milwaukee, Wisc.: Marquette University Press, 1956. 101p.

1800.   Karukin, David S. "Partisans, Guerrillas, and War in Depth: A Soviet Tactical Doctrine." *Marine Corps Gazette,* XLVI (June 1962), 28–31.

1801.   Khrushchev, Nikita S. *Khrushchev Remembers.* Translated from the Russian. Boston: Little, Brown, 1970. 636p.

1802.   Kobrin, N. "In the Enemy Rear." *Soviet Military Review,* no. 2 (February 1972), 40–42.

1803.   ———. "Moscow Region Partisans." *Soviet Military Review,* no. 10 (October 1971), 41–43.

1804.   Kournakoff, Sergei N. *Russia's Fighting Forces.* Translated from the Russian. New York: Duell, Sloan and Pearce, 1942. 258p.

1805.   Kovpak, Sydir A. *Our Partisan Course.* Translated from the Russian. London and New York: Hutchinson, 1947. 126p.

1806.   Krokhmalwik, Yurii. *U.P.A. Warfare in the Ukraine: Strategical, Tactical, and Organizational Problems of Ukrainian Resistance in World War II.* New York: Society of Veterans of the Ukrainian Insurgent Army, 1972.

1807.   Kveder, D. "Territorial War: The New Concept of Resistance." *Military Review,* XXXIV (July 1954), 46–58.

1808.   Makarov, N. "'Operation Rail Warfare.'" *Soviet Military Review,* no. 3 (March 1968), 38–41.

1809.   Medvedev, Dmitrii N. *Stout Hearts.* Translated from the Russian. Moscow: Foreign Languages Publishing House, [195–?] 237p.

1810.   Moats, Alice L. "Courage to Burn: Russian Partisan Detachments." *Collier's,* CVIII (September 27, 1942), 24+.

Mollow, Andrew, jt. author. *See* Buss, Philip H.

1811. Polyakov, Alexi. "Red Guerrillas: Tough Russians Fight Nazis Far behind the Front Lines." *Life,* XI (November 10, 1941), 126–128+.

1812. Pronin, Alexander. "Guerrilla Warfare in the German-occupied Soviet Territories, 1941–1944." Unpublished Ph.D. dissertation, Georgetown University, 1965.

1813. Reitlinger, Gerald R. *The House Built on Sand: The Conflicts of German Policy in Russia, 1939–1945.* New York: Viking Press, 1960. 459p.

1814. Rizzo, Paul J. "The Soviet Partisan: A Reappraisal." *Infantry,* LVII (July–August 1967), 3–6.

1815. Simpson, Keith. "The German Experience of Rear Area Security on the Eastern Front, 1941–1945." *Journal of the Royal United Service Institution for Defence Studies,* CXXI (December 1976), 39–46.

1816. "Soviet Partisan Warfare." *Army Information Digest,* VI (February 1951), 62+.

1817. Steenberg, Sven. *Vlasov.* Translated from the German. New York: Knopf, 1970. 230p.

1818. Strik–Strikfeldt, Wilfried. *Against Stalin and Hitler: Memories of the Russian Liberation Movement, 1941–1945.* Translated from the German. London: Macmillan, 1970. 270p.

1819. United States. Army. Historical Division. *Combat in Russian Forests and Swamps.* D. A. Pam. 20–231. Washington, D. C.: Department of the Army, 1951. 39p.

1820. _____ . _____ . _____ . *Rear Area Security in Russia: The Soviet Second Front behind German Lines.* D. A. Pam. 20–240. Washington D. C.: Department of the Army, 1951. 39p.

1821. _____ . War Department. Office of Strategic Services, Research and Analysis Branch. *The Soviet Union.* Part VI of *O.S.S./State Department Intelligence and Research Reports.* 8 reels, 35mm microfilm. Washington, D. C.: University Publications of America, 1976–1977.

1822. Vaupshasov, S. "Enveloped in the Flames of Partisan Warfare." *Soviet Military Review,* no. 4 (April 1970), 24–27.

1823. Werth, Alexander. "The Partisans in the Soviet–German War." In: his *Russia at War, 1941–1945.* New York: Dutton, 1964. pp. 649–665.

1824. Yeremeyev, L. "Scorched Earth under the Enemy's Feet." *Soviet Military Review,* no. 4 (April 1975), 15–17+.

Ukrainian partisans.

1825. Zawodny, Janusz K. "Soviet Partisans." *Soviet Studies,* XVII (January 1966), 368–377.

1826. Zvi Bar–On, A. "The Jews in the Soviet Partisan Movement." *Yad Vasham Studies,* IV (1964), 176+.

c. Jewish Resistance

1827. Ainsztein, Reuben. *Jewish Resistance in Nazi-occupied Eastern Europe, with a Historical Survey of the Jew as Fighter and Soldier in the Diaspora.* New York: Barnes and Noble, 1975. 970p.

1828. Apensziak, Jakob, and Mozzesz Polakiewicz. *Armed Resistance of the Jews in Poland.* New York: American Federation of Polish Jews, 1944. 80p.

1829. Braun, A. Z., and Dov Levin. "Factors and Motivations in Jewish Resistance." *Yad Vashem Bulletin,* no. 2 (December 1957), 4+.

1830. Dawidowicz, Lucy S. "Resistance: A Doomed Struggle." In: her *The Jewish Presence: Essays on Identity and History.* New York: Holt, Rinehart and Winston. 1977. pp. 280–288.

1831. Eckman, Lester S., and Hayim Lazar. *The Jewish Resistance: The History of the Jewish Partisans in Lithuania and White Russia during the Nazi Occupation, 1940–1945.* New York: Shengold Publications, 1977. 282p.

1832. Elkins, Michael. *Forged in Fury.* New York: Ballantine Books, 1971. 312p.

1833. Garlinski, Josef. *Fighting Auschwitz: The Resistance Movement in the Concentration Camp.* New York: Holmes and Meier, 1975. 327p.

1834. Kahanovich, Moshe. "Why No Separate Jewish Partisan Movement Was Established during World War II." *Yad Vashem Studies,* I (1960), 164+.

1835. Kowalski, Isaac. *A Secret Press in Nazi Europe: The Story of the Jewish United Partisan Organization.* New York: Central Guide, 1969. 416p.

Lazar, Hayim, jt. author. *See* Eckman, Lester S.

1836. Levin, Dov. "Life and Death of Jewish Partisans." *Yad Vashem Bulletin,* no. 18 (April 1966), 44–45+.

———, jt. author. *See* Braun, A. Z.

1837. Levin, Nora. "Resistance in the Forests." In: her *The Holocaust: The Destruction of European Jewry, 1933–1945.* New York: Crowell, 1968. pp. 362–389.

1838.   Mark, Bernard. "Problems Related to the Study of the Jewish Resistance Movement in the Second World War." *Yad Vashem Studies*, III (1963), 54+.

1839.   Michel, Henri. "The Allies and the [Jewish] Resistance." *Yad Vashem Studies*, V (1965), 317+.

1840.   Nirenstein, Albert, ed. *A Tower from the Enemy: Contributions to a History of the Jewish Resistance in Poland.* Translated from the Polish, Yiddish, and Hebrew. New York: Orion Press, 1959. 372p.

1841.   "On the Agenda, Death: A Document of the Jewish Resistance [in Bialystok]." Translated from the Polish. *Commentary*, VIII (August 1949), 105–109.

   Polakiewicz, Mozzesz, jt. author. *See* Apensziak, Jakob

1842.   Poliakov, Leon. "Jewish Resistance in France." *YIVO Annual*, VIII (1953), 252–259.

1843.   Smoliar, Hersh. *Resistance in Minsk.* Berkeley, Calif.: Judah L. Magnes Memorial Museum, 1966. 109p.

1844.   Steinberg, Lucien. *Not as a Lamb: The Jews against Hitler.* Translated from the French. Boston: D. C. Heath, 1974. 358p.

1845.   Steiner, Jean F. *Treblinka.* Translated from the French. New York: Simon and Schuster, 1967. 415p.

1846.   Sukl, Yuri, ed. *They Fought Back: The Story of the Jewish Resistance in Nazi Europe.* Translated from the Yiddish. New York: Crown, 1967. 327p.

1847.   Syrkin, Marie. *Blessed Is the Match: The Story of Jewish Resistance.* New York: Knopf, 1947. 361p. Rpr. 1977.

Further References

Readers will find additional information relative to this subsection scattered throughout all of the sections above and below. As a result of the activities covered in this part, many biographies and autobiographies exist and are entered for "highlighting" purpose in section VIII, subsection B, below. To find appropriate personnel, check the national listing in the introduction to that subsection and note the section/subsection numbers placed in parentheses alongside each person's name.

C. The Far East

1. General Works

1848. Potter, John D. *Yamamoto: The Man Who Menaced America.* New York: Viking Press, 1965. 332p.

1849. Samson, Gerald. *The Far East Ablaze.* London: Joseph, 1945. 183p.

1850. Singer, Kurt D. *Spy Stories from Asia.* New York: Funk and Wagnalls, 1955. 336p.

1851. Taylor, Edmond. *Awakening from History.* Boston: Gambit, 1969. 552p.

1852. United States. War Department. Office of Strategic Services, Research and Analysis Branch. *China and India.* Part III of *O.S.S./State Department Intelligence and Research Reports.* 16 reels, 35 mm microfilm. Washington, D. C.: University Publications of America, 1976–1977.

1853. _____ . _____ . _____ . *Japan and Its Occupied Territories During World War II.* Part I of *O.S.S./State Department Intelligence and Research Reports.* 16 reels, 35mm microfilm. Washington, D. C.: University Publications of America, 1976–1977.

2. Pacific Islands

a. Philippines

1854. Agoncillo, Teodoro A. *The Fateful Years: Japan's Adventure in the Philippines, 1941–1945.* 2 vols. Quezon City, P.I.: R. P. Garcia Publishing Co., 1965.

1855. Allied Forces. Southwest Pacific Area. *Guerrilla Resistance Movements in the Philippines.* [Melbourne?], 1945. 143p.

1856. Bolton, Grania. "Military Diplomacy and National Liberation: Insurgent–American Relations after the Fall of Manila." *Military Affairs,* XXXVI (October 1972), 99–108.

1857. Cannon, M. Hamlin. *Leyte: The Return to the Philippines.* United States Army in World War II: The War in the Pacific. Washington, D.C.: Office of the Chief of Military History, Department of the Army, 1954. 420p.

1858. Doromal, Jose D. *The War in Panay: A Documentary History of the Resistance Movement in Panay during World War II.* Manila, P. I.: Diamond Historical Publications, 1952. 313p.

1859.   Falk, Stanley L. *Decision at Leyte.* New York: W. W. Norton, 1966. 330p.

1860.   Gunnison, R. A. "Filipino Firebrands." *Collier's,* CXIV (December 16, 1944), 11+.

1861.   Harkins, Philip. *Blackburn's Headhunters.* New York: W. W. Norton, 1955. 326p.

1862.   Hernandez, Al. *Bahála Na, Come What May: The Story of Mission I.S.R.M. (I Shall Return MacArthur), an Army–Navy Intelligence Mission in the Pacific.* Berkeley, Calif.: Howell–North, 1961. 315p.

1863.   Keats, John. *They Fought Alone.* Philadelphia: Lippincott, 1963. 425p.

1864.   Kuder, E. M. "The Philippines Never Surrendered." *Saturday Evening Post,* CCXVII (February 10–March 10, 1945), 9–11+, 22–23+, 22–23+, 20+, 20+.

1865.   Lear, Elmer N. "Western Leyte Guerrilla Warfare Forces: A Case Study in the Non-legitimation of a Guerrilla Organization." *Southeast Asian History,* IX (March 1968), 69–94.

1866.   Peterson, A. H., ed. *Symposium on the Role of Air Power in Counterinsurgency and Unconventional Warfare: Allied Resistance to the Japanese on Luzon, World War II.* RAND Memorandum RM–3655–PR. Santa Monica, Calif.: RAND Corporation, 1963. 61p.

1867.   Pontius, Dale. "MacArthur and the Filipinos." *Asia,* XLVI (November 1946), 509–512.

1868.   Smith, Robert H. *Triumph in the Philippines.* United States Army in World War II: The War in the Pacific. Washington, D. C.: Office of the Chief of Military History, Department of the Army, 1963. 756p.

1869.   United States. Navy Department. Pacific Fleet, Seventh Fleet Intelligence Center. "Submarine Activities Connected with Guerrilla Operations." Unpublished paper, Type Commands File, Operational Archives, U. S. Navy Historical Center, 1945. 42p.

1870.   Willoughby, Charles A., comp. *The Guerrilla Resistance Movement in the Phillippines, 1941–1945.* New York: Vantage Press, 1972. 702p.

b. Other

　　Chamberlain, John, jt. author. *See* Willoughby, Charles A.

1871.   Davis, Burke. *Get Yamamoto.* New York: Random House, 1969. 231p.

　　Shot down as the result of Allied intelligence.

1872. Donovan, Robert J. *PT-109.* New York: McGraw–Hill, 1961. 247p.

Much on the coastwatchers.

1873. Feldt, Eric A. *The Coastwatchers.* New York and London: Oxford University Press, 1946. 246p.

1874. Falk, Stanley L. "The Ambush of Admiral Yamamoto." *Navy*, VI (April 1963), 32–34.

1875. Great Britain. Colonial Office. *Among Those Present: The Official Story of the Pacific Islands at War.* London: H. M. Stationery Office, 1946. 95p.

1876. Gurney, Gene. "How They Got Yamamoto." *American Legion Magazine*, LXVI (January 1959), 12–13+.

1877. Horton, Dick C. *Fire over the Islands: The Coastwatchers of the Solomons.* Sydney, Australia: Reed, 1970. 256p.

1878. Howlett, R. A., comp. *The History of the Fiji Military Forces, 1939–1945.* London: Published by the Crown Agents for the Colonies on Behalf of the Government of Fiji, 1948. 267p.

1879. Ind, Allison. *Allied Intelligence Bureau: Our Secret Weapon in the War against Japan.* New York: McKay, 1958. 305p.

1880. Karig, Walter. "The Makin Island Raid." *U. S. Naval Institute Proceedings*, LXXII (1946), 1277–1282.

1881. Laughlin, Austen. *Boots and All: The Inside Story of the Secret War.* Melbourne, Australia: Colorgravure Publications, 1951. 208p.

1882. Le François, Wilfred S. "We Mopped Up Makin Island." *Saturday Evening Post*, CCXVI (December 4–11, 1943), 20–21+, 28–29+.

1883. Lord, Walter. *Lonely Vigil: The Coastwatchers of the Solomons.* New York: Viking Press, 1977. 322p.

1884. Mansfield, Alan, comp. *A Brief History of the New Guinea Air Warning Wireless Company (A.I.F.).* Melbourne, Australia: James, 1961. 96p.

1885. Michel, Marshall. "To Kill an Admiral." *Aerospace Historian*, XIV (Spring 1966), 25–29.

1886. Miller, Thomas G. *The Cactus Air Force.* New York: Harper & Row, 1969. 242p.

1887.   Steinberg, Rafael. "The Allies' 'Eyes and Ears': A Picture Essay." In: his *Island Fighting.* World War II Series. New York: Time–Life, Inc., 1978. pp. 36–58.

1888.   United States. Army. Far East Command, Military Intelligence Section. *Operations of the Allied Intelligence Bureau, G.H.Q., S.W.P.A.* 3 vols. Tokyo, 1948.

1889.   Whipple, A. B. Chandler. *"Code Word Ferdinand": Adventures of the Coastwatchers.* New York: Putnam, 1971. 160p.

1890.   Wible, John T. "The Yamamoto Mission." *American Aviation Historical Society Journal,* XII (Fall 1967), 159–167.

1891.   Willoughby, Charles A., and John Chamberlain. "MacArthur's Cloak-and-Dagger Men." In: their *MacArthur, 1941–1951.* New York: McGraw–Hill, 1954. Chapter VIII.

3. China–Burma–India

a. Burma and Malaya

1892.   Alison, John R. "Glider Invasion, a Jungle Epic: American [1st Air Commando] Fliers Landed British Troops behind the Japanese in Burma." *New York Times Magazine,* (May 14, 1944), 12+.

1893.   _____ . "The Most Unforgettable Character I've Ever Met: Philip Cochran." *Reader's Digest,* LXXIII (October 1958), 130–132+.

1894.   Arnold, Henry H. "The Aerial Invasion of Burma." *National Geographic Magazine,* LXXXVI (August 1944), 129–148.

1895.   Baggaley, James A. *A Chindit Story.* London: Souvenir Press, 1954. 163p.

1896.   Barrett, Neil H. *Chinapaw.* New York: Vantage Press, 1962. 173p.

OSS in Burma.

Brelis, Dean, jt. author. *See* Peers, William R.

1897.   Chapman, Frederick S. *The Jungle Is Neutral.* New York: W. W. Norton, 1949. 384p.

Resistance in Malaya.

1898.   Connell, Brian. *Return of the Tiger: An Account of Ivan Lynn's Surprise World War II Raid on Japanese Shipping in Singapore.* London: Evans, 1960. 282p.

1899.   Cross, John. *Red Jungle.* London: Hale, 1957. 244p.

1900. Davidson, Nancy E. D. I. *Winning Hazard.* By Noel Wynyard, pseud. London: Low, 1947. 181p.

Commando canoe attacks on shipping at Singapore.

1901. Denny, John H. *Chindit Indiscretion.* London: Johnson, 1956. 256p.

1902. Dugan, James. "The Aqua Lung." *U. S. Naval Institute Proceedings,* LXXXIII (1957), 779.

The sinking of IJN *Takao* by *XE-3* in July 1945.

1903. Evans, Geoffrey C. *The Johnnies.* London: Cassell, 1964. 231p.

Resistance in Burma.

1904. Fellowes–Gordon, Ian. *Amiable Assassins: The Story of the Kachin Guerrillas in North Burma.* London: Hale, 1957. 159p.

1905. ———. *The Magic War: The Battle for North Burma.* New York: Scribner's, 1972. 180p.

1906. Fergusson, Bernard E. *Beyond the Chidwin.* London: Collins, 1951. 256p.

1907. Fraser, Ian. "The Attack on *Takao.*" In: John Winton, ed. *The War at Sea: The British Navy in World War II.* New York: Morrow, 1967. pp. 379–390.

1908. Friend, John F. *The Long Trek.* London: Muller, 1957. 187p.

Chindits.

1909. Halley, David. *With Wingate in Burma.* London: Hodge, 1945. 189p.

1910. Hampshire, A. Cecil. "The Exploits of 'Force Viper.'" *Journal of the Royal United Service Institution,* CXIII (February 1968), 41–50.

Some 106 R. M. Commandos in Burma, 1942.

1911. Henderson, Ralph E. "Jungle of Hidden [Kachin] Friends." In: *Reader's Digest,* Editors of. *Secrets and Spies: Behind-the-Scenes Stories of World War II.* Pleasantville, N. Y.: Reader's Digest Association, 1964. pp. 263–273.

1912. Hilsman, Roger. "Burma Ambush." *Marine Corps Gazette,* XLVI (January 1962), 12–13.

1913. Jeffrey, William F. *Sunbeams Like Swords.* London: Hodder and Stoughton, 1951. 176p.

Chindits.

1914. Johnston, George H. "Meet the Kachins." *Saturday Evening Post,* CCXVII (July 15, 1944), 6+.

1915. Kathigasu, Sybil D. *No Dram of Mercy.* London: Spearman, 1954. 237p.

Burma.

1916. Kittredge, George W. "Stalking the *Takao* in Singapore Harbor." *U. S. Naval Institute Proceedings,* LXXXIII (1957), 392–395.

1917. Leasor, James. *Boarding Party.* Boston: Houghton, Mifflin, 1979. 225p.

British commandos hit German shipping at Goa in 1943.

1918. McKie, Ronald C. H. *The Heroes.* Sydney and London: Angus and Robertson, 1960. 285p.

Canoe raids on Singapore harbor.

1919. Mead, P. W. "The Chindit Operation of 1944." *Journal of the Royal United Service Institution,* C (May, August, November 1955), 250–262, 468, 622–625.

1920. Moore, James A. "X–Craft." *U. S. Naval Institute Proceedings,* LXXXIII (1957), 663.

1921. Mosley, Leonard. *Gideon Goes to War.* London: Barker, 1955. 256p.

Chindits.

1922. Neely, F. R. "The Silent Invasion." *Collier's,* CXIII (June 2, 1944), 14+.

1923. Peers, William R. "Guerrilla Operations in Northern Burma." *Military Review,* XLIV (October 1964), 86–98.

1924. _____ , and Dean Brelis. *Behind the Burma Road: The Story of America's Most Successful Guerrilla Force.* Boston: Little, Brown, 1963. 246p.

OSS Detachment 101.

1925. Prasad, Bisheshwar, ed. *The Reconquest of Burma.* Official History of the Indian Armed Forces in the Second World War, 1939–1945: Campaigns in the Eastern Theater. New Delhi, India: Combined Inter-service Historical Section, 1952. 501p.

1926. Rolo, Charles J. "Commando of the Skies." *Saturday Evening Post,* CCXVII (March 3, 1945), 22–23+.

1927. _____. "Wingate's Burma Raid." *Atlantic Monthly,* CLXXII (October 1943), 91–94.

1928. _____. *Wingate's Raiders.* London: Harrap, 1944. 129p.

1929. Romanus, Charles F., and Riley Sunderland. *Stilwell's Command Problems.* United States Army in World War II: China–Burma–India. Washington, D. C.: Office of the Chief of Military History, Department of the Army, 1954. 518p.

1930. _____. *Stilwell's Mission to China.* United States Army in World War II: China–Burma–India. Washington, D. C.: Office of the Chief of Military History, Department of the Army, 1954. 441p.

1931. Shaw, James. *The March Out: The End of the Chindit Adventure.* London: Hart–Davis, 1953. 206p.

Sunderland, Riley, jt. author. *See* Romanus, Charles F.

1932. Sykes, Christopher. *Orde Wingate: A Biography.* Cleveland, Ohio: World Publishing Co., 1959. 575p.

1933. Trenowden, Ian. *Operations Most Secret: S.O.E., the Malayan Theater.* London: Kimber, 1978. 231p.

1934. Tulloch, Derek. *Wingate in Peace and War.* London: MacDonald, 1972. 300p.

1935. Tulloch, T. C. "Kachins in the War in Burma." *Asiatic Review,* XLII (July 1946), 248–250.

1936. Wilcox, W. A. *Chindit Column 76.* London: Longmans, Green, 1945. 139p.

Wynyard, Noel, pseud. *See* Davidson, Nancy E. D. I.

b. China–Siam–Indochina

1937. Adamson, Ian. *The Forgotten Men.* New York: Roy Publishers, 1965. 195p.

British/Australian commandos in China.

1938. Band, Claire, and William Band. *Two Years with the Chinese Communists.* New Haven, Conn.: Yale University Press, 1948. 347p.

1939. Barrett, David. *Dixie Mission: The United States Army Observer Group in Yenan.* Berkeley: Center for Chinese Studies, University of California, 1970. 96p.

1940. Boyle, John H. *China and Japan at War, 1937–1945: The Politics of Collaboration.* Stanford, Calif.: Stanford University Press, 1972. 430p.

1941.   Caldwell, Oliver J. *A Secret War: Americans in China, 1944–1945.* Carbondale: Southern Illinois University Press, 1972. 218p.

1942.   Chakrabandhu, M. C. Kardwik. "Force 136 and the Siamese Resistance Movement." *Asiatic Review,* CXLIII (April 1947), 168–170.

1943.   Chao, Chin–chen. "These, Too, Serve China: The Epic of China's Resistance." *Asia,* XLII (July 1942), 414–415.

1944.   Drachman, Edward R. *United States Policy towards Vietnam, 1940–1945.* Rutherford, N. J.: Fairleigh Dickinson University Press, 1970. 186p.

1945.   Fitzgerald, Oscar P. "Naval Group China: A Study of Guerrilla Warfare during World War II." Unpublished paper, Operational Archives, U. S. Navy Historical Center, 1968. 119p.

1946.   Garrett, C. W. "In Search of Grandeur: France and Vietnam, 1940–1946." *Review of Politics,* XXIX (July 1967), 303–323.

1947.   Haseman, John B. *Thai Resistance Movements during the Second World War.* Dekalb: Published for the Northern Illinois University Center for Southeast Asia Studies by Northern Illinois University Press, 1978. 192p.

1948.   Hess, Gary R. "Franklin Roosevelt and Indochina." *Journal of American History,* LIX (September 1972), 353–368.

1949.   McMahon, John T., Jr. "Vietnam: Our World War II Legacy." *Air University Review,* XIX (May 1968), 59–66.

1950.   Mansfield, Walter R. "Ambush in China." *Marine Corps Gazette,* XXX (March 1946), 12–16, 39–42.

USMC/OSS operations with the Chinese resistance.

1951.   Mao Tse–tung. *On Guerrilla Warfare.* Translated from the Chinese. New York: Praeger, 1961. 114p.

1952.   Miles, Milton E. *A Different Kind of War: The Little-known Story of the Combined Guerrilla Force Created in China by the U. S. Navy and the Chinese during World War II.* Garden City, N. Y.: Doubleday, 1967. 629p.

1953.   _____. "U. S. Naval Group, China." *U. S. Naval Institute Proceedings,* LXXII (1946), 921–931.

1954.   Millar, J. G. "The Mad Monks." *Marine Corps Gazette,* LII (November 1968), 45–48.

The Sino–American Cooperative Organization.

1955.   Noonan, William. *The Surprising Battalion: Australian Commandos in China.* Sydney, Australia: Bookstall Co., 1945. 194p.

1956.   Schaller, Michael. *From War to Revolution: The United States and China, 1938–1945.* New York: Columbia University Press, 1978. 352p.

1957.   "SACO! The United States Navy's Secret War in China." *Pacific Historical Review,* XLIV (November 1975), 527–553.

1958.   Snow, Edgar. "Secrets from Siam." *Saturday Evening Post,* CCXVIII (January 12, 1946), 13+.

OSS operations.

1959.   Stratton, Roy O. "Navy Guerrilla." *U. S. Naval Institute Proceedings,* LXXXIX (1963), 83–87.

1960.   United States. Congress. Senate. Committee on Foreign Relations. *The United States and Vietnam, 1944–1947:* Staff Study, no. 2. 92d Cong., 2d session. Washington, D. C.: U. S. Government Printing Office, 1972.

1961.   Vallat, Antoine. "Resistance in Indochina." *Asiatic Review,* XLI (July 1945), 311–314.

1962.   Walker, C. Lester. "China's Master Spy." *Harper's Magazine,* CXCIII (August 1946), 162–169.

OSS operations.

1963.   Ward, Francis K. "Siamese Dusk." *Blackwood's Magazine,* CCLV (May 1944), 309–321.

Further References

Additional information relative to this subsection will be found throughout this guide. As a result of the activities covered in this part, many biographies and autobiographies exist and are entered for "highlighting" purpose in section VIII, subsection B, below. To find appropriate personnel, check the national listing in the introduction to that subsection and note the section/subsection numbers placed in parentheses alongside each person's name.

D. The Western Hemisphere

1964.   Aswell, Edward C. "The Case of the Ten Nazi Spies." *Harper's Magazine,* CLXXXV (June 1942), 1–21.

1965.   Behrendt, Richard F. *Fascist Penetration in Latin America.* Washington, D. C.: American Council on Public Affairs, 1941. 27p.

1966.   Bryan, George S. *The Spy in America*. Philadelphia: Lippincott, 1943. 256p.

Carlson, John R. pseud. *See* Derounian, Arthur

1967.   Cave–Brown, Anthony, and Charles B. McDonald. *The Secret History of the Atomic Bomb*. New York: Dial Press, 1977. 788p.

Looks at Allied intelligence and counterintelligence as well as Soviet and foreign espionage.

1968.   Compton, James V. *The Swastika and the Eagle: Hitler, the United States, and the Origins of World War II*. Boston: Houghton, Mifflin, 1967. 297p.

1969.   Cox, Albert L. "The Saboteur Story." *Columbia Historical Society Records*, LVII–LIX (1960), 16–25.

1970.   Dasch, George J. *Eight Spies against America*. New York: McBride, 1959. 241p.

1971.   Divine, Robert A. *The Reluctant Belligerent: American Entry into World War II*. New York: Wiley, 1965. 172p.

1972.   Donovan, William J., and Edgar Mowrer. *Fifth Column Lessons for America*. Washington, D. C.: American Council on Public Affairs, 1941. 17p.

1973.   Dorounian, Arthur. *Under Cover: My Four Years in the Nazi Underworld of America—The Amazing Story of How Axis Agents and Our Enemies Within Are Now Plotting to Destroy the United States*. By John R. Carlson, pseud. New York: Dutton, 1943. 544p.

1974.   Drummond, Donald F. *The Passing of American Neutrality, 1937–1941*. Ann Arbor: University of Michigan Press, 1955. 409p.

1975.   Elliott, Laurence. "Hitler's Secret Invasion of the United States." *Reader's Digest*, LXXVI (March 1960), 162–164+.

1976.   Etzold, Thomas H. "The (F)utility Factor: German Information-gathering in the United States, 1933–1941." *Military Affairs*, XXXIX (April 1975), 77–82.

1977.   Farago, Ladislas. *The Game of the Foxes: The Untold Story of German Espionage in the United States and Great Britain during World War II*. New York: McKay, 1972. 696p.

1978.   Fernandez–Artucio, Hugo. *The Nazi Underground in South America*. New York: Farrar, Straus, 1942. 311p.

1979.   Fitzgibbon, Russell H. "The Axis Advance-guard in Latin America." In: *Problems of Hemispheric Defense*. Berkeley, Calif.: University of California Press, 1942. pp. 25–52.

1980.   Friedländer, Saul. *Prelude to Downfall: Hitler and the United States, 1939–1945*. Translated from the German. New York: Knopf, 1967. 338p.

1981.   Frye, Alton. *Nazi Germany and the American Hemisphere, 1933–1941*. Yale Historical Studies, Miscellany 86. New Haven, Conn.: Yale University Press, 1967. 229p.

1982.   Gouzenko, Igor. *The Iron Curtain*. New York: Dutton, 1948. 279p.

Soviet spies seek A-bomb secrets.

1983.   Gunther, John. *Inside Latin America*. New York: Harper, 1941. 498p.

1984.   Hoover, J. Edgar. "Alien Enemy Control." *Iowa Law Review*, XXIV (March 1944), 396–408.

1985.   _____ . "The Big Scare: The Menace of Cooked-up Hysteria." *American Magazine*, CXXXII (August 1941), 24–25+.

1986.   _____ . "How the Nazi Spy Invasion Was Smashed." *American Magazine*, CXXXVIII (September 1944), 20–21+.

1987.   _____ . "The War Begins at Home: New Methods of Destruction by Saboteurs and Spies." *American Magazine*, CXXXII (September 1941), 28–29+.

1988.   Hynd, Alan. *Betrayal from the East: The Inside Story of Japan's Spies in America*. New York: McBride, 1943. 287p.

1989.   _____ . *Passport to Treason: The Inside Story of Spies in America*. New York: McBride, 1943. 306p.

1990.   Jenner, William E. "Who Scuttled the Navy's Spy Hunt during the War?" *U. S. News and World Report*, XXXVI (February 5, 1954), 39–40.

Kahn, Ely J., jt. author. *See* Sayers, Michael

1991.   Lavine, Harold. *The Fifth Column in America*. Garden City, N. Y.: Doubleday, Doran, 1940. 240p.

MacDonald, Charles B., jt. author. *See* Cave-Brown, Anthony

1992.   Martin, L. S. "Nazi Intrigues in Central America." *American Mercury*, LIII (July 1941), 66–73.

1993. Modesto, Don. *Spies and Saboteurs in Argentina.* News Background Reports, no. 7. New York: News Background, 1942. 18p.

1994. Moorehead, Alan. *The Traitors.* Rev. ed. New York: Harper, 1963. 236p.

Mowrer, Edgar, jt. author. *See* Donovan, William J.

1995. "Nazi Spies: F.B.I. Smashes Gang." *Life*, XI (December 29, 1941), 24–27.

1996. Pilat, Oliver. *The Atom Spies.* New York: Putnam, 1952. 312p.

1997. Prior, Leon O. "German Espionage in Florida during World War II." *Florida Historical Quarterly*, XXXIX (April 1961), 374–377.

1998. _____. "The Nazi Invasion of Florida." *Florida Historical Quarterly*, XLIX (October 1970), 129–139.

1999. Rachlis, Eugene. *They Came to Kill: The Story of Eight Nazi Saboteurs in America.* New York: Random House, 1961. 306p.

2000. Riess, Curt. "Hitler's U-boat Espionage: Rubber Boats Launched from Nazi Subs." *Saturday Evening Post*, CCXIV (May 16, 1942), 16–17+.

2001. Rogge, O. John. *The Official German Report: Nazi Penetration, 1924–1942.* New York: Yoseloff, 1961. 478p.

2002. Rowan, Richard W. *Secret Agents against America.* Garden City, N.Y.: Doubleday, Doran, 1939. 267p.

2003. Sayers, Michael, and Ely J. Kahn. *Plot against the Peace: A Warning to the Nation.* New York: Dial Press, 1945. 258p.

2004. _____. *Sabotage! The Secret War against America.* New York: Gleason Publications, 1944. 98p.

2005. _____ . _____ . *Reader's Digest*, XLI (October 1942), 159–176.

2006. Sondern, Frederick, Jr. "Catching Spies." *American Mercury*, LIV (February 1942), 209–216.

2007. Swanberg, W. A. "The Spies Who Came In from the Sea." *American Heritage*, XXI (April 1970), 66–69, 87–91.

2008. Terrell, J. U. "The Untold Story of the Nazi Saboteurs." *Newsweek*, XXVI (November 12, 1945), 38+.

2009. Trefousse, Hans L. "The Failure of German Intelligence in the United States, 1935–1945." *Mississippi Valley Historical Review*, XLII (June 1955), 84–100.

2010. Turrou, Leon G. *Nazi Spies in America.* New York: Random House, 1939. 299p. Rpr. 1970.

2011. United States. Congress. House, Committee on Un-American Activities. *The Shameful Years: Thirty Years of Soviet Espionage in the United States.* 85th Cong., 1st sess. Washington, D. C.: U. S. Government Printing Office, 1951. 70p.

2012. _____ . _____ . Special Subcommittee to Investigate Un-American Activities and Propaganda in the United States. *Hearings.* 16 vols. 75th Cong., 2d sess. to 77th Cong., 2d sess. Washington, D. C.: U.S. Government Printing Office, 1939–1942.

2013. _____ . Navy Department. Office of the Chief of Naval Operations, Office of Naval Intelligence. "German Espionage and Sabotage against the United States." *ONI Review,* I (January 1946), 33–38.

2014. _____ . War Department. Manhattan Project. *Manhattan Project: Official History and Documents.* 12 reels, 35 mm microfilm. Washington, D. C.: University Publications of America, 1977.

2015. Wall, Carl B. "The Hunt for a Spy [Ernest F. Lehmitz]." In: *Reader's Digest,* Editors of. *Secrets and Spies: Behind-the-Scenes Stories of World War II.* Pleasantville, N. Y.: Reader's Digest Association, 1964. pp. 186–191.

2016. Wise, William. *When the Saboteurs Came: The Nazi Sabotage Plot against America in World War II.* New York: Dutton, 1967. 127p.

Further References

More citations relative to the material covered in this subsection will be found in certain of the sections and subsections noted above, especially section III, subsection C. As a result of the activities covered in this part, many biographies and autobiographies exist and are entered for "highlighting" purposes in section VIII, subsection B, below. To find appropriate personnel, like William J. Donovan or J. Edgar Hoover, check the national listing in the introduction to that subsection and note the section/subsection numbers placed in parentheses alongside each person's name.

VIII/ Some Personalities of the Secret Wars

Introduction

The purpose of this section is to bring together in a single unit many of the most useful and interesting biographies and autobiographies available on the 1939–1945 secret war.

Section A is devoted to collective biography while section B is an alphabetically arranged guide to specific personalities.

A. General Biography

Introduction

The citations in this subsection are all concerned with either collected biography or reference tools that may be employed to keep abreast of the publication of new biographical sources. A few of the titles here are further analyzed in subsection B below.

2017.   *Army Times,* Editors of. *Heroes of the Resistance.* New York: Dodd, Mead, 1967. 133p.

2018.   Barzin, Betty. "Unsung Heroines of the Underground." *Independent Woman,* XXIII (January 1944), 2–3+.

2019.   Boehm, Eric, ed. *We Survived: The Stories of Fourteen of the Hidden and Hunted in Nazi Germany.* New Haven, Conn.: Yale University Press, 1949. 308p.

2020.   Denniston, Elinor. *Famous American Spies.* By Rae Foley, pseud. New York: Dodd, Mead, 1962. 158p.

2021.   Fest, Joachim C. *The Face of the Third Reich.* Translated from the German. London: Weidenfeld and Nicolson, 1970. 402p.

Foley, Rae, pseud. *See* Denniston, Elinor

Franklin, Charles, pseud. *See* Usher, Frank H.

2022.   Gleeson, James. *They Feared No Evil: The Women Agents of Britain's Secret Armies, 1939–1945.* London: Hale, 1976. 173p.

2023.   Great Britain. Ministry of Information, Reference Division. *Who's Who in Nazi Germany.* 3d ed. London: H. M. Stationery Office, 1942. 38p.

2024.   Gribble, Leonard R. *Stories of Famous Spies.* London: Barker, 1964. 208p.

2025.   Hoehling, Adolph A. *Women Who Spied.* New York: Dodd, Mead, 1967. 204p.

2026.   Hoover, J. Edgar. "Hitler's Spying Sirens." *American Magazine,* CXXXVIII (December 1944), 40–41+.

2027.   Hutton, Joseph B. *Women in Espionage.* New York: Macmillan, 1972. 192p.

2028.   Institut zur Erforschung der U.S.S.R., Munich. *Who Was Who in the U.S.S.R.* [1917–1967]: *A Biographic Directory Containing 5,015 Biographies of Prominent Soviet Historical Personalities.* Metuchen, N. J.: The Scarecrow Press, 1972. 687p.

2029. *The International Who's Who.* London: Europa Publications, 1939–. v. 4–.

2030. Jackson, Robert. *Heroines of World War II.* London: Barker, 1976. 170p.

2031. Keegan, John, ed. *Who Was Who in World War II.* New York: Crowell, 1978. 244p.

2032. Mason, David. *Who's Who in World War II.* Boston: Little, Brown, 1978. 363p.

2033. *New York Times,* Editors of. *New York Times Obituary Index, 1958– 1968.* New York: New York Times Co., 1970. 1,136p.

2034. Newman, Joseph. *Famous Soviet Spies: The Kremlin's Secret Weapon.* Washington, D. C.: Books by *U. S. News and World Report,* 1976. 223p.

2035. Orsag, Carol. "An International Array of Spies." In: David Wallechinsky and Irving Wallace. *The People's Almanac.* Garden City, N.Y.: Doubleday, 1975. pp. 644–650.

2036. Pinto, Oreste. "The Secrets of Super Spies." *Science Digest,* XXXV (May 1954), 57–62.

2037. Schneider, Jost W. *Their Honor Was Loyalty: An Illustrated and Documented History of the Knight's Cross Holders of the Waffen SS and Police, 1940–1945.* Translated from the German. New York: Roger James Binder Co., 1977. 480p.

2038. Singer, Kurt D. *The Men in the Trojan Horse.* Boston: Beacon Press, 1953. 258p.

2039. _____. *Spies and Traitors of World War II.* New York: Prentice– Hall, 1945. 295p.

2040. _____. *The World's Thirty Greatest Women Spies.* New York: Holt, 1951. 318p.

2041. Sinokop, N. *Letters from the Dead: Letters and Documents Written in the Last Minutes of Their Lives in a Gestapo Cell, 1941 to 1945.* New York: Universal, 1965. 233p.

2042. Sparrow, Gerald. *The Great Spies.* London: Long, 1949. 183p.

2043. Strong, Kenneth W. D. *Men-of-Intelligence: A Study of the Roles and Decisions of Chiefs-of-Intelligence from World War I to the Present Day.* London: Cassell, 1970. 183p.

2044. Taylor, Telford. *Sword and Swastika: Generals and Nazis in the Third Reich.* New York: Simon and Schuster, 1952. 431p.

2045.   *The Times*, Editors of. *Obituaries from The Times, 1961–1970*. Reading, Berks., Eng.: Newspaper Archive Developments, 1976. 952p.

2046.   Tunny, Christopher. *A Biographical Dictionary of World War II*. New York: St. Martin's Press, 1972. 216p.

2047.   Usher, Frank H. *The Great Spies*. By Charles Franklin, pseud. New York: Hart, 1967. 272p.

2048.   Von Waldheim–Emmerick, Ragnhild S. *In the Footsteps of Joan of Arc: True Stories of Heroines of the French Resistance in World War II*. Translated from the French. New York: Exposition Press, 1959. 153p.

2049.   Weyl, Nathaniel. "'Female Turncoats' and 'Hitler's Radio Traitors.'" In: his *Treason: The Story of Disloyalty and Betrayal in American History*. New York: Public Affairs Press, 1950. pp. 361–389.

2050.   Whyte, A. P. Luscombe. *Escape to Fight Again: Stories of Men and Women Who Refused to Accept Defeat*. London: Harrap, 1943. 258p.

2051.   Wighton, Charles. *The World's Greatest Spies: True-life Dramas of Outstanding Secret Agents*. New York: Taplinger, 1966. 319p.

2052.   Wilkinson, J. Burke, ed. *Cry Sabotage! True Stories of Twentieth Century Saboteurs*. Scarsdale, N. Y.: Bradbury Press, 1972. 265p.

2053.   _____ . *Cry Spy! True Stories of Twentieth Century Spies and Spy Catchers*. Scarsdale, N. Y.: Bradbury Press, 1969. 271p.

B. Specific Personalities

Introduction

The purpose of this subsection is to highlight some of the more interesting individuals who participated in the secret aspects of World War II. Most of these people were agents, some were resistance fighters, and a few were commando or other military personalities. The list of references is arranged alphabetically by surname with cross-references between some aliases.

To facilitate the use of this subsection, the following national breakdown is provided: numbers after a name refer to those sections and subsections of the bibliography above where a given person was active.

American

Hartvig Anderson (3:C:4; 7:B:2:e)

Carol Bache (3:C:4; 7:C:1)

Richard Baker (3:C:4; 7:B:2:a)

Morris "Moe" Berg (3:C:4; 7:B:2:e)

John C. Caldwell (3:C:4; 7:C:3:b)

Howard Chappell (3:C:4; 7:B: 3:a)
William E. Colby (3:C:4; 7:B)
William J. Donovan (3:C:4)
Wiiliam Dreux (3:C:4; 7:B:2:e)
Allen W. Dulles (3:C:4; 7:B)
Carl F. Eifer (3:C:4)
Eric S. Erickson (3:C:4; 7:B:2:e)
John Ford (3:C:4)
William F. Friedman (3:B:1; 4:C; 5:B)
Ricardo C. Galang (5:B; 7:C:2:a)
J. P. Gallagher (3:C:4; 7:B:3:a)
Mark Gayn (3:C:4; 7:C:3:b)
William Grell (3:C:4)
James E. Haggerty (7:C:2:a)
Roger Hall (3:C:4)
Frank Hirt (7:D)
Stuart Hood (3:C:4; 7:B:3:a)
Aldo Icardi (3:C:4; 7:B:3:a)
J. Edgar Hoover (3:C:4; 7:D)
George R. Jordan (4:B; 7:D)
Tyler Kent (7:D)
William L. Langer (3:B:3; 3:C:4)
Elizabeth P. MacDonald (3:C:4)
Sidney F. Mashbir (3:B:3; 4:B; 5:C:5:a; 7:C:2:b)
Gerald Mayer (3:C:4; 7:B:2:e)
Milton E. Miles (4:C; 7:C:3:b)
Thomas N. Moon (3:C:4)
John H. Moore (4:C; 5:B:2)
William J. Morgan (3:C:4; 7:B: 2:a; 7:B:2:b)
Saul K. Padover (3:C:4; 7:B:2:e)
Charles Parsons (4:B; 7:C:2:a)
Claire Phillips (4:B; 7:C:2:a)
William Phillips (3:C:4; 7:B:2:a)
David G. Prosser (3:C:4; 7:B: 2:b)
Iliff D. Richardson (4:B; 7:C: 2:a)
Agnes Smedley (7:C:3:b)
Nicol Smith (3:C:4; 7:C:3:b)
Louis R. Spencer (4:B; 7:C:2:a)

Robert Storey (3:C:4; 7:B:2:a)
Edmond Taylor (3:C:4; 5:C:2:b; 7:B:3:b; 7:C:3:b)
Elliott A. Thorpe (3:C:4; 4:B; 7:C:2)
Peter Tompkins (3:C:4; 7:B:3:a)
George R. Tweed (5:C; 7:C:2:b)
Russell W. Volckman (4:B; 7:C:2:a)
Ellis M. Zacharias (2;4:C;5:B; 5:C:5; 7:C:1)

Australian

Wilfred G. Burchett (4:B:C:D; 7:C:1; 7:C:2:b)
Martin Clemens (4:B:C:D; 7:C:1; 7:C:2:b)
Jock McLaren (4:B:C:D; 7:C:1; 7:C:2:b)
Mary Murray (4:B:C:D; 7:C:1; 7:C:2:b)
Malcolm Wright (4:B:C:D; 7:C:1; 7:C:2:b)

British

Ralph Arnold (3:C:1; 7:B; 7:C)
Peter Baker (3:C:1; 7:B:2:a)
Derek G. Barnes (4:D:1)
John Beamish (3:C:1; 7:C:3:a)
Branko Bokum (3:C:1; 7:B:3:a)
Pierre Boulle (3:C:1; 7:B:2:b)
Amy E. Brousse (3:C:1; 7:B:2:b)
Anne Brusselmans (3:C:1; 7:B:2:b)
Robert Burdett (3:C:1; 7:B:2:b)
Ewan Butler (3:C:1; 7:B:3:b)
James Caffin (7:B:3:e)
Francis Cammaerts (3:C:1; 7:B:2:b)
Mathilde Carré (3:C:1; 3:C:2; 7:B:2:b)
Donald C. Caskie (3:C:1; 7:B:2:b)

Marek Celt (3:C:1; 7:B:4:a)

Edward A. Chapman (3:C:1; 7:B:2:b)

Robert Crystal (3:C:1; 7:C:3:a)

Odette Churchill (3:C:1; 7:B:2:b)

Peter Churchill (3:C:1; 7:B:2:b)

Dudley Clarke (6A)

Dick Cooper (3:C:1; 7:B:2:a)

Benjamin Cowburn (3:C:1; 7:B:2:b)

James V. Davidson-Hunter (3:C:1; 7:B:2:b)

Emmanuel De La Vigerie (3:C:1; 7:B:2:a)

Sefton Delmar (3:C:1; 7:B:2:b)

Elizabeth Denham (3:C:1; 7:B:2:b)

Donald Downes (3:C:1; 7:B:3:b)

Anthony Duke (3:C:1; 7:B:2:b)

Edmund G. Edlemann (3:C:1; 7:B:2:a)

Jack Evans (3:C:1; 7:B:2:b)

Jack L. Fairweather (3:C:1; 7:B:2:b)

Roy Farran (3:C:1; 7:B:2:b)

Jan Felix (3:C:1; 7:B:2:a)

Xan Fielding (3:C:1; 7:B:2:a; 7:B:3:d)

John Fox (3:C:1; 7:C:3:b)

Norman Franks (3:C:1; 7:B:2:b)

Roman Garby–Czerniawski (3:C:1; 7:B:2:b)

Stefan Gazel (3:C:1; 7:B:4:a)

Andrew Gilchrist (3:C:1; 7:C:3:b)

Maria Ginter (3:C:1; 7:B:4:a)

John Goldsmith (3:C:1; 7:B:2:b)

F. C. Griffiths (3:C:1; 7:B:2:b)

John W. Hackett (5:C:4:c; 7:B:2:c)

William Hall (3:B:1; 3:C:1)

Donald Hamilton–Hill (3:C:1; 7:B:2:e; 7:B:3:b)

Thomas Harrisson (3:C:1; 4:B; 7:C:2:b)

Leo Heaps (5:C:4:c; 7:B:2:c)

Cyril V. Hearn (3:C:1; 7:B:3:b)

Sybil Hepburn (3:C:1; 7:b:2:b)

Richard Heslop (3:C:1; 7:B:2:b)

Leslie Howard (3:C:1; 7:B:2:a)

Meyrich E. C. James (4:B)

Reginald V. Jones (3:B:2; 3:b:3; 3:C:1)

Edita Katona (3:C:1; 7:B:2:b)

Peter K. Kemp (3:C:1; 7:C:3:b)

John Kennett (3:C:1; 7:B:2:d:1)

Alexander W. L. Kessell (3:C:1; 7:B:2:c)

Roger Keyes (6A)

Noor Inayat Khan (3:C:1; 7:B:2:b)

Roger Landes (3:C:1; 7:B:2:b)

George Langelaan (3:C:1; 7(B:2:b)

James M. Langley (3:C:1; 7:B:2:a)

Mary Lindell (3:C:1; 7:B:2:b)

Judith Hare, Countess of Listowel (3:C:1; 7:B:2:b)

Robert H. B. Lockhart (3:C:1; 7:B:2:a)

John G. Lomax (3:C:1; 7:B:2:a)

Lydia Love (3:C:1; 7:B:2:e)

Ronald C. H. McKie (3:C:1; 7:B:2:b)

Tony Mains (4:B; 7:C:3:a)

George A. Millar (3:C:1; 7:B:2:b)

Merlin Minshall (3:C:1; 7:B:2:a)

Bernard Newman (3:C:1; 7:B:2:a)

Alfred and Henry Newton (3:C:1; 7:B:2:b)

Elizabeth Nichols (3:C:1; 7:B:2:b)

Leslie A. Nicholson (3:C:1; 7:B:2:a)

Pat O'Leary (3:C:1; 7:B:2:b)
Arthur Owens (3:C:1; 7:B:2:a)
Geoffrey Parker (3:C:1; 7:B:2:a)
Jocelyn Pereira (4:B)
Oreste Pinto (3:C:1; 7:B:2:a)
Eric Piquet–Wicks (3:C:1; 7:B:2:b)
Roxane Pitt (3:C:1; 7:B:2:b)
Dusko Popov (3:C:1; 7:B; 7:D)
Harry Ree (3:C:1; 7:B:2:b)
Francis Reid (3:C:1; 7:B:3:d)
Alexander M. Rendel (3:C:1; 7:B:3:d)
Lloyd Rhys (4:B; 7:C:2:b)
Georgette Robinson (3:C:1; 7:B:2:b)
Devereaux Rochester (3:C:1; 7:B:2:b)
Lindsay Rogers (7:B:3:e)
Alaine Romans (3:C:1; 7:B:2:b)
A. W. Sansom (3:C:1; 4:B; 7:B:3:b)
George Sava (3:C:1; 7:B:2:a)
A. P. Scotland (3:C:1; 7:B:2:e)
Lionel Scott (3:C:1; 7:B:2:b)
Ronald Seth (3:C:1; 7:B:2:b)
Percy Sillitoe (3:C:1; 7:B:2:a)
J. M. Stagg (3:B:3; 4:D:1; 5:C:4:b)
John Starr (3:C:1; 7:B:2:b)
William Stevenson (3:C:1; 7:D)
Kenneth W. D. Strong (4:B; 5:4)
Bickham Sweet–Escott (3:C:1; 7:B:2:a)
Violette Szabo (3:C:1; 7:B:2:b)
Dorothy Tartière (3:C:1; 7:B:2:b)
Thomas D. G. Teare (3:C:1; 7:B:2:b)
John Toyne (3:C:1; 7:B:4)
Serge Vaculik (3:C:1; 7:B:2:b)
Jack M. Veness (3:C:1; 7:B:2:b)
Nancy Wake (3:C:1; 7:B:2:b)
David E. Walker (3:C:1; 7:B:2:a)

Anne M. Walters (3:C:1; 7:B:2:b)
Friedrich Wetzel (3:C:1; 7:B:2:a)
Charles Wighton (3:C:1; 7:B:2:b)
James F. Wilde (7:B:3:a)
J. Elder Wills (3:C:1; 7;B:2:b)
Frederick W. Winterbotham (3:C:1; 7:B:2:a; 7:B:2:e)
F. F. E. Yeo–Thomas (3:C:1; 7:B:2:b)

Burmese

U. Nu (7:C:3:a)
Yay Panlilio (7:C:3:a)

Chinese

Pin–fei Loo (7:C:3:b)

Cretan

George Psychoundakis (7:B:3:d)

Czech

Frantiseh Moravec (7:B:2:e)

Dutch

Georges Delfanne (3:C:1; 3:C:2; 7:B:2:c)
Pieter Dourlein (3:C:1; 3:C:2; 7:B:2:c)
Hubertus Lauwers (7:B:2:c)
Flemming B. Muus (7:B:2:c)
Theo Van Duren (7:B:2:c)
Albert Van Loop (3:C:1; 3:C:2; 7:B:2:c)

French

Marie Benoit (7:B:2:b)
Georges Bidault (7:B:2:b)
Jean Dutourd (7:B:2:b)
Henri Frenay (7:B:2:b)

Phillippe   Ganier–Raymond
(7:B:2:b)
Pierre Guillain de Benouville
(7:B:2:b)
Michael Hollard (3:C:5:c; 5:A:4;
7:B:2:b)
Gilbert Renault–Roulier (3:C:
5:c; 7:B:2:b)
Lily Sergueiew (3:C:1; 3:C:2;
7:B:2:b)
Helene Vagliano (7:B:2:b)

German

Ruth Andreas–Friedrich (7:B:
2:e)
Elyesa Bazna (3:C:2; 5:B;
7:B:3:b)
Ludwig Beck (7:B:2:e)
Hugo E. Bleicher (3:C:2;
7:B:2:e)
Dietrich Bonhoffer (7:B:2:e)
Wilhelm Canaris (3:C:2; 7:B:
2:e)
Johann Eppler (3:C:2; 7:B:3:b)
Reinhard Gehlen (4:B; 5:C:3)
Kurt Gerstein (7:B:2:e)
Erich Gimpel (3:C:2)
H. J. Giskes (3:C:2; 7:B:2:b;
7:B:2:c)
Joseph Goebbels (2)
Carl Goerdeler (7:B:2:e)
Hermann Goertz (3:C:2; 7:B:
2:a)
Hermann Haupt (3:C:2; 7:D)
Hans Hauser (3:C:2; 7:B:2:d:1)
Reinhard Heydrich (3:C:2;
7:B:2:e)
Heinrich Himmler (3:C:2;
7:B:2:e)
Wilhelm Höttl (3:C:2; 7:B:2)
William Joyce (2)
Ernst Kaltenbrunner (3:C:2;
7:B:2:e)

Erwin Lahousen (3:C:2; 7:B:
2:e)
Hermann Lang (3:C:2; 7:B:2:a)
Alfred Naujocks (3:C:2; 7:B:
4:a)
Peter Neumann (3:C:2; 7:B:4:b)
Wolfgang Putlitz (3:C:2; 7:B:
2:a)
Hans Scharff (4:D:1)
Walter Schellenberger (3:C:2;
7:B:2:e)
Hans Schmidt (3:C:2)
Harro Schulze–Boysen (3:C:2)
Bernard Schulze–Holthus (3:C:
2; 7:B:3:b)
Otto Skorzeny (3:C:2; 5:C:2:c;
5:C:4:d; 7:B:3:a; 7:B:4:a)
Ulrich Von Hassell (7:B:2:e)
Ursula Von Kardorff (7:B:2:e)
Helmuth Von Moltke (7:B:2:e)
Fabian Von Schlabrendorff (7:B:
2:e)
Klaus Von Stauffenberg (7:B:
2:e)

Italian

Franco Mangeri (4:C)
Giovanni Pesce (7:B:3:a)

Japanese

Olga Cane (3:C:5:b; 4:C; 5:B:3)
Kenji Doihara (3:C:5:b)
Ruth Kuhn (3:C:5:b; 4:C; 5:B:3)
Surumato Susio (3:C:5:b)
Takeo Yoshikawa (3:C:5:b; 4:C;
5:B:3)

Jewish

Emil Brigg (7:B:4:c)
Chanah Szenes (7:B:4:c)

Malayan

Mahmood K. Durrani (7:C:3:a)
Gurchan Singh (7:C:3:a)

Norwegian

Helen Astrup (7:B:2:d:1)
Paal Berg (7:B:2:d:1)
Eiliv O. Hauge (7:B:2:d:1)
Brede Klefos (7:B:2:d:1)
"Shetlands" Larsen (7:B:2:d:1)
Kim Malthe–Bruun (7:B:2:d:1)
Max Manus (7:B:2:d:1)
Asja Mercer (7:B:2:d:1)
Oluf R. Olsen (7:B:2:d:1)

Philippino

Celedanio A. Ancheta (7:C:2:a)
Higinio De Uriarte (7:C:2:a)
Joey Guerrero (7:C:2:a)

Polish

Stefan Gazel (7:B:4:a)
Maria Ginter (7:B:4:a)

Stasjek Jackowski (7:B:4:a)
Wladyslaw Sikorski (7:B:4:a)

Russian

Lavrentz P. Beria (3:C:3; 7:B:4:b)
Alexander Foote (3:C:3; 7:B:2)
Igor Gouzenko (3:C:3; 7:D)
Anatoli Granovsky (3:C:3; 7:D)
Ilya Kuzin (7:B:4:b)
Harold "Kim" Philby (3:C:1; 3:C:3; 7:B:2:a)
Rudolf Roessler (3:C:3; 4:B; 5:C:3:d; 7:B)
Richard Sorge (3:C:3; 4:B; 5:3:a; 7:C:1)
Leopold Trepper (3:C:3; 4:B; 7:B:2:c)
Andrey Vaslov (7:B:4:b)

Swiss

Henri Guisan (3:C:1; 3:C:2; 3:C:3; 3:C:4)

"Alfred," pseud. *See* Friedrich Wetzel

Celedanio A. Ancheta

2054. Ancheta, Celedanio A. "The Chinese Guerrillas in World War II." *Philippine Historical Association History Bulletin,* XII (1976), 251–259.

2055. ———. *The Escape.* Manila, P. I.: R. P. Garcia, 1966. 41p.

Hartvig Anderson

2056. Anderson, Hartvig. *The Dark City: A True Account of the Adventures of a Secret Agent in Berlin.* New York: Rinehart, 1954. 314p.

Ruth Andreas–Friedrich

2057. Andreas–Friedrich, Ruth. *Berlin Underground, 1939–1945.* Translated from the German. New York: Holt, 1945. 312p.

"Armand," pseud. *See* Roman Garby–Czerniawski

Ralph Arnold

2058. Arnold, Ralph. *A Very Quiet War.* New York: Macmillan, 1962. 176p.

Helen Astrup

2059. Astrup, Helen. *Oslo Intrigue: A Woman's Memoir of the Norwegian Resistance.* New York: McGraw–Hill, 1954. 237.

Carol Bache

2060. Bache, Carol. *Paradox Isle.* New York: Knopf, 1943. 184p.

Peter Baker

2061. Baker, Peter. *My Testament.* By Colin Strang, pseud. London: Calder, 1955. 288p.

Richard Baker

2062. Baker, Richard. *The Year of the Buzz Bomb.* New York: Exposition Press, 1952. 118p.

Derek G. Barnes

2063. Barnes, Derek G. *Cloud Cover: Recollections of an Intelligence Officer.* London: Rich and Cowan, 1943. 176p.

Elyesa Bazna

2064. Bazna, Elyesa. *I Was Cicero.* Translated from the German. New York: Harper & Row, 1962. 212p.

2065. _____ . _____ . In: Burke Wilkinson, ed. *Cry Spy!* New York: Bradbury Press, 1969. pp. 120–129.

2066. Franklin, Charles. "Cicero." In: his *Great Spies.* London: Hart–Davis, 1967. pp. 137–145.

2067. Halacy, Dan. "Cicero." In: his *Master Spy.* New York: McGraw–Hill, 1968. pp. 159–174.

2068. Kempner, Robert M. W. "The Highest Paid Spy in History." *Saturday Evening Post,* CCXXII (January 28, 1950), 17–19+.

2069. _____ . _____ . *Reader's Digest,* LVI (June 1950), 91–95.

2070. Moyzisch, L. C. "In the Ankara Spy Jungle." In: Alfred Perelis, ed. *Great True Spy Stories.* New York: Arco Press, 1957. pp. 117–123.

2071. ———— . *Operation Cicero.* New York: Coward–McCann, 1950. 208p.

2072. Wighton, Charles. "Cicero." In: his *World's Greatest Spies.* New York: Taplinger, 1965. pp. 258–271.

John Beamish

2073. Beamish, John. *Burma Drop.* London: Bestseller Library, 1958. 222p.

Ludwig Beck

2074. Reynolds, Nicholas. *Treason Was No Crime: Ludwig Beck, Chief of the German General Staff.* London: Kimber, 1976. 317p.

Marie Benoit

2075. Leboucher, Fernande. *Incredible Mission.* Translated from the French. Garden City, N. Y.: Doubleday, 1969. 165p.

Morris "Moe" Berg

2076. Kaufman, Louis, Barbara Fitzgerald, and Tom Sewell. *Moe Berg: Athlete, Scholar , Spy.* Boston: Little, Brown, 1975. 274p.

2077. Sheppard, R. Z. "Catcher in the Reich." *Time,* CV (February 3, 1975), 65–66.

Paal Berg

2078. "Paal Berg, Underground Leader." *American–Scandinavian Review,* XXXIII (September 1945), 198–202.

Lavrentz P. Beria

2079. Wittlin, Thaddeus. *Commisar: The Life and Death of Lavrentz Pavlovich Beria.* New York: Macmillan, 1972. 566p.

Georges Bidault

2080. Bidault, Georges. *Resistance: A Memoir.* Translated from the French. New York: Praeger, 1967. 348p.

Hugo E. Bleicher

2081. Bleicher, Hugo E. *Colonel Henri's Story: The War Memories of Hugo Bleicher , Former German Secret Agent.* Translated from the German. London: Kimber, 1954. 200p.

Branko Bokun

2082. Bokun, Branko. *Spy in the Vatican, 1941–1945.* New York: Praeger, 1973. 259p.

Dietrich Bonhoffer

2083. Bethge, Eberhard. *Bonhoffer: Exile and Martyr.* Sommers, Conn.: Seabury Press, 1976. 191p.

2084. _____. *Dietrich Bonhoffer: Man of Vision, Man of Courage.* Translated from the German. New York: Harper & Row, 1970. 867p.

2085. Bonhoffer, Dietrich. *Letters and Papers from Prison.* Edited by Eberhart Bethge. Enl. ed. New York: Macmillan, 1971. 437p.

2086. Bosanquet, Mary. *The Life and Death of Dietrich Bonhoffer.* New York: Harper & Row, 1968. 287p.

2087. Gill, Theodore A. *Memorandum for a Movie: A Short Life of Dietrich Bonhoffer.* New York: Macmillan, 1971. 268p.

2088. Goddard, Donald. *The Last Days of Dietrich Bonhoffer.* New York: Harper & Row, 1976. 245p.

2089. Marle, René. *Bonhoffer: The Man and His Work.* Translated from the French. New York: Newman Press, 1968. 141p.

2090. Zimmermann, Wolf D. *I Knew Dietrich Bonhoffer.* Translated from the German. New York: Harper & Row, 1966. 238p.

George Borodin, pseud. *See* George Sava

Pierre Boulle

2091. Boulle, Pierre. *My Own River Kwai.* Translated from the French. New York: Vanguard Press, 1967. 214p.

Emil Brigg

2092. Brigg, Emil. *Stand Up and Fight: His Story.* London: Harrap, 1972. 176p.

Amy E. Brousse

2093. Hyde, H. Montgomery. *Cynthia: The Spy Who Changed the Course of History.* New York: Farrar, Straus and Giroux, 1965. 240p.

Anne Brusselmans

2094. Brusselmans, Anne. *Rendez-vous 127: Diary, September 1940– September 1944.* New York: McClelland, 1954. 173p.

2095.   Duncan, Sylvia, and Peter Duncan. *Anne Brusselmans, M.B.E.* London: Benn, 1959. 207p.

Wilfred G. Burchett

2096.   Burchett, Wilfred G. *Democracy with a Tommygun.* Melbourne, Australia: Cheshire, 1946. 291p.

Robert Burdett

2097.   LeChene, Evelyn. *Watch For Me by Moonlight: A British Agent with the French Resistance.* London: Methuen, 1973. 224p.

Ewan Butler

2098.   Butler, Ewan. *Amateur Agent.* New York: W. W. Norton, 1963. 240p.

James Caffin

2099.   Caffin, James. *Partisan.* Auckland, New Zealand: Collins, 1945. 186p.

John C. Caldwell

2100.   Caldwell, John C., and Mark Gayn. *American Agent.* New York: Holt, 1947. 220p.

Francis Cammaerts

2101.   Spiro, Edward. *They Came from the Sky: The Stories of Lieutenant Colonel Francis Cammaerts, D.S.O., Legion of Honour; Major Roger Landes, M.C. and Bar, Legion of Honour; and Captain Harry Ree, D.S.O., O.B.E.* London: Heinemann, 1965. 264p.

Wilhelm Canaris

2102.   Abshagen, Karl H. *Canaris.* Translated from the German. London: Hutchinson, 1956. 264p.

2103.   Amort, Cestmir, and I. M. Jedlicka. *The Canaris File.* London: Wingate, 1970. 158p.

2104.   Brissand, André. *Canaris: The Biography of Admiral Canaris, Chief of German Military Intelligence in the Second World War.* Translated from the French. New York: Grosset and Dunlap, 1974. 347p.

2105.   Colvin, Ian G. *Canaris, Chief of Intelligence.* London: Mann, 1973. 224p.

2106.   _____ . *Master Spy: The Incredible Story of Admiral Wilhelm Canaris, Who, While Hitler's Chief of Intelligence, Was a Secret Ally of the British.* New York: McGraw–Hill, 1952. 286p.

2107. Deri, Emery. "The Super Spy Who Fooled Hitler." *Coronet,* XXXVII (January 1955), 40–45.

2108. Gumbel, E. J. "The Life and Death of a Spy Chief." *Social Research,* XIX (September 1952), 381–387.

2109. Singer, Kurt D. "Admiral Canaris." In: his *Gentlemen Spies.* London: Allen and Unwin, 1952. pp. 36–53.

2110. _____ . _____ . In: Alfred Perles, ed. *Great True Spy Stories.* New York: Arco Press, 1957. pp. 83–89.

2111. _____ . "The Spy Who Never Wore a Uniform." In: his *Three Thousand Years of Espionage.* New York: Prentice–Hall, 1948. pp. 335–353.

2112. Sternfeld, W. "Canaris: Chief of the German Intelligence Service." *Contemporary Review,* CLXIII (May 1943), 296–300.

2113. Trevor–Roper, Hugh. "Admiral Canaris." *Cornhill Magazine,* (Summer 1950), *passim.*

2114. _____ . _____ . In: his *The Philby Affair.* London: Kimber, 1968. pp. 101–126.

2115. Whiting, Charles. *Canaris.* New York: Ballantine Books, 1973. 265p.

Olga Cane

2116. Singer, Kurt D. "The Case of the Crazy Countess." In: his *Spies over Asia.* London: W. H. Allen, 1956. pp. 170–223.

Mathilde Carré

2117. Carré, Mathilde. *I Was "The Cat": The Truth about the Most Remarkable Woman Spy since Mata Hari.* Translated from the French. London: Souvenir Press, 1960. 223p.

2118. Franklin, Charles. "Mathilde Carré." In: his *Great Spies.* London: Hart–Davis, 1967. pp. 98–102.

2119. Minney, Rubeigh J. *Carve Her Name with Pride.* London: Collins, 1965. 187p.

2120. Paine, Lauren. *Mathilde Carré, Double Agent.* London: Hale, 1976. 192p.

2121. Singer, Kurt D. "The Cat." In: his *Spies for Democracy.* Minneapolis, Minn.: Dennison, 1960. pp. 105–120.

2122. Soltikow, Michael. *"The Cat": A True Story of Espionage.* Translated from the German. London: MacGibbon and Kee, 1957. 227p.

2123.   Wighton, Charles. "Mathilde Carré." In: his *World's Greatest Spies*. New York: Taplinger, 1965. pp. 135–158.

2124.   Young, Gordon. *The Cat with Two Faces*. London: White Lion Publications, 1975. 223p.

Donald C. Caskie

2125.   Caskie, Donald C. *The Tartan Pimpernel*. London: Oldbourne, 1957. 270p.

Marek Celt

2126.   Celt, Marek. *By Parachute to Warsaw*. London: Crisp, 1945. 88p.

Howard Chappell

2127.   White, William L. "The Great Ambush." In: *Reader's Digest*, Editors of. *Secrets and Spies: Behind-the-Scenes Stories of World War II*. Pleasantville, N. Y.: Reader's Digest Association, 1964. pp. 485–506.

Edward A. Chapman

2128.   Chapman, Edward A. *The Eddie Chapman Story*. New York: Julian Messner, 1954. 242p.

2129.   _____ . *Free Agent: Being the Further Adventures of Eddie Chapman*. London: Wingate, 1955. 223p.

2130.   Owen, F. "The Mysterious Mr. Eddie Chapman." In: Alfred Perles, ed. *Great True Spy Stories*. New York: Arco Press, 1957. pp. 97–101.

2131.   "Portrait of a Hero." *Time*, LXIII (January 18, 1954), 36+.

Robert Chrystal

2132.   Holman, Dennis. *The Green Torture: The Ordeal of Robert Chrystal*. London: Hale, 1962. 190p.

Odette Churchill

2133.   Tickell, Jerrard. *Odette: The Story of a British Agent*. London: Chapman and Hall, 1949. 334p.

2134.   _____ . "Odette Will Not Confess." In: Alfred Perles, ed. *Great True Spy Stories*. New York: Arco Press, 1957. pp. 131–139.

Peter Churchill

2135.   Churchill, Peter. *Duel of Wits*. London: Hodder and Stoughton, 1953. 319p.

2136. _____ . *Of Their Own Choice.* London: Hodder and Stoughton, 1952. 218p.

2137. _____ . *The Spirit in the Cage.* London: Hodder and Stoughton, 1954. 251p.

"Cicero," pseud. *See* Elyesa Bazna

Dudley Clarke

2138. Clarke, Dudley. *Seven Assignments.* London: Cape, 1948. 262p.

Martin Clemens

2139. Clemens, Martin. "Coastwatcher's Diary, Guadalcanal." *American Heritage,* XVII (February 1966), 104–110.

William E. Colby

2140. Colby, William E., and Peter Forbath. *Honorable Men: My Life in the C.I.A.* [and O.S.S.]. New York: Simon and Schuster, 1978. 493p.

"Colonel Henri," pseud. *See* Hugo E. Bleicher

Dick Cooper

2141. Cooper, Dick. *Adventures of a Secret Agent.* London: Muller, 1957. 256p.

"Coro," pseud. *See* Harro Schulze–Boysen

Benjamin Cowburn

2142. Cowburn, Benjamin. *No Cloak, No Dagger.* London: Jarrolds, 1960. 192p.

"Cynthia," pseud. *See* Amy E. Brousse

Manfred Czernin, pseud. *See* Norman Franks

James V. Davidson–Houston

2143. Davidson–Houston, James V. *Armed Pilgrimage.* London: Hale, 1949. 313p.

Emmanuel De La Vigerie

2144. De La Vigerie, Emmanuel. *Seven Times Seven Days.* Translated from the French. London: MacGibbon and Kee, 1958. . 221p.

Georges Delfanne

2148. Pinto, Oreste. "The Traitor of Arnhem." *Coronet*, XXXIV (June 1953), 127–132.

2149. Renault–Roulier, Gilbert. *Portrait of a Spy.* By "Remy," pseud. Translated from the French. New York: Roy, 1955. 224p.

Sefton Delmar

2150. Delmar, Sefton. *The Counterfeit Spy.* New York: Harper & Row, 1971. 256p.

Elizabeth Denham

2151. Denham, Elizabeth. *I Looked Right.* London: Cassell, 1956. 191p.

Higinio De Uriarte

2152. De Uriarte, Higinio. *A Basque among the Guerrillas of Negros.* Translated from the Spanish. Bacolod City, P. I.: Civismo Weekly, 1962. 316p.

William J. Donovan

2153. Dulles, Allen W. "William J. Donovan and National Security: A Speech to the Erie County Bar Association, Buffalo, New York, May 4, 1959." *Congressional Record*, CV (May 14, 1959), 8103–8105.

2154. Ford, Corey. *Donovan of O.S.S.* Boston: Little, Brown, 1970. 366p.

Kenji Doihara

2155. Gollomb, J. "Spymaster of the Rising Sun." In: Kurt D. Singer, ed. *Three Thousand Years of Espionage.* New York: Prentice–Hall, 1948. pp. 283–296.

Pieter Dourlein

2156. Dourlein, Pieter. *Inside North Pole: A Secret Agent's Story.* Translated from the Dutch. London: Kimber, 1954. 206p.

Donald Downes

2157. Downes, Donald. *The Scarlet Thread: Adventures in Wartime Espionage.* London: Verschoyle, 1953. 207p.

William Dreux

2158. Dreux, William. *No Bridges Blown.* Notre Dame, Ind.: Notre Dame University Press, 1971. 322p.

Anthony Duke

2159.   Duke, Madelein. *Slipstream: The Story of Anthony Duke*. London: Evans, 1955. 243p.

2160.   ———. *Top Secret Mission*. London: Evans, 1954. 208p.

Allen W. Dulles

2161.   "Allen W. Dulles." *Current Biography*, X (March 1949), 13–15.

2162.   Edwards, Robert, and Kenneth Dunne. *A Study of a Master Spy, Allen Dulles*. London: Housmans, 1961. 79p.

2163.   Franklin, Charles. "Allen Dulles." In: his *Great Spies*. London: Hart–Davis, 1967. pp. 252–255.

Mahmood K. Durrani

2164.   Durrani, Mahmood K. *The Sixth Column: The Heroic Personal Story of Lt. Colonel Mahmood K. Durrani, G.C.* London: Cassell, 1955. 367p.

Jean Dutourd

2165.   Dutourd, Jean. *The Taxis of the Marne*. Translated from the French. New York: Simon and Schuster, 1957. 244p.

Edmund G. Edlemann

2166.   Edlemann, Edmund G. *With My Little Eye*. London: Jarrolds, 1961. 240p.

Carl F. Eifter. *See* Thomas N. Moon

Johann Eppler

2167.   Mosley, Leonard. *The Cat and the Mice*. London: Barker, 1958. 160p.

Eric S. Erickson

2168.   Klein, Alexander. *The Counterfeit Traitor*. New York: Holt, 1958. 301p.

Jack Evans

2169.   Evans, Jack. *The Face of Death*. New York: Morrow, 1958. 220p.

Jack L. Fairweather

2170.   Bird, William R. *The Two Jacks: The Amazing Adventures of Major Jack M. Veness and Major Jack L. Fairweather.* Toronto and New York: Ryerson Press, 1954. 209p.

Roy Farran

2171.   Farran, Roy. *Winged Dagger: Adventures on Special Service.* London: Collins, 1948. 384p.

Jan Felix

2172.   Duke, Madelein. *No Passport: The Story of Jan Felix.* London: Evans, 1957. 222p.

Xan Fielding

2173.   Fielding, Xan. *Hide-and-Seek: The Story of a Wartime Agent.* London: Secker and Warburg, 1954. 255p.

2174.   _____ . *Stronghold: An Account of Four Seasons in the White Mountains of Crete.* London: Secker and Warburg, 1953. 317p.

Alexander Foote

2175.   Foote, Alexander. *Handbook for Spies.* London: Museum Press, 1949. 223p.

2176.   "The Inconspicuous Man." *Time,* LIII (May 30, 1949), 90.

John Ford

2177.   Sinclair,, Andrew. *John Ford: A Biography.* New York: Dial Press, 1979. 288p.

John Fox

2178.   Fox, John. *Afghan Adventure, as Told to Roland Goodchild.* London: Hale, 1958. 190p.

Norman Franks

2179.   Franks, Norman. *Double Mission.* London: Kimber, 1977. 192p.

Henri Frenay

2180.   Frenay, Henri. *The Night Will End.* Translated from the French. New York: McGraw–Hill, 1975. 469p.

William F. Friedman

2181. Clark, Ronald W. *The Man Who Broke Purple: The Life of Colonel William F. Friedman, Who Deciphered the Japanese Code in World War II.* Boston: Little, Brown, 1977. 271p.

Ricardo C. Galang

2182. Galang, Ricardo C. *Secret Mission to the Phillippines.* Manila, P. I.: University Publishing Co., 1948. 234p.

J. P. Gallagher

2183. Gallagher, J. P. *Scarlet Pimpernel of the Vatican.* New York: Coward–McCann, 1968. 184p.

Philippe Ganier–Raymond

2184. Ganier–Raymond, Philippe. *The Tangled Web.* Translated from the French. New York: Pantheon, 1968. 203p.

Roman Garby–Czerniawski

2185. Garby–Czerniawski, Roman. *The Big Network.* London: Ronald, 1961. 248p.

Mark Gayn

2186. Gayn, Mark. *American Agent* [in China]. New York: Holt, 1947. 220p.

Stefan Gazel

2187. Gazel, Stefan. *To Live and Kill.* Translated from the Polish. London: Jarrolds, 1958. 215p.

Reinhard Gehlen

2188. Gehlen, Reinhard. *The Service: Memoirs.* Translated from the German. Cleveland, Ohio: World Publishing Co., 1972. 386p.

2189. Hohne, Heinz, and Herman Zolling. *The General Was a Spy: The Truth about General Gehlen and His Spy Ring.* Translated from the German. New York: Coward–McCann, 1972. 347p.

2190. Spiro, Edward. *Gehlen, Spy of the Century.* By E. H. Cookridge, pseud. New York: Random House, 1972. 402p.

Kurt Gerstein

2191. Joffroy, Pierre. *A Spy for God: The Ordeal of Kurt Gerstein.* London: Collins, 1971. 319p.

Henri Guisan

2192. Kimich, Jon. *Spying For Peace: General Guisan and Swiss Neutrality.* New York: Roy, 1962. 186p.

Andrew Gilchrist

2193. Gilchrist, Andrew. *Bangkok Top Secret: Being the Experiences of a British Officer in the Siam Country Section of Force 136.* London: Hutchinson, 1970. 231p.

Erich Gimpel

2194. Gimpel, Erich, with Will Berthold. *Spy for Germany.* Translated from the German. London: Hale, 1957. 238p.

Maria Ginter

2195. Ginter, Maria. *Life in Both Hands.* Translated from the Polish. London: Hodder and Stoughton, 1964. 254p.

H. J. Giskes

2196. Giskes, H. J. *London Calling North Pole.* London: Kimber, 1953. 208p.

2197. _____ . "'Operation Nordpol.'" *Reader's Digest,* LXIII (August 1953), 161–168.

2198. _____ . "Operation North Pole." In: *Reader's Digest,* Editors of. *Secrets and Spies: Behind-the-Scenes Stories of World War II.* Pleasantville, N.Y.: Reader's Digest Association, 1964. pp. 207-216.

Joseph Goebbels

2199. Ebermayer, Erich, and Hans O. Meissner. *Evil Genius.* Translated from the German. London: Wingate, 1954. 207p.

2200. Goebbels, Joseph. *Final Entries, 1945: The Diaries of Joseph Goebbels.* Edited, introduced, and annotated by Hugh Trevor–Roper. Translated from the German. New York: Putnam, 1978. 368p.

2201. _____ . *The Goebbels Diaries, 1942–1943.* Edited by L. P. Lochner. Translated from the German. Garden City, N. Y.: Doubleday, 1948. 496p.

2202. Heiber, Helmut. *Goebbels.* Translated from the German. New York: Hawthorn Books, 1972. 387p.

2203. Manvell, Roger, and Heinrich Fraenkel. *Doctor Goebbels: His Life and Death.* London: Heinemann, 1960. 320p.

2204. Riess, Curt. *Joseph Goebbels: A Biography.* London: Hollis and Carter, 1949. 460p.

2205. Semmler, Rudolf. *Goebbels: The Man Next to Hitler.* Translated from the German. London: Westhouse, 1947. 234p.

2206. Wykes, Alan. *Goebbels.* Ballantine's Illustrated History of the Violent Century: War Leader Book. New York: Ballantine Books, 1973. 160p.

Carl Goerdeler

2207. Ritter, Gerhard. "A German Professor in the Third Reich: The Character of the Anti-Nazi Opposition Maintained by National-minded Groups." Translated from the German. *Review of Politics,* VIII (April 1946), 242–254.

2208. _____ . *The German Resistance: Carl Goerdeler's Struggle against Tyranny.* Translated from the German. New York: Praeger, 1959. 330p.

Hermann Goertz

2209. O'Callaghan, Sean. *The Jackboot in Ireland.* New York: Roy, 1958. 157p.

John Goldsmith

2210. Goldsmith, John. *Accidental Agent.* New York: Scribner's, 1971. 192p.

Igor Gouzenko

2211. Gouzenko, Igor. *This Was My Choice.* 2d ed. Montreal, Canada: Palm Publishers Press Service, 1968. 238p.

Anatoli Granovsky

2212. Granovsky, Anatoli. *All Pity Choked: The Memoirs of a Soviet Secret Agent.* Translated from the Russian. London: Kimber, 1955. 248p.

William Grell

2213. Grell, William. "A Marine with O.S.S." *Marine Corps Gazette,* XXIX (December 1945), 14–18.

F. C. Griffiths

2214. Griffiths, F. C. "In the Marquis." *Blackwood's Magazine,* CCLVII (June 1945), 361–375.

Joey Guerrero

2215. Johnson, Thomas M. "Joey's Quiet War." In: *Reader's Digest,* Editors of. *Secrets and Spies: Behind-the-Scenes Stories of World War II.* Pleasantville, N. Y.: Reader's Digest Association, 1964. pp. 180–186.

Pierre Guillain de Bénouville

2216. Guillain de Bénouville, Pierre. *The Unknown Warriors: A Personal Account of the French Resistance.* Translated from the French. New York: Simon and Schuster, 1949. 372p.

John W. Hackett

2217. Hackett, John W. *I Was a Stranger.* Boston: Houghton, Mifflin, 1978. 219p.

James E. Haggerty

2218. Haggerty, James E. *Guerrilla Padre of Mindanao.* Detroit, Mich.: Cellar Book Shop, 1964. 257p.

Roger Hall

2219. Hall, Roger. *You're Stepping on My Cloak and Dagger.* New York: W. W. Norton, 1957. 219p.

William Hall

2220. James, William. *The Code-breaker of Room 40: The Story of Sir William Hall, Genius of British Counterintelligence.* London: Methuen, 1955. 207p.

Donald Hamilton–Hall

2221. Hamilton–Hall, Donald. *S.O.E. Assignment.* London: Kimber, 1973. 186p.

Thomas Harrisson

2222. Harrisson, Thomas. *World Within.* London: Cresset Press, 1959. 349p.

Hermann Haupt

2223. Martin, John. "The Making of a Nazi Saboteur: Hermann Haupt." *Harper's Magazine,* CXCV (April 1943), 532–540.

Eiliv O. Hauge

2224. Hauge, Eiliv O. *Salt-water Thief.* Translated from the Norwegian. London: Duckworth, 1958. 159p.

Hans Hauser

2225.   Burt, S. "Secret Agent on Skis." *Harper's Magazine,* CCIV (February 1952), 84–92.

Leo Heaps

2226.   Heaps, Leo. *Escape from Arnhem: A Canadian among the Lost Paratroops.* Toronto, Canada: Macmillan, 1945. 159p.

2227.   _____. *The Grey Goose of Arnhem.* Toronto, Canada: Paperjacks, 1977. 239p.

Cyril V. Hearn

2228.   Hearn, Cyril V. *Desert Assignment.* London: Hale, 1963. 192p.

2229.   _____. *Foreign Assignment.* London: Hale, 1961. 191p.

Sybil Hepburn

2230.   Hepburn, Sybil. *Wingless Victory.* London: Ian Allan, 1969. 190p.

Richard Heslop

2231.   Heslop, Richard. *"Xavier": The Famous British Agent's Dramatic Account of His Work in the French Resistance.* London: Hart–Davis, 1970. 272p.

Reinhard Heydrich

2232.   Burgess, Alan. *Seven Men at Daybreak.* New York: Dutton, 1960. 231p.

2233.   Fay, Stephen B. "The Nazi Hangman's End." *Current History,* II (July 1942), 361–365.

2234.   "Former Gestapo Officer," pseud. *Heydrich the Murderer.* London: Quality, 1942. 62p.

2235.   Ivanov, Miroslav. *Target: Heydrich.* Translated from the French. New York: Macmillan, 1974. 292p.

2236.   Wiener, Jan G. *The Assassination of Heydrich.* New York: Grossman, 1969. 177p.

2237.   Wighton, Charles. *Heydrich: Hitler's Most Evil Henchman.* Philadelphia: Chilton, 1962. 288p.

2238.   Wykes, Alan. *Heydrich.* Ballantine's Illustrated History of the Violent Century: War Leader Book. New York: Ballantine Books, 1973. 160p.

Heinrich Himmler

2239. Axelsson, George. "Hitler's Hatchet Man: Heinrich Himmler." *New York Times Magazine,* (February 28, 1943), 12–13+.

2240. Combs, George. *Himmler: Nazi Spider–Man.* Philadelphia: McKay, 1942. 64p.

2241. Frischauer, Willi. *Himmler: The Evil Genius of the Third Reich.* Boston: Beacon Press, 1953. 269p.

Frank Hirt

2242. "G.I. Spy." *Newsweek,* XXVII (January 7, 1946), 24–25.

Michael Hollard

2243. Halacy, Don. "Michael Hollard." In: his *Master Spy.* New York: McGraw–Hill, 1968. pp. 113–123.

2244. Martelli, George. *The Man Who Saved London: The Story of Michael Hollard.* Garden City, N. Y.: Doubleday, 1961. 258p.

Stuart Hood

2245. Hood, Stuart. *Pebbles from My Skull.* New York: Dutton, 1963. 153p.

J. Edgar Hoover

2246. Demaris, Ovid. *The Director: An Oral Biography of J. Edgar Hoover.* New York: Harper & Row, 1975. 405p.

2247. De Toledano, Ralph. *J. Edgar Hoover: The Man and His Times.* New Rochelle, N. Y.: Arlington House, 1973. 384p.

Wilhelm Höttl

2248. Bloom, Murray T. "The World's Greatest Counterfeiters." *Harper's Magazine,* CCXV (July 1957), 47–53.

2249. Höttl, Wilhelm. *Hitler's Paper Weapon.* Translated from the German. London: Hart–Davis, 1955. 187p.

2250. _____ . *The Secret Front: The Story of Nazi Political Espionage.* By Walter Hagen, pseud. Translated from the German. New York: Praeger, 1954. 327p.

2251. Pirie, Anthony. *"Operation Bernhard": The Greatest Forgery of All Time.* New York: Morrow, 1962. 303p.

Leslie Howard

2252. Colvan, Ian G. *Flight 777.* London: Evans, 1957. 212p.

Aldo Icardi

2253.   Icardi, Aldo. *Aldo Icardi: American Master Spy*. New York: University Books, 1956. 275p.

"Intrepid," pseud. *See* William Stevenson

Staszek Jackowski

2254.   Gruber, Ruth. "The Heroism of Staszek Jackowski." *Saturday Review of Literature*, L (April 15, 1967), 19–21+.

Meyrick E. C. James

2255.   James, Meyrick E. C. *I Was Monty's Double*. London and New York: Rider Press, 1954. 192p.

Jean Gilbert, pseud. *See* Leopold Trepper

"Jim," pseud. *See* Alexander Foote

Reginald V. Jones

2256.   Jones, Reginald V. "Scientific Intelligence." *Journal of the Royal United Service Institution*, XCII (1947), 352–369.

2257.   ———. ———. *Research*, IX (September 1956), 347–352.

2258.   ———. *The Wizard War: British Scientific Intelligence, 1939–1945*. New York: Coward–McCann, 1978. 556p.

George R. Jordan

2259.   Jordan, George R., with Richard Stokes. *From Major Jordan's Diaries*. New York: Harcourt, 1952. 284p.

William Joyce

2260.   Cole, John A. *Lord Haw–Haw and William Joyce: The Full Story*. New York: Farrar, Straus and Giroux, 1965. 316p.

2261.   Fairfield, Cicily I. *The Meaning of Treason*. By Rebecca West, pseud. New York: Viking Press, 1947. 307p.

2262.   Graves, Harold N., Jr. "Lord Haw Haw of Hamburg." *Public Opinion Quarterly*, IV (September 1940), 429–450.

2263.   Hall, J. W., ed. *The Trial of William Joyce, Lord Haw–Haw*. London: Hodge, 1946. 372p.

2264.   Roberts, C. E. B., ed. *The Trial of William Joyce*. London: Jarrolds, 1946. 191p.

Ernst Kaltenbrunner

2265. Kelly, Douglas M. "Ernst Kaltenbrunner." In: his *22 Cells in Nuremberg.* Philadelphia: Chilton, 1947. pp. 100–105.

Edita Katona

2266. Katona, Edita, and Patrick Macnaghton. *Code Name Marianne: An Autobiography.* London: Collins, 1977. 212p.

Peter K. Kemp

2267. Kemp, Peter K. *Alms for Oblivion.* London: Cassell, 1961. 188p.

2268. ———. *No Colours or Crest.* London: Cassell, 1958. 305p.

John Kennett

2269. Kennett, John. *Two Eggs on My Plate: Secret Service and Underground Movements in Norway.* Glasgow, Scotland: Blackie, 1972.

Tyler Kent

2270. Snow, John H. *The Case of Tyler Kent.* New York and Chicago: Domestic and Foreign Affairs and Citizens Press, 1946. 59p.

Alexander W. L. Kessell

2271. Kessell, Alexander W. L. *Surgeon at Arms.* By Daniel Paul, pseud. London: Heinemann, 1958. 227p.

Roger Keyes

2272. Aspinall–Oglander, Cecil. *Roger Keyes.* London: Hogarth Press, 1951. 478p.

2273. Daniell, Francis R. "Chief of the Commandos." *New York Times Magazine,* (May 3, 1942), 15+.

Noor Inayat Khan

2274. Fuller, Jean O. *Madeleine: The Story of Noor Inayat Khan.* London: Gollancz, 1952. 192p.

2275. Hoehling, Adolph A. "Noor Inayat Khan." In: his *Women Who Spied.* New York: Dodd, Mead, 1967. pp. 123–132.

Brede Klefos

2276. Klefos, Brede. *They Came in the Night: The Wartime Experiences of a Norwegian–American.* Greenlawn, N. Y.: Harian, 1959. 206p.

Alexander Klein

2277. Klein, Alexander. *The Counterfeit Traitor.* New York: Holt, 1958. 301p.

2278. Shearer, Lloyd. "Master Spy." *Parade Magazine,* (August 21, 1960), 6–8.

Ruth Kuhn

2279. Hendrickson, Robert. "The Eight-eyed Spy: The Family That Gave You Pearl Harbor." In: David Wallechinsky and Irving Wallace, eds. *The People's Almanac.* Garden City, N. Y.: Doubleday, 1975. pp. 650–654.

Ilya Kuzin

2280. Kuzin, Ilya. *Notes of a Guerrilla Fighter, with a Biographical Sketch.* Translated from the Russian. Moscow: Foreign Languages Publishing House, 1942. 63p.

Erwin Lahousen

2281. Wighton, Charles, and Günter Peis. *Hitler's Spies and Saboteurs: Based on the German Secret Service War Diary of General Lahousen.* New York: Holt, 1958. 285p.

Roger Landes. *See* Francis Cammaerts

Hermann Lang

2282. Franklin, Charles. "Hermann Lang." In: his *Great Spies.* New York: Hart–Davis, 1967. pp. 122–123.

2283. Wighton, Charles. "Hermann Lang." In: his *World's Greatest Spies.* New York: Taplinger, 1965. pp. 112–122.

George Langelaan

2284. Langelaan, George. *The Masks of War.* Garden City, N. Y.: Doubleday, 1959. 284p.

William L. Langer

2285. Langer, William L. *In and Out of the Ivory Tower.* New York: Neale Watson Academic Publications, 1977. 268p.

James M. Langley

2286. Langley, James M. *Fight Another Day.* London: Collins, 1974. 254p.

"Shetlands" Larsen

2287. Saelen, Frithjof. *None But the Brave: The Story of "Shetlands" Larsen.* Translated from the Norwegian. London: Souvenir Press, 1955. 232p.

2288. Wilkinson, J. Burke. "As Brave as Any Man Can Be." *U. S. Naval Institute Proceedings,* LXXVI (1950), 838–845.

Hubertus Lauwers

2289. *Army Times,* Editors of. "Nordpol." In: J. Burke Wilkinson, ed. *Cry Spy!* New York: Bradbury Press, 1969. pp. 130–139.

Mary Lindell

2290. Wynne, Barry. *No Drums . . . No Trumpets: The Story of Mary Lindell.* London: Barker, 1961. 278p.

Judith Hare, Countess of Listowel

2291. Listowel, Judith Hare, Countess of. *Crusader in the Secret War.* London: Johnson, 1952. 287p.

Robert H. B. Lockhart

2292. Lockhart, Robert H. B. *Comes the Reckoning.* London: Putnam, 1947. 384p.

John G. Lomax

2293. Lomax, John G. *The Diplomatic Smuggler.* London: Barker, 1965. 288p.

Pin–fei Loo

2294. Loo, Pin–fei. "How We Learned to Kill Traitors." *Harper's Magazine,* CLXXXVII (May 1943), 565–572.

2295. _____. *It Is Dark Underground.* New York: Putnam, 1946. 200p.

Lydia Love

2296. Izbicki, John. *The Naked Heroine: The Story of Lydia Love.* London: Spearman, 1963. 189p.

"Lucy," pseud. *See* Rudolf Roessler

Elizabeth P. MacDonald

2297. MacDonald, Elizabeth P. *Undercover Girl.* New York: Macmillan, 1947. 305p.

Ronald C. H. McKie

2298. McKie, Ronald C. H. *Heroes.* New York: Ryerson Press, 1960. 285p.

Jock McLaren

2299. Richardson, Hal. *One-man War: The Jock McLaren Story.* Sydney and London: Angus and Robertson, 1957. 189p.

"Madeleine," pseud. *See* Noor Inayat Khan

Tony Mains

2300. Mains, Tony. *The Retreat from Burma.* London: Foulsham, 1973. 151p.

Kim Malthe–Bruun

2301. Malthe–Bruun, Kim. *Heroic Heart: The Diary and Letters of Kim Malthe–Bruun, 1941–1945.* Edited by Vibeko Malthe-Bruun. Translated from the Russian. New York: Random House, 1955. 177p.

Max Manus

2302. Manus, Max, with Dorothy Giles. *Nine Lives before Thirty.* Garden City, N. Y.: Doubleday, 1947. 328p.

"Marianne," pseud. *See* Edita Katona

Sidney F. Mashbir

2303. Mashbir, Sidney F. *I Was an American Spy.* New York: Vantage Press, 1953. 374p.

"Masuy," pseud. *See* Georges Delfanne

Franco Maugeri

2304. Maugeri, Franco. *From the Ashes of Disgrace.* Edited by Victor Resen. Translated from the Italian. New York: Reyal and Hitchcock, 1948. 376p.

Gerald Mayer

2305. Morgan, Edward P. "The Spy the Nazis Missed." *True Magazine,* XXXI (July 1950), *passim.*

Asja Mercer

2306. Mercer, Asja, with Robert Jackson. *One Woman's War.* London: Wingate, 1958. 220p.

Milton E. Miles

2307. Stratton, Roy. "Navy Guerrilla." *U. S. Naval Institute Proceedings,* LXXXIX (July 1963), 83–87.

George R. Millar

2308. Millar, George R. *Waiting in the Night: A Story of the Marquis, Told by One of Its Leaders.* Garden City, N. Y.: Doubleday, 1946. 377p.

Merlin Minshall

2309. Minshall, Merlin. *Guilt-edged.* London: Bachman and Turner, 1975. 319p.

Thomas N. Moon

2310. Moon, Thomas N., and Carl F. Eifter. *The Deadliest Colonel.* New York: Vantage Press, 1975. 342p.

John H. Moore

2311. Moore, John H. "Getting Fritz to Talk." *Virginia Quarterly Review,* LIV (Spring 1978), 263–280.

Frantisek Moravec

2312. Jefferson, M. "Czechmating the Nazis." *Newsweek,* LXXXV (June 2, 1975), 70+.

2313. Moravec, Frantisek. *Master of Spies: The Memoirs of General Frantisek Moravec.* Garden City, N. Y.: Doubleday, 1975. 240p.

William J. Morgan

2314. Morgan, William J. *The O.S.S. and I.* New York: W. W. Norton, 1957. 281p.

Mary Murray

2315. Murray, Mary. *Hunted: A Coastwatcher's Story.* San Francisco, Calif.: Tri–Ocean Books, 1967. 240p.

Flemming B. Muus

2316. Muus, Flemming B. *The Spark and the Flame.* Translated from the Danish. London: Museum Press, 1956. 172p.

Alfred Naujochs

2317. Blackstock, Paul W. "Covert Operations and Policy Sabotage." In: his *The Strategy of Subversion: Manipulating the Politics of Other Nations.* Chicago: Quadrangle Books, 1964. pp. 208–213.

2318.   Peis, Günther. *The Man Who Started the War.* Translated from the German. London: Odham's Press, 1960. 233p.

Peter Neumann

2319.   Neumann, Peter. *The Black March: The Personal Story of an SS Man.* Translated from the French. New York: Sloane, 1959. 278p.

Bernard Newman

2320.   Newman, Bernard. *Spy and Counter-spy: Bernard Newman's Story of the British Secret Service.* Edited by I. O. Evans. London: Hale, 1970. 255p.

Alfred and Henry Newton

2321.   Thomas, John. *No Banners: The Story of Alfred and Henry Newton.* London: W. H. Allen, 1955. 346p.

Elizabeth Nichols

2322.   Nichols, Elizabeth. *Death Be Not Proud.* London: White Lion, 1972. 294p.

Leslie A. Nicholson

2323.   Nicholson, Leslie A. *British Agent.* London: Kimber, 1966. 224p.

U. Nu

2324.   Nu, U. *Burma under the Japanese.* Translated from the Burmese. London: Macmillan, 1954. 132p.

Pat O'Leary

2325.   Bromme, Vincent. *The Way Back: The Story of Lt. Commander Pat O'Leary, G.C., D.S.O., R.N.* 2d ed. New York: W. W. Norton, 1958. 249p.

Oluf R. Olsen

2326.   Olsen, Oluf R. *Two Eggs on My Plate.* Translated from the Norwegian. London: W. H. Allen, 1952. 301p.

Arthur Owens

2327.   Franklin, Charles. "Arthur Owens." In: his *Great Spies.* London: Hart–Davis, 1967. pp. 116–122.

2328.   Wighton, Charles. "Arthur Owens." In: his *World's Greatest Spies.* New York: Taplinger, 1965. pp. 123–134.

Saul K. Padover

2329. Padover, Saul K. *Experiment in Germany: The Story of an American Intelligence Officer.* New York: Duell, Sloane and Pearce, 1946. 408p.

Yay Panlilio

2330. Panlilio, Yay. *The Crucible: An Autobiography.* New York: Macmillan, 1950. 348p.

Geoffrey Parker

2331. Parker, Geoffrey. *The Black Scalpel.* London: Kimber, 1968. 157p.

Charles Parsons

2332. Ingham, Travis. *Rendezvous by Submarine: The Story of Charles Parsons and the Guerrilla Soldiers in the Phillippines.* Garden City, N. Y.: Doubleday, 1945. 255p.

2334. Wise, William. *Secret Mission to the Philippines.* New York: Dutton, 1969. 160p.

Daniel Paul, pseud. *See* Alexander W. L. Kessell

Jocelyn Pereira

2335. Pereira, Jocelyn. *A Distant Drum: War Memories of the Intelligence Officer of the 5th Battalion, Coldstream Guards, 1944–1945.* Aldershot, Eng.: Gale and Polden, 1948. 213p.

Giovanni Pesce

2336. Pesce, Giovanni. *And No Quarter: An Italian Partisan in World War II.* Translated from the Italian. Athens: Ohio University Press, 1972. 292p.

Harold A. R. "Kim" Philby

2337. Page, Bruce, David Leitch, and Phillip Knightley. *The Philby Conspiracy.* Garden City, N. Y.: Doubleday, 1968. 300p.

2338. Philby, Harold A. R. *My Silent War.* New York: Grove Press, 1968. 164p.

2339. Seale, Patrick, and Maureen McConville. *Philby: The Long Road to Moscow.* New York: Simon and Schuster, 1973. 282p.

2340. Trevor–Roper, Hugh R. *The Philby Affair: Espionage, Treason, and Secret Services.* London: Kimber, 1968. 126p.

Claire Phillips

2341. Phillips, Claire. "I Was an American Spy." *American Mercury,* LX (May 1945), 592–598.

2342. _____ , and Myron B. Goldsmith. *Manila Espionage.* Portland, Ore.: Binfolds and Mort, 1947. 226p.

William Phillips

2343. Phillips, William. *Venture in Diplomacy.* Boston, Beacon Press, 1952. 477p.

Oreste Pinto

2344. "Oreste Pinto." *Newsweek,* LVIII (October 2, 1961), 50.

2345. _____ . *Time,* LXXVIII (September 29, 1961), 86.

2346. Pinto, Oreste. *Friend or Foe?* New York: Putnam, 1953. 245p.

2347. _____ . *Spycatcher.* London: Laurie, 1952. 175p.

2348. _____ . *Spycatcher 2.* London: Landsborough, 1960. 160p.

2349. _____ . *Spycatcher 3.* London: Four Square, 1960. 160p.

2350. _____ . *The Spycatcher Omnibus: The Spy and Counter-spy Adventures of Lt. Colonel Oreste Pinto.* London: Hodder and Stoughton, 1962. 479p.

Eric Piquet–Wicks

2351. Piquet–Wicks, Eric. *Four in the Shadow: A True Story of Espionage in Occupied France.* London: Jarrolds, 1957. 206p.

Roxane Pitt

2352. Pitt, Roxane. *Courage of Fear.* New York: Duell, Sloan and Pearce, 1957. 242p.

2353. _____ . *Operation Double-life: An Autobiography.* London: Bachman and Turner, 1976. 183p.

Dusko Popov

2354. Popov, Dusko. "An Interview." Edited by H. R. Lottman. *Publisher's Weekly,* CCV (April 22, 1974), 12–13.

2355. _____ . _____ . In: *Publisher's Weekly,* Editors of. *The Author Speaks: Selected Publisher's Weekly Interviews, 1967–1976.* New York: R. R. Bowker, 1977. pp. 323–325.

2356. _____ . *Spy/Counterspy: An Autobiography.* New York: Grosset and Dunlap, 1974. 339p.

David G. Prosser

2357. Prosser, David G. *Journey Underground.* New York: Dutton, 1945. 347p.

George Psychoudakis

2358. Psychoudakis, George. *Cretan Runner: His Story of the German Occupation.* Translated from the Cretan. New York: Transatlantic Books, 1955. 242p.

Wolfgang Putlitz

2359. Putlitz, Wolfgang. *The Putlitz Dossier.* Translated from the German. London: Wingate, 1957. 252p.

Harry Ree. *See* Francis Cammaerts

Francis Reid

2360. Reid, Francis. *I Was in Noah's Ark.* London: Chambers, 1957. 143p.

"Remy," pseud. *See* Gilbert Renault–Roulier

Gilbert Renault–Roulier

2361. Renault–Roulier, Gilbert. *Courage and Fear.* Vol. 2 of *Memoirs of a Secret Agent of Free France.* By "Remy," pseud. Translated from the French. London: Barker, 1950. 320p.

2362. _____ . *The Silent Company, June 1940–June 1942.* Vol. 1 of *Memoirs of a Secret Agent of Free France.* By "Remy," pseud. Translated from the French. New York: McGraw–Hill, 1948. 406p.

The remaining four volumes in this set are untranslated and consist of: *Comment meurt un réseau* (Monte Carlo: Raoul Solar, 1947), *Une affaire de trahison* (Monte Carlo: Raoul Solar, 1947), *Les mains jointes* (Monte Carlo: Raoul Solar, 1948), *Mais le temple est bâti* (Monte Carlo: Raoul Solar, 1950).

Alexander M. Rendel

2363. Rendel, Alexander M. *Appointment in Crete: The Story of a British Agent.* London: Wingate, 1953. 240p.

Lloyd Rhys

2364. Rhys, Lloyd. *Jungle Pimpernell: The Story of a District Officer in Central Netherlands New Guinea.* London: Hodder and Stoughton, 1947. 239p.

Iliff David Richardson

2365.   Wolfert, Ira. *American Guerrilla in the Philippines.* New York: Simon and Schuster, 1945. 301p.

"Robin," pseud. *See* Charles Wighton

Georgette Robinson

2366.   Robinson, Georgette. *Green Avalanche: The Story of an English Girl's Adventures as a Combatant in World War II.* Translated from the French. London: Pythagorean Publications, 1960. 225p.

Devereaux Rochester

2367.   Rochester, Devereaux. *New Moon to France.* New York: Harper & Row, 1977. 256p.

Rudolf Roessler

2368.   Accoce, Pierre, and Pierre Quet. *A Man Called Lucy, 1939–1945.* Translated from the French. New York: Coward–McCann, 1967. 250p.

2369.   _____ . _____ . In: Burke Wilkinson, ed. *Cry Spy!* New York: Bradbury Press, 1969. pp. 88–97.

2370.   Franklin, Charles. "Rudolf Roessler." In: his *Great Spies.* London: Hart–Davis, 1967. pp. 145–150.

2371.   Wighton, Charles. "Rudolf Roessler." In: his *World's Greatest Spies.* New York: Taplinger, 1965. pp. 240–257.

2372.   "Would You Believe?" *Time,* LXXXIX (May 5, 1967), 102+.

Lindsay Rogers

2373.   Rogers, Lindsay. *Guerrilla Surgeon.* London: Collins, 1957. 254p.

Alaine Romans

2374.   Wynne, Barry. *The Empty Coffin: The Story of Alaine Romans.* London: Souvenir Press, 1954. 196p.

A. W. Sansom

2375.   Sansom, A. W. *I Spied Spies.* London: Harrap, 1965. 271p.

George Sava

2376.   Sava, George. *No Crown of Laurels.* By George Borodin, pseud. London: Laurie, 1950. 224p.

Hanns Scharff

2377. Frey, Royal D. "The Luftwaffe's Master Interrogator." *Air Force Magazine,* LIX (June 1976), 68–71.

2378. _____. "'Poet' Laureate of Stalag I" *Aerospace Historian,* XVI (Spring 1966), 15+.

2379. Toliver, Raymond F. *The Interrogator: The Story of Hanns J. Scharff, the Luftwaffe's Master Interrogator.* Fallbrook, Calif.: Aero Publishers, 1978.

Walter Schellenburg

2380. Schellenburg, Walter. *The Labyrinth: Memoirs.* Translated from the German. New York: Harper, 1956. 423p.

Hans Schmidt

2381. Franklin, Charles. "Hans Schmidt." In: his *Great Spies.* London: Hart–Davis, 1967. pp. 150–153.

Harro Schulze–Boysen

2382. Singer, Kurt D. "Harro 'Coro' Schulze–Boysen." In: his *Gentlemen Spies.* London: W. H. Allen, 1952. pp. 59–81.

Bernhard Schulze–Holthus

2383. Schulze–Holthus, Bernhard. *Daybreak in Iran: A Story of the German Intelligence Service.* Translated from the German. New York: De Graff, 1956. 319p.

A. P. Scotland

2384. Scotland, A.P. *The London Cage.* London: Evans, 1957. 203p.

Lionel Scott

2385. Scott, Lionel. *I Dropped In.* London: Barrie and Rochliff, 1959. 224p.

Lily Sergueiew

2386. Sergueiew, Lily. *Secret Service Rendered.* London: Kimber, 1918. 223p.

Ronald Seth

2387. Seth, Ronald. *A Spy Has No Friends.* London: Deutsch, 1952. 206p.

Wladyslaw Sikorski

2388. Ainsztein, Reuben. "The Death of General Sikorski." *World Today*, XXV (February 1969), 47–52.

2389. "The Death of General Sikorski." *After the Battle*, no. 20 (1978), 1–18.

Percy Sillitoe

2390. Sillitoe, Percy. *Cloak without Dagger*. London: Cassell, 1955. 206p.

Gurchan Singh

2391. Singh, Gurchan. *Singa, the Lion of Malaya: Being the Memoirs of Gurchan Singh*. Edited by Hugh Barnes. London: Quality Press, 1949. 255p.

Otto Skorzeny

2392. Foley, Charles. *Commando Extraordinary*. New York: Putnam, 1955. 241p.

2393. Hibbert, Christopher. "The Rescue of Mussolini." In: Bernard Fitzsimons, ed. *Warplanes and Air Battles of World War II*. New York: Beekman House, 1973. pp. 97–101.

2394. Johnson, Thomas M. "The Most Dangerous Man in Europe." In: *Reader's Digest*, Editors of. *Secrets and Spies: Behind-the-Scenes Stories of World War II*. Pleasantville, N. Y.: Reader's Digest Association, 1964. pp. 468–475.

2395. Skorzeny, Otto. "The Rescue of Mussolini." Unpublished paper, Foreign Military Studies Program, Historical Division, U. S. Army, Europe, 1954. 10p.

2396. _____. *Secret Missions: War Memoirs of the Most Dangerous Man in Europe*. Translated from the French. New York: Dutton, 1950. 256p.

2397. _____. *Skorzeny's Special Missions*. London: Hale, 1957. 221p.

2398. Whiting, Charles. *Skorzeny*. Ballantine's Illustrated History of the Violent Century: War Leader Book. New York: Ballantine Books, 1972. 160p.

Agnes Smedley

2399. Smedley, Agnes. "With the Chinese Guerrillas." *New Republic*, CVIII (April 12, 1943), 471–473.

Nicol Smith

2400. Smith, Nicol, and Thomas B. Clark. *Into Siam: Underground Kingdom.* Indianapolis: Bobbs–Merrill, 1946. 315p.

Richard Sorge

2401. Deakin, Frederick W. *The Case of Richard Sorge.* New York: Harper & Row, 1966. 373p.

2402. De Toledano, Ralph. *Spies, Dupes, and Diplomats.* New Rochelle, N. Y.: Arlington House, 1967. 258p.

2403. Franklin, Charles. "Richard Sorge." In: his *Great Spies.* London: Hart–Davis, 1967. pp. 520–525.

2404. Freed, L. I. "Russia's Master Spy." *Coronet,* XXXI (February 1952), 98–102.

2405. Halacy, Dan. "Richard Sorge." In: his *Master Spy.* New York: McGraw–Hill, 1968. pp. 177–189.

2406. Ind, Allison W. "Sorge—Synonym for Cunning." In: Burke Wilkinson, ed. *Cry Spy!* New York: Bradbury Press, 1969. pp. 77–87.

2407. Johnson, Chalmers. "Again, the Sorge Case." *New York Times Magazine,* (October 11, 1964), 89–90+.

2408. _____. *An Instance of Treason: Ozaki Hotsumi and the Sorge Spy Ring.* Stanford, Calif.: Stanford University Press, 1964. 278p.

2409. Kirst, Hans H. *The Last Card.* Translated from the German. New York: Pyramid Publications, 1967. 254p.

2410. Lamott, Kenneth. "The Career of Richard Sorge." *Nation,* CCII (June 6, 1966), 687–688.

2411. Le Carré, John. "The Spy to End Spies: On Richard Sorge." *Encounter,* XXVII (November 1966), 88–89.

2412. Meissner, Hans O. *The Man with Three Faces.* Translated from the German. New York: Rinehart, 1956. 243p.

2413. Prange, Gordon W. "Master Spy." *Reader's Digest,* XC (January 1967), 209–212+.

2414. Singer, Kurt D. "Richard Sorge." In: his *Gentlemen Spies.* London: W. H. Allen, 1952. pp. 213–224.

2415. Sorge, Richard. *Sorge's Own Story.* Translated from the Russian. Tokyo, Japan: Military Intelligence Section, General Headquarters, U. S. Far East Command, 1945. 35p.

2416. "The Sorge Story." *Newsweek*, XXXVIII (August 20, 1951), 22–23.

2417. United States. Congress. House, Committee on Un-American Activities. *Hearings on American Aspects of the Richard Sorge Spy Case, Based on Testimony of Mitsusada Yoshikawa and Major General Charles A. Willoughby.* 82d Cong., 1st sess. Washington, D. C.: U. S. Government Printing Office, 1951. 122p.

2418. _____. Department of Defense. "The Sorge Spy Ring: A Case Study in International Espionage in the Far East." *Congressional Record*, XCIV (February 10, 1949), A705–A723.

2419. Wighton, Charles. "Richard Sorge." In: his *World's Greatest Spies.* New York: Taplinger, 1965. pp. 174–209.

2420. Willoughby, Charles A. *Shanghai Conspiracy: The Sorge Spy Ring—Moscow, Shanghai, Tokyo, San Francisco.* New York: Dutton, 1952. 315p.

Louis R. Svencer

2421. Spencer, Louis R. *Guerrilla Wife.* New York: Crowell, 1945. 209p.

J. M. Stagg

2422. Stagg, J. M. *Forecast for Overlord.* New York: W. W. Norton, 1972. 128p.

John Starr

2423. Fuller, Jean O. *No. 13, Bob.* Boston: Little, Brown, 1955. 240p.

William Stevenson

2424. Hyde, H. Montgomery. *Room 3603: The Story of the British Intelligence Center in New York during World War II.* New York: Farrar, Straus, 1963. 257p.

2425. Lowenthal, Mark M. "'Intrepid' and the History of World War II." *Military Affairs*, XLI (April 1977), 88–90.

2426. Stevenson, William. *A Man Called Intrepid: The Secret War.* New York: Harcourt, Brace, Jovanovich, 1976. 486p.

James Stewart–Gordon

2427. Stewart–Gordon, James. "My Chinese Army." *Reader's Digest*, CXIII (October 1978), 247–248+.

Colin Strang, pseud. *See* Peter Baker

Kenneth W. D. Strong

2428.   Strong, Kenneth W. D. *Intelligence at the Top: The Recollections of an Intelligence Officer.* Garden City, N. Y.: Doubleday, 1969. 366p.

Robert Storey

2429.   Storey, Robert. *The Final Judgment.* San Antonio, Tex.: Naylor, 1968. 208p.

Surumato Susio

2430.   Nigra, Le Roy. "Little Man: Surumato Susio in the Japanese Intelligence Service." *Infantry Journal,* LIX (July 1946), 14–17.

Bickham Sweet–Escott

2431.   Sweet–Escott, Bickham. *Baker Street Irregular.* London: Methuen, 1965. 278p.

Violette Szabo

2432.   Hoehling, Adolph A. "Violette Szabo." In: his *Women Who Spied.* New York: Dodd, Mead, 1967. pp. 117–123.

Chanah Szenes

2433.   Levin, Meyer. "Of Chanah Szenes and Other Secret Agents." *Menorah Journal,* XXXIV (April 1946), 122–132.

Dorothy Tartière

2434.   Tartière, Dorothy, and Morris R. Werner. *The House Near Paris: An American Woman's Story of Traffic in Patriots.* New York: Simon and Schuster, 1946. 326p.

Edmond Taylor

2435.   Taylor, Edmond. *Awakening from History.* Boston: Gambit, 1969. 522p.

Thomas D. G. Teare

2436.   Teare, Thomas D. G. *Evader.* London: Hodder and Stoughton, 1954. 256p.

Elliott A. Thorpe

2437.   Thorpe, Elliott A. *East Wind Rain: A Chief of Counterintelligence Remembers Peace and War in the Pacific, 1939–1949.* Boston: Gambit, 1969. 307p.

Peter Tompkins

2438. Tompkins, Peter. *Italy Betrayed.* New York: Simon and Schuster, 1966. 352p.

2439. _____. *A Spy in Rome.* New York: Simon and Shuster, 1962. 347p.

John Toyne

2440. Toyne, John. *Win Time for Us.* Toronto: Longman's Canada, 1962. 241p.

Leopold Trepper

2441. Trepper, Leopold. *The Great Game: Memoirs of the Spy Hitler Couldn't Silence.* Translated from the French. New York: McGraw–Hill, 1977. 442p.

"Trycycle," pseud. *See* Dusko Popov

George R. Tweed

2442. Clark, Thomas B. *Robinson Crusoe, U.S.N.: The Adventures of George R. Tweed on Jap–held Guam.* New York: Whittlesey House, McGraw–Hill, 1945. 275p.

Serge Vaculik

2443. Vaculik, Serge. *Air Commando.* Translated from the French. London: Jarrolds, 1954. 303p.

Helene Vagliano

2444. Townroe, B. S. "Heroine of France: Helene Vagliano." *Blackwood's Magazine,* CCLVIII (October 1945), 281–284.

Theo Van Duren

2445. Van Duren, Theo. *Orange Above.* Translated from the Dutch. London: Staples Press, 1956. 221p.

Albert Van Loop

2446. Hoover, J. Edgar. "The Spy Who Double-crossed Hitler: An Inside Story of the Normandy Invasion." *American Magazine,* CXLI (May 1946), 23+.

Jack M. Veness. *See* Jack L. Fairweather

Andrey Vlasov

2447. Burton, Robert B. "The Vlasov Movement of World War II: An Appraisal." Unpublished Ph.D. dissertation, American University, 1963.

2448. Lyons, Eugene. "General Vlasov's Mystery Army." *American Mercury*, LXVI (February 1948), 183–191.

2449. Thorwald, Jürgen. *The Illusion: Soviet Soldiers in Hitler's Armies.* Translated from the German. New York: Harcourt, Brace, 1975. 342p.

Russell W. Volckmann

2450. Volckmann, Russell W. *We Remained: Three Years behind the Enemy Lines in the Philippines.* New York: W. W. Norton, 1954. 244p.

Ulrich Von Hassell

2451. Von Hassell, Ulrich. *The Von Hassell Diaries, 1938–1944: The Story of Forces against Hitler inside Germany.* Translated from the German. Garden City, N. Y.: Doubleday, 1947. 400p.

Ursula Von Kardorff

2452. Von Kardorff, Ursula. *Diary of a Nightmare: Berlin, 1942–1945.* Translated from the German. New York: John Day, 1966. 256p.

Helmuth Von Moltke

2453. Balfour, Michael L. G., and Julian Frisby. *Helmuth Von Moltke: A Leader against Hitler.* New York: St. Martin's Press, 1973. 388p.

2454. Van Roon, Gerhard. *German Resistance to Hitler: Count Von Moltke and the Kreisau Circle.* Translated from the German. New York: Van Nostrand, Reinhold, 1971. 400p.

2455. [Von Moltke, Helmuth J.] "A German of the Resistance: The Last Letters of Count Helmuth J. Von Moltke." *Round Table*, XXXVI (June 1946), 213–231.

Fabian Von Schlabrendorff

2456. Von Schlabrendorff, Fabian. "Our Two Tries to Kill Hitler." *Saturday Evening Post*, CCXIX (July 20–27, 1946), 16–17+, 20+.

2457. _____ . *Revolt against Hitler: The Personal Account of Fabian Von Schlabrendorff.* Edited by George V. S. Gaevernitz. Translated from the German. London: Eyre and Spottiswoode, 1948. 176p.

2458. _____ . *The Secret War against Hitler.* Translated from the German. New York: Pitman, 1965. 438p.

Klaus Von Stauffenberg

2459.   Dow, James E. "Count Von Stauffenberg and the 20th of July." *Modern Age,* XX (Spring 1976), 206–213.

2460.   Gibson, T. A. "A Teutonic Knight." *Army Quarterly,* LXXXVII (October 1963), 77–86.

2461.   Kramarz, Joachim. *Stauffenberg, the Architect of the Famous July 20th Conspiracy to Assassinate Hitler.* Translated from the German. New York: Macmillan, 1967. 255p.

Nancy Wake

2462.   Braddon, Russell. *Nancy Wake: The Story of a Very Brave Woman.* London: Cassell, 1956. 273p.

David E. Walker

2463.   Walker, David E. *Adventure in Diamonds.* London: Evans, 1955. 186p.

2464.   ———. *Lunch with a Stranger.* New York: W. W. Norton, 1957. 223p.

Anne M. Walters

2465.   Walters, Anne M. *Moondrop to Gascony.* London: Macmillan, 1946. 296p.

Friedrich Wetzel

2466.   Wetzel, Friedrich. *The Called Me Alfred.* London: Ronald, 1959. 237p.

John Whitwell, pseud. *See* Leslie A. Nicholson

Charles Wighton

2467.   Wighton, Charles. *The Pin-stripe Saboteur: The Story of Robin, British Agent and French Resistance Leader.* London: Odham's Press, 1959. 256p.

James F. Wilde

2468.   Warren, Charles E. T., and James Benson. *The Broken Column: The Story of James Frederick Wilde's Adventures with the Italian Partisans.* London: Harrap, 1966. 207p.

J. Elder Wills

2469.   Bell, Leslie. *Sabotage: The Story of Lt. Colonel J. Elder Wills.* London: Laurie, 1957. 189p.

Frederick W. Winterbotham

2470. Winterbotham, Frederick W. *The Nazi Connection*. New York: Harper & Row, 1978. 222p.

2471. _____. *Secret and Personal*. London: Kimber, 1969. 192p.

Malcolm Wright

2472. Wright, Malcolm. *If I Die: Coastwatching and Guerrilla Warfare behind Japanese Lines*. New York: Ginn, 1966. 192p.

"Xavier," pseud. *See* Richard Heslop

F. F. E. Yeo–Thomas

2473. Marshall, Bruce. *The White Rabbit: From the Story Told to Him by F. F. E. Yeo–Thomas*. London: Evans, 1966. 248p.

Takeo Yoshikawa

2474. "Remember Pearl Harbor." *Time*, LXXVI (December 12, 1960), 3.

2475. Yoshikawa, Takeo. "Top Secret Assignment." *U. S. Naval Institute Proceedings*, LXXXVI (December 1960), 27–39.

Ellis M. Zacharias

2476. "Surrender Talk: Captain Zacharias, America's Voice." *Newsweek*, XXV (June 25, 1945), 94.

2477. Wilhelm, Maria. *The Man Who Watched the Setting Sun: The Story of Admiral Ellis M. Zacharias*. New York: K. S. Giniger Co., 1967. 238p.

2478. Zacharias, Ellis M. *Secret Missions: The Story of an Intelligence Officer*. New York: Putnam, 1946. 433p.

2479. _____. "Eighteen Words That Bagged Japan." *Saturday Evening Post*. CCXVIII (November 17, 1945), 17+.

"Zigzag," pseud. *See* Edward A. Chapman

Further References

Readers will find additional biographical and autobiographical material scattered throughout this guide.

Appendix I: Late Entries, to Fall 1979

Introduction

The following citations were uncovered too late for inclusion in the main body of the bibliography. To aid you in their use, they are divided as to the type of material involved: books, articles (including articles in anthologies or collections), and documents, papers, or reports.

Books

2480.   Achin, Milos K. *The First Guerrillas of Europe: The True Stories of General Mihailovic's Warriors.* New York: Vantage Press, 1963. 181p. (VII:B:3:e)

2481.   Angelbert, Jean-Michel. *The Occult and the Third Reich.* Translated from the French. New York: Macmillan, 1974. 306p. (III:C:2)

2482.   Balfour, Michael. *Propaganda in War, 1939–1945: Organizations, Policies, and Publics in Britain and Germany.* London: Routledge, 1979. (II)

2483.   Barker, Ralph. *Blockade Busters.* New York: Norton, 1977. 224p. (VII:B:2:d)

2484.   Bramsted, Ernest F. *Dictatorship and Political Police: The Technique of* [Gestapo] *Fear.* London and New York: Oxford University Press, 1945. 275p. (III:C:2)

2485.   Cooksley, Peter G. *Flying Bomb.* New York: Scribner's, 1979. (V:A:4)

2486.   Couvaras, Costa. *Photo Album of the Greek Resistance.* San Francisco: Wire Press, 1978. 138p. (VII:B:3:d)

2487.   Dunlop, Richard. *Behind Japanese Lines: With the O.S.S in Burma.* Chicago: Rand McNally, 1979. 480p. (VII:C:3:b)

2488.   Flick, Wilhelm F. *War Secrets* [German Cryptology] *in the Ether.* 2 vols. Laguna Hills, CA.: Aegean Park Press, 1979. (III:B:1)

2489.   Hanswer, Richard. *A Noble Treason: The Revolt of the Munich Students against Hitler.* New York: Putnam, 1979. (VII:B:2:e)

2490.   Hehn, Paul N. *The German Struggle against the Yugoslav Guerrillas in World War II: German Counterinsurgency in Yugoslavia, 1941–1943.* East European Monographs, no. 57. New York: Columbia University Press, 1979. 160p. (VII:B:3:e)

2491.   Homes, Wilfred J. *Double-Edged Secrets.* Annapolis: U.S. Naval Institute, 1979. 265p. (IV:C)

2492.   Kuusinen, Aino. *Rings of Destiny: Inside Russia from Lenin to Brezhnev.* Translated from the German. New York: Morrow, 1974. 255p. (III:C:3)

2493.   Moulton, James L. *The Royal Marines.* Famous Regiments Series. London: Leo Cooper, 1972. 100p. (VI:A)

2494.   Mrazek, James E. *The Fall of Eben Emael: Prelude to Dunkirk.* London: Hale, 1972. 192p. (VII:B:2:b:2)

2495.   Ortzen, Len. *Famous Stories of the Resistance.* New York: St. Martin's Press, 1979. (VII:B:1)

2496.   Owen, David. *Battle of Wits: A History of Psychology and Deception in Modern Warfare.* New York: Crane, Russak, 1978. 207p. (II)

2497.   Solovyov, Boris. *The Battle of Kursk.* Moscow: Novosti Press Agency Publishing House, 1973. 40p. (V:C:3:d)

2498.   Steinert, Marlis G., ed. *Hitler's War and the Germans: Public Mood and Attitudes during the Second World War.* Athens: Ohio University Press, 1977. 387p. (II)

2499.   Taylor, Richard. *Film Propaganda: Soviet Russia and Nazi Germany.* New York: Harper & Row, 1979. 250p.(II)

2500.   Thomson, Oliver. *Mass Persuasion in History: An Historical Analysis of the Development of Propaganda Techniques.* Edinburgh, Scotland: Paul Harris, 1977. 142p. (II)

2501..   Villari, Luigi. *The Liberation of Italy, 1943–1947.* Translated from the Italian. Appleton, Wisc.: C. C. Nelson, 1959. 265p. (VII:B:3:a)

2502.   Young, Richard A. *The Flying Bomb.* New York: Sky Books Press, 1978. 160p. (V:A:4)

Articles

2503.   "America Deciphered Our Code: The Battle of Midway." *U.S. Naval Institute Proceedings,* CV (June 1979), 98–100. (V:B:4)

2504.   Bailey, Ronald H. "All-Seeing Eyes in the Sky." In: his *The Air War in Europe.* World War II Series. New York: Time-Life, 1979. pp. 66–79. (IV:D:2)

2505.   Ball, Desmond J. "Allied Intelligence Cooperation Involving Australia during World War II." *Australian Outlook,* XXXII (December 1978), *passim.* (VII:C:1)

2506.   Birtles, Philip J. "Wooden Warbird: The Fighter Bombers." *Air Classics,* XV (August 1979), 14–33. (VII:B:2)

2507.   Bowyer, Chaz. "The Amiens Raid." In: Anthony Robinson, ed. *Wings: The Complete Encyclopedia of Aviation.* 25 vols. London: Orbis, 1977. I, 49–52. (VII:B:2:b:2)

2508.   Esslin, Martin. "The Art of [British] Black Propaganda." *Encounter,* LII (January 1979), 42–49. (II)

2509.   Holmes, Wilfred J. "Pearl Harbor Aftermath." *U.S. Naval Institute Proceedings*, CIV (December 1978), 68–75. (IV:C)

2510.   Kahn, David. "The International Conference on Ultra." *Military Affairs*, XLIII (April 1979), 97–100. (III:B:2)

2511.   Kelly, John. "Intelligence and Counterintelligence in German Prisoner-of-War Camps in Canada during World War II." *Dalhousie Review*, XLVIII (Summer 1978), *passim*. (IV:B)

2512.   Kelly, Joseph B. "Assassination in War Time." *Military Law Review*, XXX (October 1965), 101–111. (III:A)

2513.   Koscresza, Bogumil. "Misan 5703: 1943, Warsaw Uprising." *Commonweal*, LXVII (April 1979), 57–66. (VII:B:4:a)

2514.   Little, Wendell. "The Intelligence Bookshelf." *Air University Review*, XXX (May–June 1979), 85–91. (I:A)

2515.   MacDonald, Charles A. "The Venlo Affair." *European Studies Review*, VIII (October 1978), 443–464. (VII:B:2:b:1)

2516.   Kieval, Hillel J. "The [European Resistance] Bluff That Came Off?" *American Scholar*, XLVIII (Spring 1979), 273–280. (VII:A)

2517.   Patrick, Stephen B. "Commando." *Strategy and Tactics*, no. 75 (July–August 1979), 25–32. (VI:A)

2518.   Poolman, Kenneth. "The American Volunteer Group." In: Anthony Robinson, ed. *Wings: The Complete Encyclopedia of Aviation*. 25 vols. London: Orbis, 1977. I, 44–48. (VI:B)

2519.   Possony, Stefan T. "Organized Intelligence: The Problem of the French General Staff." *Social Research*, VIII (May 1941), 213–237. (IV:B)

2520.   Pugh, Craig A. "A Man [Jacques Grillon] of Honor [in the French Resistance]." *Airman*, XXIII (February 1979), 24–30. (VII:B:2:b:1)

2521.   "The Rescue of Mussolini." *After the Battle* (November 1978), 12–31. (VII:B:3:a)

2522.   Sinclair, Andrew. "John Ford's War." *Sight and Sound*, XLVIII (Spring 1979), 99–104. (VII:B)

2523.   Steinberg, Raphael. "The Makeshift [Guerrilla] Army." In: his *Return to the Philippines*. World War II Series. New York: Time-Life, 1978. pp. 194–202. (VII:C:2:a)

2524. Tsinev, G. "Military Counterintelligence History Reviewed: Reprinted from *Kommunist Vooruzhennyke Sil,* December 1978." *Translations on U.S.S.R. Military Affairs,* no. 1421 (March 20, 1979), 1–9. (III:C:3)

2525. Twining, Stephen N. "Japanese Counterinsurgency Efforts in China." *Military Journal,* II (Spring 1979), 30–34. (VII:C:3:1)

2526. Vane, Amoury. "The Surveillance of Northern Australia—It's History: The Story of Stanner's Bush Commando." *Defence Forces Journal,* (January–February 1979), 15–30. (VI:A)

2527. Wehr, Paul."The Norwegian Resistance." In: his *Conflict Regulation.* Boulder, Colo.: Westview Press, 1979. Chpt. 4. (VII:B:2:d:1)

2528. Whittier, Henry S. "Soviet Special Operations, Partisan Warfare: Implications for Today." *Military Review,* LIX (January 1979), 48–58. (VII:B:4:b)

Documents, Papers, and Reports

2529. Auckland, Reginald G., comp. *Catalogue of British Black Propaganda to Germany, 1941–1945.* Kettering, Eng.: Psywar Society, 1977. 32p. (II)

2530. Buchsbaum, John H. *German Psychological Warfare on the Russian Front, 1941–1945.* Washington, D.C.: Office of the Chief of Military History, Department of the Army, 1953. 376p. (II)

2531. Casey, William J. "The German Resistance to Adolf Hitler." M.A. Thesis, St. John's University, 1949. (VII:B:2:e)

2532. Gardner, Hugh H. *Guerrilla and Counterguerrilla Warfare in Greece, 1941–1945.* Washington, D.C.: Office of the Chief of Military History, Department of the Army, 1962. 234p. (VII:B:3:d)

2533. Jacobsen, Hans-Adolf, ed. *July 20, 1944: The German Opposition to Hitler as Viewed by Foreign Historians.* Bonn: Press and Information Office of the Federal Government of West Germany, 1969. 338p. (VII:B:2:e)

2534. Stroop, Juergen. *The Stroop Report: The Jewish Quarter in Warsaw Is No More.* Translated from the German. New York: Pantheon, 1979. 192p. (VII:B:4:a)

2535. United States. Marine Corps. *U.S.M.C. Destruction by Demolition, Incendiaries, and Sabotage.* Boulder, Colo.: Paladin Press, 1979. 270p. (III:C:4)

2536. _____ . Office of Strategic Services. *O.S.S. Sabotage and Demolition Manual.* Boulder, Colo.: Paladin Press, 1979. 319p. (III:C:4)

2537. _____ . _____ . *O.S.S. Special Weapons Catalog.* Boulder, Colo.: Paladin Press, 1979. 100p. (III:C:4)

2538. Von Luttichau, Charles. *Some Observations on Guerrilla Warfare in Russia during World War II.* Washington, D.C.: Office of the Chief of Military History, Department of the Army, 1960. 33p. (VII:B:4:b)

2539. _____ . *Guerrilla and Counterguerrilla Warfare in Russia during World War II.* Washington, D.C.: Office of the Chief of Military History, Department of the Army, 1963. 167p. (VII:B:4:b)

Appendix II:
Magazines and Journals Containing at Least One Article Relative to This Guide

Aerospace Historian
Aerospace Safety
Air Classics
Air Force and Space Digest
Air Force Magazine
Air Power Historian
Air University Review
Airman
American Aviation Historical Society
 Journal
American Committee on the History of
 the Second World War Newsletter
American Heritage
American Historical Review
American Journal of International
 Law
American Journal of Sociology
American Legion Magazine
American Magazine
American Mercury
American Neptune
American Philosophical Society Pro-
 ceedings
American Political Science Review
American Quarterly
American–Scandinavian Review
American–Slavic Review
American Sociological Review
Annals of the American Academy of
 Political and Social Science
Army
Army Quarterly
Asia
Asiatic Review
Atlantic
Bell System Technical Journal
Blackwood's Magazine
Bulletin of the New York Public Li-
 brary
Cambridge Journal
Canadian Geographic Review
Canadian Journal of History
Catholic Historical Review
Catholic World

Cinema Journal
Coast Artillery Journal
Collier's
Columbia Historical Society Records
Combat Forces
Commentary
Commonweal
Comparative Studies in Society and
 History
Contemporary Review
Cooperation and Conflict
Coronet
Cosmopolitan Magazine
Cryptologia
Current History
Dissent
Eastern European Quarterly
Electronic Warfare
Encounter
Far Eastern Survey
Florida Historical Quarterly
Flying
Flying Review International
Foreign Affairs
Fortnightly
Fortune
Free World
Geographic Review
Harper's Magazine
Historian
History, Numbers, and War
History Today
Illustrated London News
Infantry
Infantry Journal
International Affairs (London)
Iowa Law Review
Journal of American History
Journal of the American Statistical
 Association
Journal of Central European Affairs
Journal of Contemporary History
Journal of European Studies
Journal of Modern History

Journal of Social Psychology
Journal of Southeast Asian History
Journal of the Royal United Service
    Institute for Defence Studies
Labour Monthly
Library Journal
Life
Living Age
Look
Marine Crops Gazette
Massachusetts Review
Menorah Journal
Military Affairs
Military Review
Mississippi Valley Historical Review
Modern Age
Nation
National Geographic Magazine
National Review
Naval War College Review
New Leader
New York Times Magazine
New Yorker
Newsweek
ONI Review
Pacific Spectator
Parade
Parameters
Philippine Historical Association
    History Bulletin
Plain Talk
Polish Perspectives
Polish Review
Political Quarterly
Political Science Quarterly
Political Studies
Popular Mechanics
Popular Science
Public Opinion Quarterly
Publisher's Weekly
Quarterly Review
R.A.F. Flying Review
Reader's Digest
Research

Review of Politics
Roundel
Royal Air Forces Quarterly
Russian Review
Saturday Evening Post
Saturday Review of Literature
Scandinavian Review
Science
Science and Society
Science Digest
Scientific American
Sea Classics
Signal
Slavic Review
Slavonic and East European Review
Social Forces
Social Research
Sociological and Social Research
South Atlantic Quarterly
Soviet Literature
Soviet Military Review
Soviet Studies
Strategy and Tactics
T.A.F. Review
Tactical Air Reconnaissance Digest
Time
Times Literary Supplement
The Trident
True Magazine
Ukrainian Quarterly
U.S. Army Talks
U.S. Naval Institute Proceedings
U.S. News and World Report
Virginia Quarterly Review
Vital Speeches
World Marxist Review
World Politics
World Today
World War II Journal
World War II Magazine
Yad Vashem Bulletin
Yad Vashem Studies
Yale Review

Author Index

The entries in this index are keyed to the entry numbers of references in the guide. Cross-references are provided for pseudonyms and real names.

_____ . _____ . Historical Division, 1608, 1819–1820

_____ . _____ . Military History Institute, 73

_____ . _____ . Security Agency, Historical Section, 613

_____ . Central Intelligence Agency, 542

_____ . Chief of Counsel for the Prosecution of Axis Criminality, 526–527

_____ . Congress. House. Special Committee on Un-American Activities, 327, 2011–2012, 2417

_____ . _____ . Joint Select Committee on the Pearl Harbor Attack, 867–869

_____ . _____ . Senate. Committee on Foreign Relations, 1960

_____ . _____ . _____ . Committee on the Judiciary, Subcommittee to Investigate the Administration of the Internal Security Act and Other Internal Security Laws, 1754

_____ . Department of Defense, 403, 2418

_____ . Department of State, 74

_____ . Foreign Broadcast Information Service, 328

_____ . Joint Board of Scientific Information Policy, 462–463

_____ . Library of Congress, 75

_____ . Marine Corps. Historical Branch, 899

_____ . Military Academy, Department of Military Arts and Engineering, 959

_____ . National Defense Research Committee, Division 15, 464

_____ . Navy Department. Court of Inquiry on the Pearl Harbor Attack, 869

_____ . _____ . Office of the Chief of Naval Operations. Amphibious Forces, Underwater Demolition Teams, 1163–1165.

_____ . _____ . _____ . Naval Technical Mission, Europe, 465

_____ . _____ . _____ . Office of Naval Intelligence, 384, 404, 632–633, 2013

_____ . _____ . Pacific Fleet and Pacific Ocean Area, 466, 634–636, 1118

_____ . _____ . _____ . Seventh Fleet Intelligence Center, 1869

_____ . _____ . Tenth Fleet, 637

_____ . Office of Strategic Services. Assessment Staff, 581

_____ . _____ . History Project, 582

_____ . _____ . Research and Analysis Branch, 1273, 1609, 1821, 1852–1853

_____ . Strategic Bombing Survey, 616, 763–764, 777

_____ . Superintendent of Documents, 76

_____ . War Department. Information and Education Division, Research Branch, 329

_____ . _____ . Manhattan Project, 2014

_____ . _____ . Military Intelligence Service, 112, 1119

Urquhart, Robert E., 1018

Usher, Frank H., 2047

Vaculik, Serge, 2433
Vagts, Alfred, 617
Valcher, W. H., Jr., 330
Vallat, Antoine, 1961
Van der Rhoer, Edward, 405
Van Duren, Theo, 2445
Van Roon, Gerhard, 2454
Van Woerdan, Peter, 1425
Vaupshasov, S., 1822
Verrier, Anthony, 765
Vigness, Paul C., 1464
Volckmann, Rusell W., 2450
Von der Porten, Edward P., 824
Von Hassell, Ulrich, 2451
Von Kardorff, Ursula, 2452
Von Luttichau, Charles V. P., 1031
Von Manstein, Erich, 960
Von Moltke, Melmuth J., 2455
Von Plehwe, Fredrich–Karl, 946
Von Schlabrendorff, Fabian, 2456–2458
Von Strempel, Heribert, 332
Von Waldheim–Emmerick, Ragnhild S., 2048
Voorhis, Jerry L., 1465
Vosseller, Aurelius B., 467
Vyvyan, Michael, 1557

Wachsman, Z. H., 1274
Waddington, Conrad, 468
Waddington, P. A. J., 1558
Wade, G. A., 485
Wahl, Anthony N., 1369
Waldenstrom, Stig, 1222
Waldron, Thomas J., 1165
Wales, H. G. Q., 333
Walker, C. Lester, 1962
Walker, David E., 334, 2463–2464
Walker, Roy, 1466
Walker, Wayne T., 1202
Wall, Carl B., 2015
Wallace, Robert, 1592
Walter, Gerald, 1370
Walters, Anne M., 2465
Warbey, William, 1467
Warburg, James P., 335
Ward, Francis K., 1963
Ward, Robert E., 870
Warmbrunn, Walter, 1426–1427
Warner, Philip, 1121
Warrack, Graeme, 1428
Warren, Charles E. T., 1166, 2468
Warren, Harris G., 1275–1276
Wasserman, Benno, 385
Waters, John M., 825
Watson–Watt, Robert A., 469

Subject Index

Organizations, engagements, and personnel referred to by name in the guide are cited in this index, keyed to entry numbers. National intelligence, special force military units, and other organizations appropriate to a given country are listed under that country: e.g., United States, Office of Strategic Services. Additionally, one will find indexed certain general topics such as resistance, cryptography, espionage, and intelligence.

In order for the user to associate certain persons or organizations with events or other figures, the index includes extensive cross-references. Where appropriate, the code names of agents are entered with a reference to real names.